THE TOOTH TRIP

THOMAS McGUIRE D.D.S.

AN ORAL EXPERIENCE

RANDOM HOUSE - BOOKWORKS

First Printing August 1972:   2,000 copies in cloth and
                                10,000 copies in paperback

Illustrations by Amit Pieter, Carmel, California
Front cover designed and illustrated by Linda Bennett, Pt. Richmond, California
Photographs by Joel Smith Thomas, Carmel, California
Typeset by Vera Allen Composition Service, Hayward, California
                (Special thanks to Vera and Dorothy)
Printed and Bound by The Colonial Press Inc., Clinton, Mass.
Special Editor: Hal Bennett, Pt. Richmond, California
Special Typist: Bev Horn, Monterey, California

This book is co-published by **Random House Inc.**
                              201 East 50th Street
                              New York, N.Y. 10022

                     and **The Bookworks**
                            1409 Fifth Street
                            Berkeley, California 94710

Distributed in the United States by Random House, and simultaneously published in Canada by Random House of Canada Limited, Toronto

The publishers wish to acknowledge use of the following copyrighted material:

From the book, HUNZA HEALTH SECRETS FOR LONG LIFE AND HAPPINESS by Renee Taylor. © 1964 by Renee Taylor. Reprinted with permission of the publisher, Prentice-Hall, Inc., Englewood Cliffs, New Jersey.

From the book, THE HERBALIST by Joseph E. Meyer. Reprinted with permission of the publisher, Indiana Botanic Gardens, Hammond, Indiana

Library of Congress Cataloging in Publication Data
McGuire, Thomas, 1940-
        The tooth trip.

        1. Teeth—Care and hygiene. I. Title. [DNLM:
1. Oral health—Popular works. WU 80 M148t 1972]
RK61.M215   617.6'01   72-5130
ISBN 0-394-48288-3
ISBN 0-394-70793-1 (pbk.)

Edited and designed in Berkeley and produced in New York
Manufactured in the United States of America

You could say that the Tooth Trip began with this most beautiful lady. She is my grandmother. This picture was taken around 1918. Today, at 77, she is still a very beautiful lady.

I place her here because she belongs here. Without her, the Tooth Trip would not have happened. But more than that, she is here because she is living proof of the reason there must be a book such as this one.

My lovely grandmother happens to be one of the twenty-five million living people who have lost their teeth. One of the twenty-five million who lost their teeth not because they wished to or desired it, but because they didn't have the knowledge to prevent this loss. Who lost them because they put their faith and trust in a dental profession that did little or nothing to educate them or help prevent this tragedy.

It may be too late for my grandmother, and perhaps yours, but with the spirit of prevention in mind, it need not be too late for you and your children.

To you, Delia Kinsey, I dedicate this book, hopefully fulfilling your desire to help make this world a better place to live.

CONTENTS

INTRODUCTION

The popular conception that the way to stop tooth decay is to see your dentist twice a year and pray, is not working. If that has been your idea, you'd best chuck it. To continue to follow that course means more of the same old cavities, more of the same fillings, root canals, lost teeth, bridges, dentures and plates. And more money in the dentists' pockets.

If you are one of the sufferers and you wish to change your dental trip, then the TOOTH TRIP is for you. Through the knowledge contained in this book you will be able to turn your attention to the *source* of the problem; you will learn how to focus your energy effectively on true preventive dentistry. This means that you will learn what to do before any problem starts, and also what to do if disease has already begun.

What I am going to tell you here relies not on its humor, nor on literary style, but on *results*. You know better than I whether your gums bleed, how many teeth you have lost, how many fillings you've had, how bad your breath smells or how much money you've spent on dentistry. You know all of that. I am here to tell you that this need not have occurred, that there is another way — the way of knowledge. All that is needed is for you to apply the ideas of preventive dentistry contained in thes book, plus your desire, and — presto! no more dental disease.

Look in detail at what I have to say, then look into your mouth. Spend a few weeks following the home care plan I outline, then look at the results — they should be proof enough.

This book is a path. Follow it into your mouth, and, through diet, eventually into your whole body as well. Dental health is directly related to diet, digestion and physical energy and well-being. This is a high path. May it help keep you well!

THE ANATOMY OF TOOTH DECAY

THE DECAY TRIP
A DAY IN THE LIFE OF A GERM
REFINED FOODS FOR THE GOURMET GERM
HOW GERMS RELATE TO NATURAL AND REFINED FOODS
DECAY RESEARCH GROUP "A" EXPERIMENTS
GROUP "B" EXPERIMENTS
THE BAD ACID TRIP
BYE BYE MISS AMERICAN PIE

No one should ever get tooth decay. The fact that almost every American has tooth decay proves either that people do not know how it happens and do not know how to prevent it from happening, or they do not care.

THE DECAY TRIP

All tooth decay is related to diet. When man's diet in his early history was natural and balanced, he had no tooth decay, and little or no other dental disease. When man changed his natural balanced diet and began processing and refining his natural food, he created tooth decay. This process is simple. In order for it to occur, three things are needed:

1) Germs (Bacteria) — Germs are normally found in man's mouth. More of these germs are found in man's mouth than in *any* other part of his body. Even a dog's mouth has less. Germs are so small they are rarely seen. That's why this guy is so indignant at our looking at him.

2) Food — This means the food we leave in our mouths, the most destructive being of the refined and processed variety. (To be explained shortly.)

3) Teeth — We all at least start with them, even though today there are 25 million Americans who do not have a single tooth in their heads; about 1/8 of the population of the U.S.A.

These three items need a place to come together, and your mouth fulfills this requirement perfectly. Also, so that bacteria can destroy your teeth as rapidly as possible, they need freedom and complete privacy from the brush. Thus, there exists in all of us, except the 25 million people with no teeth, the potential for tooth decay to happen.

A DAY IN THE LIFE OF A GERM

Here are some facts about germs:

1) The little buggers are super small, almost unbelievingly small. Millions of them could fit into an area the size of this dot. (·)

2) Sexually, they are amazing and you really must consider their birth rate excessive. Given the proper conditions, which most of us do give them, one germ can divide itself into millions in as little as one hour. Good reason for germ birth control education.

3) They have a very unique life style; unlike man, the germs causing tooth decay do not need to breathe oxygen to survive. This is important, for even when they get tucked into areas of the mouth where there is no air, they can still continue doing their thing.

4) They love just about every type of food we eat, and they certainly like refined and processed foods, for if we leave it in our mouths, they will eat it twenty-four hours a day, every day, for as long as it is left in there. I know a few people who really dig eating, but not twenty-four hours a day.

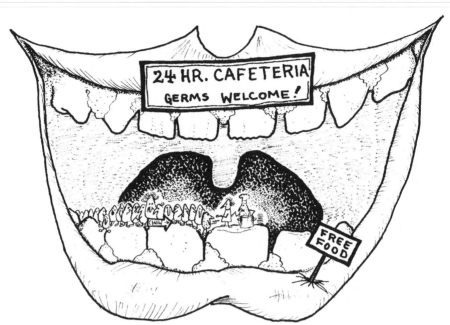

5) They need very little food to live. Thus, any excess food allows them to increase and maintain their numbers quite adequately. Once tooth or gum disease gets started, you give the germs another source of fresh food — your body. How's it feel to get eaten alive by these little cannibals?

All of the above characteristics of germs play a very important role in the decay process, as you shall soon see.

First, in order to understand the decayed state, we should have an understanding of the healthy mouth; the environment where germs cannot overproduce. A healthy mouth provides 1) practically no source of nutrition (food) for the germs, 2) with no food, very few can live in your mouth, 3) the few germs that are present are not harmful, 4) the spit (saliva) produced in a healthy mouth will protect the tooth against the harmful acid that the germs make and use to dissolve the teeth.

The only time germs can cause a healthy mouth to become diseased is when we do not keep our mouth clean, and this gives the germs the food they need to tremendously increase their numbers. The germs can then make more acid than the spit in your mouth can neutralize. When this happens, the germs can penetrate man's natural defenses — the skin of the mouth (causing gum disease), or the enamel of the tooth (causing tooth decay).

What the healthy mouth has shown us is that to be free of decay, you must keep it clean. This, in effect, means that two of the three things (food, germs, teeth) needed to initiate tooth decay are not present in sufficient quantity. Herein lies the key; *at least one of the three must be eliminated in order to prevent decay.* Of course, we do not want to eliminate our teeth. We also do not need to eliminate all germs, for in limited amounts they are normal and do not cause harm. Thus, food is the easiest and most logical of the three to either eliminate or control.

Food only has value when it gets to the stomach; it is not meant to be left in the mouth. Thus, decay occurs when we leave food (especially refined and processed food) in our mouth, with the severity of the decay being directly related to the amount, type, and length of time the food is left in the mouth.

When the germs have eaten and digested the food you've left them, their nature also demands that they eliminate the waste products of their bodies. This natural function occurs almost immediately after eating. The waste products which each of these millions of germs eliminate are very acidic, producing a substance that has the ability to dissolve certain materials it may come in contact with; sadly for us the enamel of our teeth is one of the substances this acid can dissolve.

REFINED FOODS FOR THE GOURMET GERM

Processing and refining foods changes the natural fibrous consistency of the food and reduces the size of the food particle. This reduction in size is most dramatically illustrated in the refining of white sugar.

In his natural state, the sugar beet is quite far out. Who would suspect that this round, jolly fellow would soon be transformed into one of the nastiest of all villians, white sugar? In his natural state the sugar beet is much too large to be eaten by the germs in your mouth. This is generally true of almost all foods in their natural state. If we ate the sugar beet raw, even if we chewed it up into little pieces, the particles would still be too large for the germs to eat immediately, and thus no decay could occur. But, when it is refined, the picture changes.

The refining process reduces poor Mr. Beet down to one of the smallest sizes a food can be reduced to and still be called a food, if white sugar can be called a food. This end product that Mr. Beet has now been reduced to is a carbohydrate (type of energy food man needs in his diet but can get from sources other than white sugar) which is called sucrose.

When this end product, white sugar, is placed in the mouth, the white sugar can combine with the germs and commit the crime of tooth decay. You are the victim of this crime.

Bear in mind that any refined food can be easily digested by the germs, but white sugar happens to be one of the smallest and most common of the refined foods. As long as the food is left in the mouth, the germs continue to do their dirty work; eating, digesting, producing their acid, and continually dissolving your teeth. The acid the germs produce is powerful stuff. The enamel of your teeth is the hardest substance in your body, but this acid has no trouble dissolving it.

HOW GERMS RELATE TO NATURAL AND REFINED FOODS

Natural foods (foods which have not been refined) are so much larger than the germs (even after being well chewed) that the germs could not possibly digest them during the time this food is normally left in your mouth. It takes days for the enzymes of the mouth to break down natural foods to a size the germs can eat, whereas the germs can begin to digest white sugar (and all other processed foods) immediately on contact. White sugar particles are small enough for the germs to eat. No enzymes are needed to break them down.

DECAY RESEARCH GROUP "A" EXPERIMENTS

There have been some very far out experiments done that show the relationships between natural foods, refined foods and tooth decay. The experiments point out what we might call the "trio theory" — that there must be teeth, food and germs involved together before you get tooth decay.

One set of laboratory animals were sterilized (Group A) to remove all of the germs from them and their environment, thus none were present in their mouths. A second set of the same kind of animals (Group B) were left untouched in their natural environment. Their diet was the same natural diet that normally prevented them from getting tooth decay.

Group A was fed a diet consisting only of refined and processed foods. This was done for a period of months. No decay was found, even though these foods were known to cause decay normally. The reason for this being that the germs had been removed. Thus, there was nothing present in the mouth to eat the refined foods and therefore, no acid produced and so no decay. Now, in the second part of the experiment, these same animals (Group A) were fed refined foods, but this time through a tube connected to their stomachs. The idea was to keep any food from touching the teeth and mingling with the germs that were replaced in the mouth. As the researchers found that food without bacteria did not cause decay, they now wanted to see if germs without food also would not cause decay. To make sure there were enough germs, the researchers continually pumped germs, produced in the laboratory, into the animals' mouths, so at any time there could be found more decay-causing bacteria in their mouths than would be found naturally. Again, no decay was found, and again the trio theory was proven correct. One of the trio was again missing (refined foods) and thus it demonstrated that even increased amounts of bacteria will not cause tooth decay if food is not also present.

The third phase of the experiment was then carried out. This consisted of using the same animals (Group A), but this time both the refined foods and the decay-causing germs were put back into the animals' mouths. Again, the experiment lasted the same amount of time as the previous two. The results showed that the same teeth that didn't decay in the previous experiments were now rotting out due to decay. Decay resulted because, for the first time in the experiments, all three of the things needed to initiate decay were found in the mouth: germs, food and teeth.

There was a fourth phase of the experiment, but as I think it to be cruel, I will only touch on it, and you can judge for yourself. The same animals were used, they were fed the same food and bacteria, and the test lasted the same amount of time as the previous three. The difference here was that they had their teeth pulled before the experiment started. Of course there was no tooth decay. What the hell did they expect, anyway? But, in its own stupid way, it also proves the trio theory; one of the three culprits was eliminated, the teeth. And again, no decay.

GROUP "B" EXPERIMENTS

In experiement One (Group B) the decay-causing germs were removed from the mouth, as was done in Group A's experiment, leaving natural food and teeth. The results: no decay. Reason: one of the trio was missing.

In experiment Two the natural food was taken away (they fasted the animals and the germs were put back into the animals' mouths). Results: no decay, since the trio was again incomplete. (This is getting so predictable that it could get boring, but don't get too complacent, as I've a surprise in store for you.)

In experiment Three the natural food was left for the germs to eat, the teeth were left intact, and the zillions of excess germs were pumped in. Results: no decay. Well, that seems to shoot down my trio theory, for in this experiment we find all three items present and accounted for: teeth, food and bacteria. Not quite. You see, all along I've been telling you that a natural, balanced diet will by its very nature prevent tooth decay. For, even though all three elements were seemingly present, the natural food the animals ate was not only too large for the germs to eat (thus no acid could form) but its fibrous and abrasive nature actually polished and cleaned the teeth the same as if they were brushed.

Experiment Four: The same animals (Group B) were used. Remember, their teeth were not decayed. Every phase of the previous experiments was exactly duplicated, except that the natural diet was replaced by a diet of refined foods. Results: all the teeth decayed. Why? The germs got their refined food back and proceeded

9

to pull off another decay scam. (Scam, in case you do not already know, means pulling a fast one on someone; in this case the germs and refined food pulled one on the teeth.)

Thus, we have demonstrated three things:

1) how decay happens
2) the role refined foods play in its happenings, and
3) how natural foods will help prevent decay.

The following two diagrams will help put it together:

Experiment A (+ means plus or addition of; - means not present or removed)

#1	Animals with teeth (+) refined foods (-) germs	NO DECAY
#2	Animals with teeth (-) refined foods (+) germs	NO DECAY
#3	Animals with teeth (+) refined foods (+) germs	DECAY
#4	Animals without teeth (+) refined foods (+) germs	NO DECAY

Experiment B

#1	Animals with teeth (+) natural foods (-) germs	NO DECAY
#2	Animals with teeth (-) natural foods (+) germs	NO DECAY
#3	Animals with teeth (+) natural foods (+) germs	NO DECAY
#4	Animals with teeth (+) refined foods (+) germs	DECAY

THE BAD ACID TRIP

We should know by now that the acid produced by the germs in your mouth can dissolve the enamel of your teeth. But what happens once it gets through the enamel? A drawing will help you follow the train of thought.

If the little germs are allowed enough time to produce enough acid to dissolve the enamel, you will have gone past the point of home care prevention. A visit to your dentist is now a must, for the dentin (inside the tooth) is not nearly as hard as the enamel outside and the acid can more easily dissolve it. The germs will also begin using the dentin as a source of food since about thirty per cent of the dentin exists in a form that can be very readily eaten by the germs. This is not good, of course, because now it has its own source of food (dentin) and even if you now completely remove all the food after eating, you would not be able to stop the destruction. You can stop any new decay from occurring by regular brushing, but as the hole the acid made is too small for any brush to get into, the germs can do their nasty work without interference. Remember, they don't need oxygen, so once inside your tooth, they can get into eating you twenty-four hours a day. (Take note here the teeth are as much a part of your body as your eyes or hands or breasts.)

As you have no way of knowing when the germs have reached the dentin since you can't see between your teeth — you should now be able to appreciate the value of an examination, including a full mouth series of x-rays. For even though you can see what is happening on the outsides of your teeth, by following the self-evaluation section, only an x-ray will show up decay between the teeth. Unless this is done, you won't be able to tell what is happening until the pain comes. And if that has ever happened to you, you know what a totally miserable trip dental pain can be! Aside from the suffering part, the cost grows; the longer you wait, the more it costs you. The following graph illustrates this point, based on 1972 prices:

1) Perfect tooth — *no cost.* No repair is needed.
2) Acid has etched some enamel — not true decay — can be stopped. *No Cost.*
3) One side, smallest silver filling — one surface filling: Cost $10 to $12
4) Two sides involved: Cost $15 to $17
5) Three sides involved: Costs $24 to $27
6) Too much tooth lost for silver. Needs gold cap. Costs $90 to $120
7) Nerve infected — root canal plus gold crown. Cost $300 total
8) Tooth so rotted it has to be pulled and replaced by bridge. Costs from $300 up to thousands depending on how many teeth are involved.

9) All abcessed and all must be pulled. Full plates — should be remade every three years. Cost $400 to $500. Could add up to thousands.

BYE BYE MISS AMERICAN PIE

Last year, Americans spent $4 billion dollars at the dentist's office. How much of that did you contribute? With a $4 billion dollar pie to divide up, you should be able to understand why the average dentist can spend a great deal of time at the stock market instead of getting after the germs and telling you how to prevent decay.

For how to reduce the size of this pie while reducing your own suffering, see my chapter on "Home Care." Remember, as I said in in the beginning of thic chapter, *no one should get tooth decay.*

2

HOW TO EVALUATE
THE CONDITION OF YOUR GUMS

WHAT YOU WILL NEED
WHERE TO GET THE MIRROR
WHAT TO LOOK FOR
HOW TO LOOK AT THE GUMS IN FRONT
HOW TO LOOK AT THE GUMS IN THE BACK
SECRETS - GROUP TWO
STAGES OF GUM DISEASE

In this chapter you will begin to get the feel, or intent, of the book — that being to allow you to eliminate or at least greatly reduce the need for the dentist, through home care. Thus, I will show you what the normal mouth is like so you can better understand any abnormalities in yours. I will explain just how to diagnose the conditions of your gums and how to determine the severity of your condition.

It may well be that your discoveries will require you to solicit the aid of a good dentist (which I will show you how to find later in the book), but you can do a great deal to restore your gums to a healthy state on your own.

First, you will need to know the tools that are required to perform your own diagnosis. Following a description and explanation of these tools, I will describe ideal "healthy gums." Then you can go exploring for yourself.

Okay, now that I've got you chomping at the bit, I'd better turn you loose. Here is what you'll need in the way of equipment.

WHAT YOU WILL NEED

1) You — but much better if there are two, sharing is beautiful. So why not stop now, go get your old man or lady or a friend, and do the Tooth Trip with him or her?
2) Eyes — yours, or someone else's.

3) Source of light — flashlight is groovy and necessary to look into your mouth. It's easier if someone is there to hold it, which will also prevent you from dropping the light (in case the shock of discovery is great.)

4) Mirror — bathroom mirror is best, kitchen mirror is far out, bedroom mirror or any ol' mirror will do so long as you can see your face.

5) A good place to set this book — somewhere it won't get wet — if you're into carpentry, perhaps you could you could make a book pulpit, whatever.

6) Small Dental Mirror — this little guy will allow you to see areas and things you've never seen before. Always keep it clean and in a safe place.

WHERE TO GET THE MIRROR

Some drug stores have plastic dental mirrors; if not, they can get one for you. Also, a dentist can order the inexpensive kind for you and may even have some on hand. They cost about $1.00.

Professional Secret Number One: as you may already know, mirrors fog up when you breathe on them; then you can't see very well. In order not to get bummed (upset), run warm water over the mirror just before you start. For you technically-minded people, the temperature of the water should be 98-99° Fahrenheit, equal to body temperature. If the mirror is colder than that, it will fog up.

Secret Number Two: when you look at the gums behind the front teeth, both upper and lower, shine the flashlight into the mirror and let it reflect the light onto the gums. "Let there be light." By reflecting the light rays from your flashlight you accomplish two very necessary requirements for diagnosing your gums now and your teeth later. These are:

1) The mirror serves to "bend" the light, allowing you to light up the inside of your mouth.

2) The bending of the light onto the teeth will prevent you from being blinded by the light of the flashlight, thus being able to pick up the images of your teeth and gums in the mirror — as you shall soon see.

Secret Number Three: to smile you have only to move your heart and lips. Feels good, doesn't it!

WHAT TO LOOK FOR

There are five clearly distinguishable characteristics of healthy gums:

1) Healthy gums are firm.

2) Healthy gums are a pinkish color; some may even look whitish-pink. This color should extend down about one-half inch from the highest point between the teeth to where the color ends. It should be noted that the pinkish color is not a universal criteria for healthy gums, as dark-skinned people, particularly Blacks, have pigmented skin and thus the color cannot be used as a guideline to the health of the gums. In fact, even fair-skinned people can have dark pigmented gums. The point here is to follow all of the guidelines for healthy gums and if the remaining characteristics check out okay and your gums are dark, you still have healthy gums.

3) Healthy gums fill in the spaces between the teeth and should be shaped like an inverted V at their highest point between the teeth.

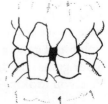

Healthy, perfect gums also have two other characteristics that are easily recognized. You can see these on either the upper or the lower gums. The lower is easier to see than the upper, especially if you are a male with a moustache.

4) Healthy gums have little dot-like indentations (stippling), especially found in the areas closest to the teeth. Your gum, in these areas, should look like the outside of an orange peel.

5) Healthy gums have a collar or a rim around the gums at the highest point the gums extend to. This collar, or rim, can be seen in the drawing, and it is nothing more than an elevated roll of gum tissue that begins where the gum meets the tooth, rises up and blends back into the gum. This collar is about one-eighth of an inch wide. Here are healthy gums with rim and stippling, and "puffy" gums without.

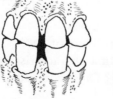

15

Okay, you know the normal, and now you should be ready to go non-stop to the mirror and see just where you fit into the dental health picture. You might say that this is your first step on the road to your oral experience!

HOW TO LOOK AT THE GUMS IN FRONT

Plant your feet firmly in front of the mirror (to help prevent you from shaking or fainting if the shock of discovery gets too heavy for you). Ready . . . lights, no camera, but action. You will now get to know your gums (the skin that surrounds your teeth). Dentists call it the Gingiva and when it's infected they call it Periodontal (around-the-tooth) disease.

1) Wash your hands, if you're into that sort of thing, if not go on to 2.

2) With your left hand, take your index and middle fingers and place them inside the left corner of your mouth (with the fingernails facing into the mouth). Do the same with the right hand. (See why it's groovy to have someone help you?)

Once both hands have been positioned, open your fingers, scissors-like. Only open and separate the fingers enough to allow you to see your gums; do not try to pull your lips apart. Your mouth is a very delicate and sensitive organ, as many of you know, so be gentle, be very gentle. A simple rule would be to stretch it only as much as you need to see what you need to see.

Once you've done this, you can move your lower jaw forward until the lower front teeth are even with the upper front teeth. In this position you should be able to see the firmness, color and general shape of your gums, the first characteristics. Are you looking? Once you get to

16

this position, you should be able to see all of the five previously mentioned signs of healthy gums. Look closely now, either you see them or you don't.

To see if you have "stippling" and a rim, we will have to change positions. With your left hand, pull your lower lip down and out of the way, far enough to allow the flashlight to shine in. You may have to open your lower jaw slightly. Gently now, these are the lips you kiss with. (Lots of light is very important here.) With the right hand take a piece of tissue paper, toilet paper, newspaper (it's very sanitary), or a wash cloth if you aren't a paper freak and you dig saving some trees. Thoroughly dry the gums around the lower front teeth. (Only takes a second so you don't have to rub them — blot them.) Now turn the flashlight on them and observe very closely. See the "stippling"? No? Blot and look again. How about the "rim"? Is it there? Take your time. Try for as accurate and dispassionate an assessment of your gums as possible. Good, that's it . . . remember, it's your body, study it, listen to the vibrations. Done . . . now to the back of your mouth.

HOW TO LOOK AT THE GUMS IN THE BACK

1) Lower Jaw — The gums around the back teeth (on the outside) can be seen by holding the flashlight in one hand and holding the cheek and lips out of the way with the other hand.

For the gums around the inside (backs) of your teeth, you can tilt your chin down to your chest and shine the light directly into your mouth. If it is difficult to see behind the lower front teeth, you can use the mirror as shown. Remember to run warm water and shine the light onto the mirror; play with the angle until you can see the area you want. But check every area and make notes of anything you think to be strange.

2) Upper Jaw — Same, except the mirror will have to be used to see the gum around the outside back teeth and behind the front teeth. For looking at the gum around the outside back teeth you can use the back of the mirror to hold the cheek back and then shine the light into the mirror. Play with it until you get the hang of it; it's easy!

SECRETS - GROUP TWO

Secret Number One: You probably saw that the pinkish gum color moving away from the teeth toward the top and bottom of the mouth ends and blends into a strange-looking region. (Both upper and lower gums will show this.) You will see what looks like and are little blood vessels. On the lower gums particularly, you may see portions of the bone that cover the roots of the teeth sticking out. Don't be alarmed, this is normal in this area. Probably the first time you've really seen it, so don't panic. The reason the blood vessels show through is that, unlike the gum around the tooth, this lower gum area cannot form extra layers of skin to protect itself.

Ideally, the gums should fill in the spaces between the teeth completely, as the previous drawings have shown. If you have spaces

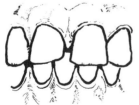 between the teeth that have occured *naturally,* the gum will not fill these in. But the gum in between should still be healthy and show the five normal characteristics.

In a normal mouth, the gum appears to be held so tightly to the tooth that the top of the gum seems to be attached to the enamel of the tooth. This is good; if it looks like it is attached below the white part of the tooth, the gum has *receded* and that is not good. This recession can be caused by several factors:

1) Gum disease, whose infectious destruction causes the gum to attach further down the root. This will show more tooth and possibly even the root.

18

2) Brushing the wrong way (from front to back instead of the way the teeth grow). This pushes the gums down and forces the gum to attach lower down the root, again with more tooth showing.

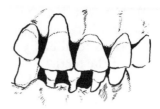

3) Excessive wearing of the teeth, via an abrasive diet, will give the appearance of receding gums. In actuality, it is the teeth growing upward in order to make up for the wearing down of the teeth. If this phenomenon didn't take place the lower jaw would continually move closer to the upper jaw, giving the unsightly appearance of the chin reaching out to touch your nose.

The enamel should always look as if it is coming out of the gum. Another drawing will show this.

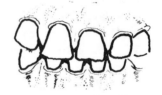

Secret Number Two: *Healthy gums do not bleed.* If your gums bleed when brushing or eating, they are *not*, I repeat, *not* normal or healthy. No matter what your friends say — your teacher, your family or anyone else. Most people's gums have been bleeding for so long that they think that bleeding is either normal or inevitable. Well, it's damn well not!

Think about it; we've established that the gums are part of your body, they are you . . . so tell me honestly, would you let any part of your body bleed? Would you let your eye or your breast bleed everyday? Please grasp fully this idea that bleeding from your body is abnormal and can even be *fatal.* Disease will result from it unless corrected. (Menstruating women excepted, of course.)

You and your mouth ought to be getting on like old friends; it's like living next door to someone all of your life and never really knowing them. Let's find out more . . .

I'll give you a list of common gum disease symptoms to look for. Look for them one at a time or all at once, but if you find one, mark down in the space provided it's exact location and the tooth or teeth where you made the discovery. (See page 32 for how to number teeth.) This will help you watch your progress later, as you develop your home treatment.

1) Are your gums shiney and smooth but have no stippling?
2) Are they swollen and puffy and reddish in color?

3) Can you see a white pus-like substance at the highest tip of the gum between the teeth (mostly around your front teeth)?

4) Does food easily get stuck or jammed into the gum between any of the teeth?

5) Do your gums bleed when brushed, when eating or any other time?

6) Do you have bad breath? Be honest; most bad breath is caused by gum infection. (Who knows, if you've had a hard time getting a chick or guy it could be gum infection — disease — and the resultant bad breath it can cause.)

7) Are your gums painful; a burning pain to the touch?

8) Do your gums feel hot; could you "melt snow" with your breath?

9) Have the gums receded (dropped below) the enamel (white part) of your tooth?

10) Have any of your teeth moved; are there now spaces where there were once none; are any teeth loose?

11) When looking behind the front teeth can you see what looks like a buildup of a stained substance (calculus or tartar) that is rough and hard to the touch?

12) Do you think you have a fever, sore throat, loss of energy, and been feeling flat out lousy?

Any of the above conditions indicate either actual disease or a condition existing just prior to the actual disease. It is important that you recognize the difference in your mouth between normal, healthy gums and diseased gums. If, after your first examination of your gums, you are not certain how to answer any of the above questions, stop, go back to the mirror, and look again. Better yet, ask your friend to look with you, then talk about it. In fact, get as many opinions as you can. Once you get your evaluation done, you can help someone else. Take your time. If you're still not sure where you stand, assume you have a pre-disease condition bordering on Stage One and follow my recommended treatment. Stages of gum disease are easier to distinguish as the condition gets worse, as you shall see.

Okay, got everything answered? Feel more at home with your gums? If you were one of the two percent of people whose gums have all of the five healthy characteristics and you gave no negative answers to the questions, you can celebrate now and go right on to the chapter on tooth exploration and evaluation. Congratulations! If not, stay with this chapter and read on until you find your niche.

Stage One — Pre-Disease, the twilight zone between healthy gums and disease. The key here is whether or not the gums have started bleeding yet. Sometimes the bleeding starts in localized areas and is hard to notice, like around one or two teeth. Thus, at first it is difficult to tell if they bleed or not. One way is to put your finger on the gum, put pressure inward and upward and see if any pus or blood comes out. If it doesn't always bleed when you push on it but does sometimes under the pressure of food or the toothbrush, you're in Stage One. If you are not sure about the bleeding, run a piece of dental floss (see page 72 for instructions) in between the two teeth and gently against the gum. If this procedure causes the gum to bleed, it means you're in Stage One.

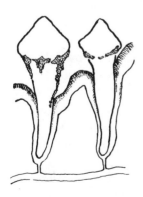

No matter what stage you find yourself in, the best way to see if you've evaluated yourself correctly is to see if you get quick results with the home care treatment found in this book. If you correctly follow my instructions on how to take care of your gums and have evaluated yourself as being in Stage One of gum disease, your gums should be back to a normal state of health in about three weeks time. Keep a constant check on them; it's a trip to watch the *miracle* of *self-healing*.

Secret Number Four: If it only takes three weeks to get gums healthy, it also only takes three weeks of non-care for them to get back to Stage One again.

Stage Two — Playing with Fire. If you have all the symptoms of Stage One and also have regular bleeding when you brush, bad breath and occasional pain or tenderness, you've just arrived at Stage Two. Too bad, the road back is a little tougher (but you can do it). Disease has now entered the picture, and it's either them little buggers or you — survival of the fittest. Anytime you suffer from *any* disease you are fighting for your life, for every disease can ultimately lead to death if left unchecked. The body's defensive mechanisms do their best to prevent and fight off disease. These heroic (especially when you give the body little or no help) efforts on the part of your body require energy – a great deal of energy. The more serious the disease the more energy needed.

The whole point here is that being high naturally means being able to draw on all your body's available energy and putting it to good use. Disease deprives you of this energy and no matter what level of consciousness you are on, disease and its subsequent drain on your energy source will bring you right down and down and down, until you stop it. Okay. That in itself is a good enough reason to get things in gear.

Approaching it a little differently and on a more physical level, the situation here can be compared to a cut, say, on your arm. If you take the proper steps as soon as you get cut, it will heal normally and you may not even know it was ever there. If you let it go and it gets infected, you'll have a much more difficult time getting it cured. Of course, the bigger the cut, the more difficult it is to cure. It is possible that if you let your cut go too far, it can actually get so infected (gangrene) that your finger, hand or arm (wherever the infection is) may have to be removed to keep the disease from spreading to the rest of your body and doing you in. (Death = bad karma.)

Same goes for your mouth; if you let it go now, the infection can get more severe and ultimately (with no care) the tooth, or teeth, will have to be removed to prevent the infection from also doing you in. End result is the same – same body, just a different place. Severe uncared-for gum infection can and has caused death.

So, if you've hit Stage Two, don't kid yourself anymore. What I've been talking about happens, maybe not to you, *yet*, but when 25 million Americans do not have a single tooth left in their heads, you'd better believe it can happen. Ask one of them, chances are you have an Aunt, Uncle or Grandparent who has no teeth; see what they have to say about it!

Best get it in gear, it isn't going to get better on its own. If you are in Stage Two, you should now supplement your home care with a dental visit. You can do a great deal on your own, but it is much easier to get your home care trip together with a cleaning. You should be able to get it back to normal in three or four weeks.

Hint: The longer your gums have been bleeding the more serious the condition.

Stage Three – You're in quicksand, best grab the rope now, if you've all the symptoms of Stages One and Two plus:

1) Your gums bleed most all the time.
2) You have bad breath.
3) You have painful burning gums.
4) The tips of the gums between the teeth are white and pus-like.
5) You may have a slight fever and you generally don't feel good.
6) Lots of crap and junk is piled up around your teeth.

You can now be sure the disease is eating your body, and digging it.

If you have most of the above symptoms you are being digested (eaten alive). If I haven't gotten through to you yet, you soon may not have any teeth or gums to worry about.

You are now diseased and need treatment immediately. Follow the directions in the home 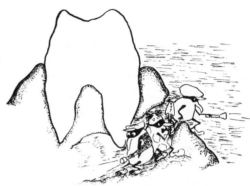 care section, page 77, and get an appointment with a dentist. Tell him it is an emergency — it is — and ask him to see you at once. If it's Sunday night, you'll survive until Monday, but the price you pay gets higher every day you wait. When he asks what is wrong, tell him you have a severe gum infection and need treatment immediately and that you are in pain. (If you have time, see my Survival Kit for the Dentist Office section on what to expect and how to handle your visit, page 143.)

You may not be able to tell if you are in late Stage Two, early Stage Three, or on the other end, late Stage Three, or early Four. No matter. That is just a problem of degree; the important thing is that you are diseased and don't have time to wait further.

In Stage Three, the bone that holds the teeth is diseased and is being dissolved by the infection process. You can't see this; it happens under the gums. Only the dentist can tell how much bone is lost by probing around and taking x-rays. (See x-rays, page 144.)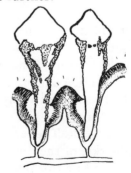

It will mean more work, but you can get back to a healthy state and keep yourself there. Allow at least six weeks from the time of your final cleaning at the dentist's to good gum health.

Secret Hint: *Do not let any dentist pull a tooth, or teeth* (wisdom teeth, page 173, are an exception) *unless he has completely explained the alternatives to your satisfaction.* He may make it sound less costly, but in the long run it is much better and cheaper to save a tooth, regardless of the immediate cost.

Many teeth that are surrounded by gum infection (disease) can be saved, even if it doesn't look like it to you; the body is an amazing healer. So tell him you absolutely want to save every one of your teeth.

Stage Four – "Help." In this stage, you've all the symptoms of Stages One, Two and Three plus *loose* teeth. You also probably have symptoms I haven't even heard of. You may not necessarily have a great deal of pain or suffering, so don't let that fool you into thinking that this Stage must be painful to be serious.

Secret Hint: The human body is an amazing creation of God and nature. It will resist and try to protect you from pain in spite of yourself. I've had patients whose disease had gone way past the point of saving their gums and teeth and yet they felt *no* severe pain. So, don't rely completely on pain to evaluate your condition, use *all* the symptoms I've listed to check yourself thoroughly.

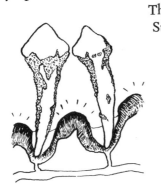

The simplest test for Stage Four is to place your fingers (looking into the mirror) on the suspected teeth (usually, at this stage, you can see some of the root of the tooth, it will give the appearance of having less gum and more teeth). See if the teeth move under *light* pressure. (The front teeth are suspect most often and are easier to examine, but Stage Four can involve any or all of your teeth.)

Make sure you can *see* the movement and not just feel it. The feel (touch) can be deceptive, as the skin of the fingers is moveable, so be careful not to confuse this finger movement with actual tooth movement.

If you find you are somewhere in this stage, it is your last stop, and unless you get it together and keep it together immediately, you won't have any teeth or gums to worry about. You may have had some teeth removed already; if so, now is the time to stop the disease from taking the rest of them, as it will if you let it go.

The help of a dentist is an absolute must in Stage Four. You have a very serious disease and you will not be able to cure it alone. You will need at least two cleanings to remove the tartar and possible gum surgery to remove severely infected gum tissue. You may end up losing some teeth, but again, make sure you have been convinced that they are not going to be pulled just because it may be cheaper at the moment. Don't panic, there is hope, if you've the desire!

The final stage is plates, dentures, false teeth, no teeth, or whatever else you want to call it, in the end it is all the same. (No choppers left.) Let's get it in gear! Be true to your teeth or they will be false to you!

Secret Hint: Most dentists are strange; for some reason (explained in chapter on "Dentist As Con Artist," page 196) they automatically assume that you don't and won't want to take care of your teeth. Because of this they think they'll be doing you a favor by pulling your teeth, assuming that because you haven't taken care of them in the past you won't in the future and will need them pulled out (extracted) later anyway. You must remember that painful teeth or gums does *not* mean you have to have the teeth pulled. Pain is only a *warning* system the body used to tell you something is wrong. It is not a diagnosis and you therefore cannot (nor should the dentist) use pain as an indication a tooth should be pulled. If he seems to, say thank you, get your coat and split to another dentist.

So, tell the dentist you want to save every tooth you can, for as long as possible, and that you have the *desire* and the *knowledge* to take care of them. Ask him for his help.

It is difficult to be anything but serious with gum disease. You should now be able to distinguish the normal gum from the abnormal gum and even the various stages of gum disease. Whatever the stage you are in, something can be done for you. The "Home Care" section of this book will tell you how to make home repairs.

3

EXAMINING YOUR TEETH

GETTING STARTED

I'm sure that in evaluating your gums you discovered some hard funny-looking whitish things sticking out of your gums. Isn't discovery far out? Well, these are called teeth.

The object of this chapter is the thorough examination of each and every one of them, following a procedure similar to but more complex than the one just used to explore your gums.

By the way, if you have not just finished reading the preceding chapter on how to examine and evaluate the condition of your gums, stop now, go back and do so. I'll wait for you to catch up before going ahead . . .

In this adventure on the teeth, we'll use all the same tools you became familiar with while working on your gums. That's a good thing, too, because you're going to have to use them more expertly than before, if you want to see everywhere around and between your teeth. So, get your light and your mirrors ready, and we'll begin.

When I said this examination will be more thorough than last chapter's, I meant you must look for smaller detail. Though you can begin this exploration anywhere in your mouth you wish, you must carefully check every tooth. I will outline one procedure to follow. You mavericks skip around if you must, but don't miss anything. First, I will tell you how to look, then what to look for. Best to read this chapter through to get the hang of it, then come back to "How To Look" when you and your mirror get it on.

HOW TO LOOK

First, brush your teeth in your normal way, then rinse very well. Always use lukewarm water to rinse (see "How To Brush Properly," page 67).

Then, run warm water over the mirror as before. This keeps your hot, excited, clammy breath from steaming it up.

Now, confront the large mirror and look yourself right in the mouth. Get as close as you can to the mirror while still being able to use the flashlight and focus your eyes clearly. You'll tilt your head down to check the lower, and back slightly to review the upper jaw.

LOWER JAW

Let's begin your examination with the last tooth on your left side, and look at the front or "outside" surfaces of all these lower teeth. Place your left index finger inside your mouth and gently pull your cheek and lip out, down, and away from your teeth. Your mouth should be open about half way. This will allow you to pull your cheek out further. (Oops, don't forget to wash your fingers.)

With your right hand, you can now shine your light at that back tooth on

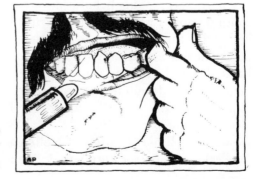

your left. Now move your finger slowly (slow enough to allow you to evaluate what you see) toward the front of your mouth, always holding your cheek clear of your teeth. The light should move in the same direction and at the same rate of speed. Keep moving your finger around toward your right side, holding back your cheek, stopping only at the last tooth on your right. Please notice that as you swing around the outside surfaces of your front teeth, you stop and change hands before proceeding to check out the teeth on

your right. This is a simple matter. Remove your left index finger from your mouth, put your light in that hand, insert your right index finger into your mouth, gently pull the right cheek away, focus your light on the lower front right teeth and continue on to that last tooth. With a little practice you'll get the hang of it. But patience, go slow, and enjoy!

Whenever you're ready, let's go on to view the backs or "inside" surfaces of the lower teeth. To do this smoothly will take skill and coordination with the dental mirror and the light. Also, at times you may feel you are running out of hands to hold everything with. But patience and practice; you'll master it.

Open wide and carefully place the dental mirror far enough into your mouth to enable you to see *behind* your last tooth. If you're now looking behind the last tooth on your right (as I am), you'll be holding the dental mirror in your left hand and visa versa. With your free hand, direct the light to shine into the dental mirror. If you learned this technique well in the "gums" chapter, you'll clearly see the back of the tooth — all lit up. No? Too Bad! Slowly adjust the pitch and yawl (angles) of the mirror until you do see it. Have you got it? Good!

To check the "insides" of the lower teeth, you can begin moving the mirror from the last tooth on the right side around toward the last tooth on the left side checking the backs of each of your lower teeth in turn. You can also use the mirror to hold your curious tongue back out of the way. Don't forget to keep shining the light *on* the mirror and moving light and mirror along together.

When you get to your front teeth, you may have to juggle the mirror to see the backs of them. This is usually where you see most of the garbage. After you have freaked out on the backs of the front teeth, you can now switch hands, mirror now in right and light in left, and move on left to finish looking at the insides of the lower left teeth. Remember to keep your chin tucked into your chest.

Finally, you can check out the tops of the lower teeth. If you keep your head down and your tongue out of the way, you most likely won't need the hand mirror. But take your time and look carefully here, too.

HINTS

1) If you have missing teeth, you may have to adjust the mirror to see the exposed backs of the teeth next to these spaces.
2) If you seem to have lots of spit in your mouth, you can wipe your teeth with a cloth or paper towel before continuing. This sometimes makes it easier to see.

UPPER JAW

The basic procedure here is about the same, but everything is a little harder to see. Again, let's start with the left side and examine the front or "outside" surfaces of these upper teeth. Tilt your head back, but not so far back you'll have to strain your eyes. To see the back teeth on the upper jaw, your mouth will have to be almost closed, because your lower jaw bone will obstruct your line of vision if your mouth is wide open.

Use the mirror in your right hand to hold back your left cheek and, placing it so the mirror's glass is facing the outside of your last left tooth, shine the light into the mirror and view a never-before-seen tooth! You can use the mirror like this until you get to the front teeth, which you can see without it. As you move around to the right side of your upper jaw, you can switch the mirror to the right hand and the flash-light to the left. View the out-sides of the right side teeth in the same manner, adjusting the angle of the mirror as needed to see clearly.

While the mirror is still in the right hand, position it so you can see behind your last upper right tooth. Then, switch hands and take a peek be-hind your last upper left tooth. You can also check your upper wisdom teeth now.

After checking both upper wisdom teeth, you can begin checking the "insides" of your upper teeth. I prefer to continue from where I left off — namely from the last upper right tooth working toward the

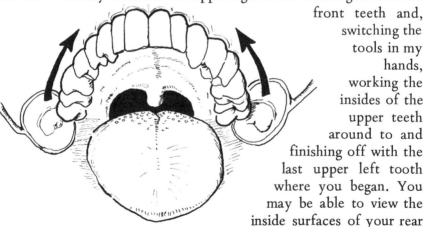

front teeth and, switching the tools in my hands, working the insides of the upper teeth around to and finishing off with the last upper left tooth where you began. You may be able to view the inside surfaces of your rear teeth without using the dental mirror, but as you move toward the front teeth, you will have to switch from direct viewing (i.e., shining your light directly on the tooth's surface) to refractive viewing (i.e., shining your light into the dental mirror, as before) in order to see everything you need to see.

Okay, done the insides? All that remains is to check the "tops" of the upper teeth. For these, too, you'll need to use your dental mirror and light. Go slowly and look carefully in the natural crevices of the big rear molars.

There, you've done it. With a few more practice runs, this business will seem natural to you and you will begin to get through. Always go slow, don't rush, and remember to:

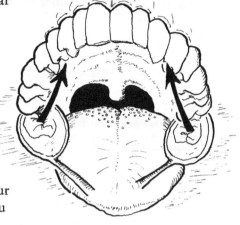

1) see all the parts of every tooth, and
2) follow some order in your exams which insures that you don't skip any teeth.

WHAT TO LOOK FOR

Briefly, as you follow the above procedure, you should be looking at your teeth to determine:
1) How many do you have?
2) Are there cavities in them?
3) Are there broken or lost fillings?
4) Is there stain?
5) What is the general shape, form and size of your teeth?
6) Is there food on your teeth?
7) Is there tartar on your teeth?
8) Are there spaces between the teeth?
9) Are there broken, chipped or cracked teeth?.
10) Is your bite irregular?
11) Are any teeth crooked?
12) What is the condition of your wisdom teeth?

Obviously, this is such a comprehensive list you will not be able to check for all of these things on each tooth on your first exam. Try checking all of your teeth first just to see if my instructions make any sense to you, and to see if you can see all the surfaces of every tooth. Then redo the exam, checking for part of the above list, and do it yet again to complete the list. If it seems too much to do all this at one sitting, schedule yourself to do it over a period of several days. Whatever. Believe that, like anything else, once you have a little practice, the whole routine will come naturally and easily. Persevere through this early period of resistance. The benefits will be yours!

A good way to remember the stuff you find on this little exam is to mark it down on a tooth chart, which will help you locate the tooth, the specific part of the tooth with the problem, and the nature of the problem. For instance, if you find a cavity on the "top" surface of your lower second-from-the-rear molar, you could mark it down with an "X." Use any system you like; so long as it works, it's fine. Here's a couple of sets of choppers to serve as tooth charts; one for the upper and one for the lower.

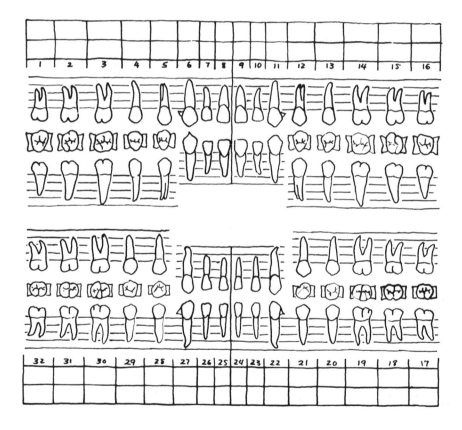

Most dentists use the same numbering system, and if you use it, you will be able to communicate to them in their language. The upper right last tooth is Number One; the enclosed drawing will show you where to go from there.

Now, let's take a more detailed look at each of the kinds of problems you're likely to find.

1: NUMBER OF TEETH

Count all of your teeth; you may have done that when examining the gums. Remember you should have thirty-two, counting your four possibly hidden wisdom teeth. If you have them all, you can skip ahead. If not, pay very close attention. Look to see:

a) if you have less than twenty-eight teeth

b) if the teeth immediately behind the missing spaces have moved or look like they are moving into the empty space. This seems to happen more often and more seriously on the lower jaw. If you see this, ask your dentist what can be done, for it can really mess up your biting and cause mucho problems. It may be easier to see this by turning your face slightly sideways.

c) if a lower tooth (or teeth) is missing. If so, check the upper to see if the upper tooth (or teeth) above the empty space has grown or is growing into the void left on the lower. You can do this by closing your teeth together, as you would normally. Then, with the fingers of your left or right hand, separate your lips and see if the upper tooth protrudes past the rest of the upper ones next to it and looks like it is growing into the empty space (see drawing). Any missing teeth will have to be replaced, and the sooner the better.

If any of your teeth have begun to move or grow into a space where a tooth was pulled, your problem is more serious than if teeth adjoining such a space seem to be normal and upright. Either way, unless you have this tooth or teeth replaced, *you will lose more teeth.* There are no other possibilities. So, read my guidebook for dealing with the dentist and hie thee thither!

2: SHAPE, FORM AND SIZE OF TEETH

There are a wide variety of sizes, forms and shapes found in nature. This, for the most part, means simply that God or Nature doesn't like doing everyone up exactly the same way.

We have been conditioned to believe that unless we have "perfect" teeth we are ugly and should somehow be ashamed and embarrassed for them. This is nonsense. You have heard that beauty is only skin deep. The same idea holds true for teeth. So don't worry if you have a crooked tooth or two. As I will point out, all it will mean is that the more your teeth differ from "the ideal," the more difficult it will be to keep them clean.

Dentists say that their *normal, ideal, tooth standard* is found in only 2% of the population. You do not have to be a math genius to figure out that it may be ideal, but that 2% is surely not average. It is wise though, to become aware of extreme exceptions, so if after checking the drawings (page 33) you find that your teeth are really too far from that ideal, you should then ask your dentist what he thinks can be done. If you have the money, there are many corrections that can be made. If you don't, well there are still some things you can do. I will tell you more about what can be done in the chapter titled "Survival in The Dental Office," page 143.

3: SPACES BETWEEN THE TEETH

There are natural and unnatural spaces found in the mouth. Most natural ones are harmless and you need not be concerned. This is not true of the unnatural ones. The *unnatural* spaces can best be felt rather than seen. For example, if after eating (especially meat and other fibrous foods, like rope or string) you feel something stuck between your teeth, that even a good brushing will not remove, you can be pretty certain that you have an *unnatural* space or spaces. It may also feel as if something is wedged between your teeth, pushing them apart. After a few days, the food stuck between your teeth begins to break down and usually starts to smell rotten; always nice for your breath! I've been through that trip myself, and it is a pain. It must be fixed, as it can help cause both decay and gum disease. Until you can get in to have this done, dental floss will be a big help to you in removing the food (see chapter on "Home Care," page 66).

Natural spaces can and often do exist. Nature works its wonders in many ways, and often it may be beneficial to have a space between teeth, especially in children. Normally, natural spaces are wide enough apart so that food will not get stuck in between them, and this is fine, as long as the space did not result from having a tooth pulled or a filling lost, which is not natural. If you have all of your teeth and you do find these spaces, just make sure you check the areas out well. Look to see if you have any sign of gum disease. If all looks well, don't worry. Again, if you are not positive, have the dentist check it out for you to be sure.

4: CROWDED OR CROOKED TEETH

This is an easy one to recognize. About 98% of us have at least one or more crooked teeth. Most of us will have more than one. This condition causes one or more of the following problems:

a) Difficulty in keeping your teeth clean.
b) It can mess up your bite and cause chewing problems.
c) It can cause speech problems.
d) You may not think they look too good.
e) In small children it can cause their permanent teeth to come in all screwed up. (Parents should keep an eyeball out for this. It could save you thousands ($) in braces.)

There can be many causes for crowded teeth. Some people are unfortunate enough to suffer from more than one of the causes. Some of these are — and you mothers and expectant mothers will do a lot for your children by paying close attention to these:

a) thumb sucking
b) sucking on poorly designed nipples — man-made bottles, not God's
c) some children push out their teeth with their tongue when nervous
d) birth defects, or other inherited abnormalities

e) having too much pressure on the developing child's facial region, like sleeping always on the same side, or holding your child in the same position all the time.

There will be more about kids in the chapter on your kid's trip, page 104.

Orthodontists, the dentists who are into straightening teeth, can fix this, in most cases, for anyone. Thus, you can be almost any age and still get your teeth straightened if that's your trip. So, although my rap on orthodontists is in the chapter on kids, don't take that to mean that you're excluded if you're past puberty. Just turn to that section and realize that what it says there applies as much to adults as it does to children.

5: FUNNY-TYPE BITES (JAW CLOSURES)

Many of you have this problem, whether you are aware of it or not. Bite problems can range from minor problems, involving only an improperly placed filling (which is very easily corrected), to major ones which involve all of your teeth and even muscles operating the jaws. Things to watch and feel for here are:

a) If when you bite down without food in your mouth you seem to be hitting first on just one side of your mouth,

b) or if again when closing you feel like you are hitting first on just one tooth or the filling in a tooth.

c) If your teeth seem to be sore for no reason and are especially tender and sore when you chew.

d) If the muscles toward the back of your jaw are sore, possibly making it difficult to open and close your jaws without discomfort (but this could also be wisdom teeth).

e) If when opening your jaws you hear a cracking or popping sound.

f) If your jaw slides out of its socket when you open wide.

g) If you notice you seem to be chewing differently than you used to chew.

h) If when you check the teeth with the light and the mirror shows you a shiny *wear spot* on any of your fillings. This shows up most clearly on silver fillings, as you'll see a bright spot on an otherwise dull filling.

i) If you notice *any* change in the way your teeth come together. A simple way to test this is to lightly tap your teeth together, trying to close as far back as you can and trying to touch all the back teeth at the same time. If the sound you hear is *even* and it feels like you are evenly touching *all* teeth while tapping lightly, you probably are in good shape. Assuming, of course, that you do not have any of the other problems listed above.

It is important to verify any suspicions with your dentist, for it could be something very minor and if caught early enough, it could be easily corrected. On the other hand, if you let it go, the problem could become very serious and the average dentist may not be qualified to work on it. Advanced bite problems are one of the *least* understood aspects of dentistry. So don't let it go to the advanced stage. Most bite problems start as simple problems and get complex through neglect. You could thus pay a very heavy price for delaying its correction. If it is determined that you have an advanced condition, ask your local dentist to recommend you to a specialist in bite problems. Do not let him experiment with you unless he promises to get results. Once you ask him to commit himself as to the outcome, he may think twice about using you as a guinea pig. This is one good way of making sure he really knows what he is doing, and doesn't just think or hope he does. Whatever, this is one dental problem that should not be put off.

6: STAINS

Stains on teeth are caused by outside sources, and work on your teeth from the outside. You may confuse some stains for decay, but point them out to your dentist and he will verify this for you. Stains are most often found in the same areas that decay is found, so you could very easily have both. Thus, if you see a hole with stain around it, you can bet you have just discovered two for the price of one. The evident lesson is that the better you take care of your mouth, the less stain you will have. Generally stains are harmless, if stain is all you have; it's an aesthetic problem. The point is to use stain as a guide to how well you are taking care of your mouth. Normally, a routine office cleaning will remove most stains, but always ask your dentist to verify all of your discoveries.

Stains can be many colors — yellow, orange, black, brown, red and even green. Nice earthy colors, right? This is what these stains are all about:

a) Natural Stains

The general rule here is that the teeth start out bluish white when you are young, and get yellow to greyish-yellow as you get older. So, if you used to have white teeth and they are now yellow, don't freak out, you are just facing the thing most of us hide — ageing. Here is how it happens.

The white part of your teeth (enamel) gets worn with age, and as it can actually be seen through (transparent), the more enamel that is worn off means the more the yellow portion of the tooth (dentin), which is underneath the enamel, can show through. Thus, as enamel wears off, the tooth gets more yellow.

This is normal unless it wears off too rapidly. The dentist should be asked about this if you think yours is wearing off too fast. (There are some rare diseases that can cause the enamel to wear too fast, or you could be using too much of an abrasive toothpaste. See my rap on toothpaste in the "Home Equipment" section of this book.)

The tops of the teeth normally wear much faster, as they are always being chewed on, especially if your diet is very abrasive — like chewing on beetle nuts or sand. Therefore, do not be alarmed too much if the tops look a little yellow. But again, check this with the dude in the white coat. You don't want them worn off completely while you are still walking around using them.

b) Green

This color stain is most often found on children's teeth. Usually seen at and around the point where the tooth and gum meet, it is more easily seen on the front teeth. This is not serious and can usually be removed by a simple dental cleaning. It is caused by a membrane that helps form the teeth and happens to stick around after they erupt (break through the gum). If you see this stain, point it out to the dentist.

c) Black Lines

If you do not smoke, are a woman and really take good care of your gums and teeth, and *still* have a black line around your teeth (mostly on the backs of the teeth, down by the gum) you have one of those things that dentistry does not know about. Nice, huh? But do not worry, it doesn't cause any damage, even though it usually comes back a few days after its removal. It is my personal opinion that this phenomenon is related to your diet. Experiment by investigating with your diet to see if you can come across anything that might be the cause of it. Don't worry ... and keep on brushing. I'm sure that by having a good cleaning and then maintaining good home care you will keep it off.

d) Brownish

This stain usually is caused by smoking (cigarettes, cigars or grass). Make sure your dentist is not a narcotics agent, because if you tell him you do not smoke cigarettes and he sees grass stains, well ...! Also, no sense leaving tell-tale evidence around; this in itself is good enough reason for brushing. This stain can also be caused by chewing tobacco or drinking coffee or tea. Usually the stain is most severe in dirty mouths, for it also stains the tartar (solidified food) that sticks to your teeth much more and much faster than it will stain a nicely cared-for tooth or teeth. I have patients who will smoke a lot of whatever they can get their hands on, but they also get off on taking care of their teeth and consequently have very little or no stain of this type visible.

e) Orange to Orange-Red

This is the normal color of down to earth natural stain which you get if you do not drink or smoke or do any of the things that cause abnormal staining (that which masks the normal orange stain). Nothing to feel that good about, though, for almost all stain means you are not doing the job you should be doing on your mouth. Think about it — do you want your teeth to be orange all of your life?

f) Dark Grey, Yellow, Brown or Black

There is another type of discoloration that you all should be very much aware of since it is very common, especially in children. The discoloration can range from grey to yellow to brown or black. What is important to note is whether this change in color *recently* occurred, and whether the tooth used to be white. It can be caused by certain well-placed blows and it does not necessarily need to be a powerful one. This particular discoloration means that you have a dead or dying tooth. Almost any blow can kill the nerve of the tooth. In the process of dying, the tooth changes color. Thus, if you recently fell off your horse onto your face, or if your best friend's best friend just punched you in the mouth, you may be noticing a change of color in your teeth. Young children are always taking weird falls, so you mothers be aware of their teeth changing color.

This discoloration is one of your dental emergencies, and unless it is corrected by the dentist, it can lead to serious abcesses (infections) of the teeth and can cause the tooth or teeth to be pulled. Check this with your dentist as soon as possible.

g) Too much fluoride can also cause the tooth to change color. This abnormal amount of fluoride can cause the teeth to have dense looking (cloudy and opaque) areas usually colored yellow or brown. Although this is somewhat unsightly-looking, you won't find decay in any of the teeth. It means that the person has received too much fluoride, usually from the water supply. This situation is found most often in the southwestern United States, where the fluoride content of natural water is very high. There are also certain other abnormalities that can cause this type of discoloration, so it's good to verify your suspicions with the dentist.

The use of fluoride is at best a controversial subject; one I feel is important enough to rate a chapter by itself. So, rather than digressing onto fluoride here, I refer you to the fluoride chapter. Now, back to the teeth.

7: JUNK ON YOUR TEETH

If you do not brush your teeth properly, you will begin to notice a buildup of a hard yellowish material, especially on the backs of your front teeth. This junk may look innocent, but it is a killer of teeth and an enemy to your gums. Here are the things to look out for if you want to keep your mouth in good shape:

a) Materia Alba

This is the dentist's nice, sterile, sophisticated term for the garbage you leave between your teeth and around your teeth where they meet the gum after you finish eating. You can recognize it because it looks soft and mushy and is whitish grey in color. It resembles particles of white bread chewed up.

While *materia alba* is in its soft, mushy stage, it can be scraped off your teeth with your fingernail. But within one to three days it becomes hard enough that you can no longer scrape it off. In its hardened stage, it is called *tartar* or *calculus.*

b) Tartar or Calculus

There are other dental words for *materia alba* after it has been left in your mouth long enough to combine with the many minerals, germs and other things found in your spit. In one to three days it becomes very sticky and extremely hard, binding to your teeth like epoxy glue! It is at this point that you can best recognize it, for it cannot be removed by scraping with your fingernail, nor by brushing.

b) *Tartar* and *calculus* usually become stained (yellowish), and are rough to the touch of both finger and tongue. It is most readily seen on the backs of the lower front teeth, but can also be found around every tooth, close to the gums (irregular in shape and rough to the touch). In advanced cases you would have to be blind to miss it.

If you do find tartar or calculus on your teeth, understand that it will not go away by itself. In fact, it just keeps growing and growing, much like an ant hill. This junk is the number one contributor to gum destruction and subsequent loss of teeth. Once you get it, only a cleaning at the dentist's office will take it off — short of having your mouth sandblasted, that is.

It is a fact, my friends, that tartar is mainly what helped 25 million Americans to lose all their teeth. That amounts to around 800 million lost teeth, and that's a mountain of them. All this happened because these people failed to remove food particles from their mouth after eating. Am I talking about you?

Some people seem to naturally form this tartar faster than others. If you are one of these people, you must be more careful as to your diet and the home care of your teeth. (See my chapters on "Diet and Home Care" for more information.) But tartar is not — I repeat — *not normal;* any amount that you form is bad, and it must be removed to prevent problems with your gums and teeth. Here are a few things that will cause you to form more tartar at a faster rate:

1) Smoking: This means smoking anything — tobacco, grass or dried cabbage leaves. Anything smoked will irritate your mouth, and it is generally true that any substance that will

41

irritate your salivary (spit) glands can make you form more tartar — but *only if you leave food in your mouth to allow it to form tartar.*

2) Refined and Processed Foods: briefly, refined and processed foods tend to stick to your teeth much more than do natural and raw foods. This, combined with the fact that you may not have been taking good care of your teeth, means more tartar formed at a faster rate. (More about this in my chapter on diet.)

3) Crowded and/or Crooked Teeth: being more difficult to clean, more food will stick in areas hard to reach because of overlapping teeth. Thus, more tartar forms at a faster rate.

Except for rare birth defects, accidents, and rare inherited defects, every dental problem that you now suffer, or have suffered in the past, was caused by not removing leftover food from your mouth and teeth after eating. Leftover food particles (call it *materia alba* or just plain *garbage*) not only leads to the buildup of tartar, it is also a prime breeding ground for unwanted, and often dangerous bacteria. This goes for everybody you know — your friends, your husband, your senator, your wife, your lover, your kids . . .

8: CAVITIES IN YOUR TEETH

Cavities are normally found in *three* areas:
1) in between the teeth
2) where the gum and tooth meet
3) in the grooves on the tops of the teeth

Look closely. Cavities are caused by decay (rot), or whatever you'd like to call it. All cavities first show a small hole, usually stained a blackish color. You should be made aware that the hole on the outside is much smaller than the hole being made inside the tooth. Since large cavities endanger the tooth itself, eating away the tooth until an abcess occurs (disease), and since there is no known process to reverse the growth of a cavity once it begins, you'll have to have all cavities filled. Catch them early; the fillings are smaller and cheaper. Better still, once you have this batch filled at the dentist, prevent their future occurrence in your mouth.

You cannot give too much attention to examining your teeth. Take your time. Mark carefully on your tooth chart the location of each cavity you find. It is your mouth and no one should know or care for it better than you, okay?

9: BROKEN OR LOST FILLINGS

Depending on their age, how carefully they were put in and how well you've taken care of them, fillings can have an indeterminate age, but they can fracture or fall out as they wear in your mouth, especially the silver and plastic ones. Often there is no pain, so you may not know they are gone. Some fillings, the old fashioned white ones in the front teeth, will eventually dissolve in the spit from your mouth. Thus, after a time a hole will develop and food will get stuck in the hole. If you see a hole that has a well-defined outline, or perhaps one in which one-half of the filling is left, it must be repaired. (Note: Sometimes it is best first to dry the areas you are looking at with a towel or cloth so that you can better see what's going on in there. You may also discover that food sometimes gets stuck in these holes, making them harder to see. Therefore, it is important to brush and rinse well before beginning this exam.)

Keep a sharp eye out for cracked fillings. A crack in the filling (almost always happens with silver ones) can be seen as a line running across the top of the filling.

Some chipped fillings, if they are not too serious, can be smoothed out and given added life. Ask the dentist if he feels yours should be repaired or replaced.

Almost every broken filling should be replaced. A general rule of thumb is that the larger the break, the more likely are the chances it should be replaced.

10: BROKEN, CHIPPED OR CRACKED TEETH

You should now know, by looking at the drawings of natural, ideal teeth what the shape of each tooth looks like. Go over every tooth, starting with Number One, comparing yours with the drawing. If one or any of yours looks different, there is a good chance you have a broken or chipped tooth. Keep in mind that this can happen without any pain to you, and thus unless you check it out, it may go unnoticed. Mark down any findings and report them to the dentist. The best guideline for looking for fractured teeth is to check the fronts of the teeth, and look especially hard at any teeth that may be sensitive to hot, cold or sweets. (Bad, sweets are bad!)

Cracks and fractures may or may not be difficult for you to see. If it is a big crack or fracture, you will readily be able to find it, but there often exist very minute cracks that are very hard to find, even for the dentist. These little ones are most often recognized by the symptoms they exhibit rather than their visual appearance. What to feel for is sensitivity in a tooth that seems to be perfectly okay. In other words, if you or even the dentist can find no logical or apparent reason for the sensitivity of the tooth, you should look for a small crack. For some reason, most dentists do not include this in their list of examination possibilities. For sure, do *not* let him tell you that the sensitivity is all your imagination. It is the dentist's job to tell you *why* something is happening, not to convince you that you're crazy and what you feel isn't real; most dentists are insensitive enough as it is.

If you find it difficult to examine your own teeth for cracks because of too much moisture in your mouth, dry off your teeth by damping them with a piece of paper towel. And bear in mind that if you do find cracked or damaged teeth, you should not despair; but you *should* get yourself to the dentist's office. These teeth can be nicely repaired if you take your mouth to the man in the white jacket soon enough.

11: EROSION AND ABRASION

These terms simply mean that your teeth are being worn abnormally by various things that have no business being in your mouth. It could also mean that things that should be put in your mouth are being used improperly. End results being about the same – not too good. What actually is erosion and abrasion, and what causes it?

    a) Erosion

This is abnormal wear due to action by a *chemical* process. This means you do not have much to do with it other than putting something in your mouth – but that's enough. A good example of this would be lemon sucking. Lemons, as well as other citrus fruits, contain a natural acid in their juices. This acid is strong enough, in almost every case I've seen, to dissolve the enamel and dentin of your teeth completely away. I have seen advanced cases where the tooth was nearly worn in half; somewhat like a river does to rocks over the years. Of course, it happens much faster in the mouth, and if you are a moderate to heavy lemon sucker, it could happen in just a few years. Some of the things to watch for here would be:

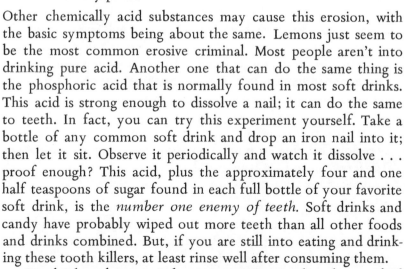

1) If the gum gives the appearance of having *receded* down the tooth, thus showing more tooth than before.
2) If your teeth seem to be getting yellow at a very rapid rate, particularly where the tooth meets the gum.
3) If your teeth are sensitive to foods or drink or brushing, again particularly by the gum line. Sweet things really seem to irritate this condition and can even be very painful.

Other chemically acid substances may cause this erosion, with the basic symptoms being about the same. Lemons just seem to be the most common erosive criminal. Most people aren't into drinking pure acid. Another one that can do the same thing is the phosphoric acid that is normally found in most soft drinks. This acid is strong enough to dissolve a nail; it can do the same to teeth. In fact, you can try this experiment yourself. Take a bottle of any common soft drink and drop an iron nail into it; then let it sit. Observe it periodically and watch it dissolve . . . proof enough? This acid, plus the approximately four and one half teaspoons of sugar found in each full bottle of your favorite soft drink, is the *number one enemy of teeth*. Soft drinks and candy have probably wiped out more teeth than all other foods and drinks combined. But, if you are still into eating and drinking these tooth killers, at least rinse well after consuming them.

But back to lemons, I do not mean to say that they are bad for you; the fact is they are very good for you, but only when the juice gets to your stomach. Lemon juice is not meant to be left in your mouth, as you can see, and it is a good policy to get into the habit of rinsing after drinking or sucking *anything.*

Another fairly valuable aid in detecting both the erosion I've just talked about and the abrasion I will shortly speak of is your visit to the dentist. When the dentist starts poking around with his little poker (explorer) and he touches one or more of these worn areas, you will immediately feel a sensation that some of you recognize as pain. Thus, if your own home examination happened to miss erosion, you may discover it at the dental office. Tell the doc at once, in case your scream did not already inform him. Be sure you tell him, because in its early stages it is easier to feel it than see it. Many times this can be corrected by simply finding out and eliminating what caused it in the first place. When you catch this in the early stages, there are also a few special kinds of toothpastes that can help prevent the sensitivity, either *Sensodyne* or *Thermodent.* If it has gone too far for this cure, you may have to have these areas filled. But first try eliminating the *cause*, for unless you eliminate the cause, it will in time also dissolve the fillings you get to replace the eroded area! Always keep in mind that the best and easiest way to tackle any problem is to get to its *source.*

b) Abrasion
This can happen anywhere in the mouth and it can be caused by anything that exerts its action by *mechanical* means. The basic principle here is like that of sandpaper rubbing on wood. Very abrasive sandpaper rubbing on soft wood will wear the wood very rapidly. Same goes for the teeth. If you use something very abrasive in your mouth, it will also wear your teeth, the rate of wear depending on how strong your teeth are, how often you do it, and how abrasive the material you are using is.

The end result is very similar to that of erosion, so you can look for the same symptoms and signs that I mentioned with erosion, keeping in mind that you may have to look toward a *different* cause of the problem. Some of the more common causes of abrasion are:

1) Brushing the wrong way
I have seen cases where wrong brushing has worn teeth in half. It looks as if a super small Paul Bunyan got into your mouth and chopped your tooth like he would a tree. This can happen with just about any toothpaste substance you may use, but it happens much faster if the paste is very abrasive (more on this in chapter

on tools, page 81). It is of value for you to note that you should never brush sideways when brushing. This is what I mean by brushing the wrong way: teeth should always be brushed in the direction that the teeth grow; upward on the lowers and downward on the uppers.

As this particular type of abrasion is very common and being that I also have suffered from it, I will explain to you how it takes place. Hopefully this will give you a better idea as to how to avoid it.

The closer the enamel gets to the gum, the thinner it becomes. This enamel ends at the same point at which the gum normally attaches to the tooth. A simple drawing will show this point. The enamel has a type of grain to it, like wood. The tooth is more able to resist wear that moves up and down, and less able to resist wear that moves against it (in a sideways manner). Thus, by brushing your teeth sideways, you are not only brushing against the grain of the tooth (which causes it to wear faster), but also heavily wearing the areas where the enamel is the thinnest (closest to the gum). Along with this, you push the gum out of the way and eventually break it loose from the point where it is attached. Thus, you are in effect pushing the gum further and further down the tooth. When this happens, you expose the sensitive and much softer part of the tooth (dentin) to the abrasive action of the paste and brush. As this part of the tooth wears much faster than the white part, it can be "chopped" through with improper brushing. As is the case with erosion, the tooth is now usually very sensitive to foods and liquids, especially sweets. Again, this should stop when you begin to brush the right way. (See chapter on "Home Care" for more information.)

2) Toothpicks

If used all of the time, toothpicks can push the gum down between the teeth and wear the tooth down in the same manner as the toothbrush does when used in the wrong way. I do not see as many abuses with the toothpick as I do with the

47

brush, but I have seen enough to make note of it here. If you use toothpicks it is easy to discover the abuses caused by tooth-pick abrasion; just pull one out from between your teeth and look into the "void." The drawing will show you what advanced toothpick abuse looks like. By pushing the gum down and wearing the tooth and gum away you create new areas where food can stick. An occasional use of the pick is okay as you may be stuck somewhere without your brush. But, as you will see, there are other and better ways of keeping your pearly whites clean. *"ABUSE AND YE SHALL LOSE."*

3) Thread biting and Hairpin biting

Abuse of these two items is very easy to spot. Thread biting almost always occurs on the top part of the front teeth. The effects of thread biting are difficult to miss — especially if you know you bite thread. This is not good for your teeth. That seemingly small notch you have created can set up a fracture line that if hit the right way can split your tooth down the middle and

possibly require it to be pulled. It may also cause the teeth involved to become sensitive. Best treatment here is to have your dentist smooth and polish the notched areas, usually most *good* dentists will do this free of charge. If you stop biting thread, but if he charges you . . . well, grin and bear. It is much wiser and in the long run much cheaper to get a pair of scissors and use them.

For you bobby pin freaks: Opening bobby pins with your front teeth can cause the same type of notching as does thread biting. The problems caused by these "hair holders" got so outrageous that some time ago the dental association had the bobby pin manufacturers put plastic tips on the ends of the pins. It seems to have helped alot, but there are still some who insist on removing the rubber tips, and thus we still see this notching problem. So, if your teeth are notched, use your fingernails to open your bobby pins. And next time you see your dentist, have him smooth and polish your notches for you.

4) Pipestem Biters

This wear takes place on the front teeth
— mostly on the front teeth of the lower
jaw. It is easily recognized by the
wearing of usually one tooth, which
is also generally quite stained. This
staining and wear is not good for
your teeth, and can cause them to be
sensitive, to chip, or even to split
down the middle. You may not care,
but it looks bad, too. As we all know
that tobacco is addicting, I am not asking you to stop smoking a pipe; just try holding it with your hand, or maybe get your lower tooth capped in steel! Whatever, just know that your tooth probably wishes you'd treat it better. Pipe smoking is very distinguished looking; a notched, stained tooth is not.

5) The Odds and Ends of Wear

There are other types of wear and other things that cause it. Some of these are beetle nuts, chewing tobacco, almost all seeds and nuts. If these are chewed all the time and over a long period, check for wear on the tops of your teeth. Even occupational hazards, such as working in a sand factory, etc., can cause wear by exposing your teeth to the abrasive material you work with. When you eat the abrasives mingle with your food and wear down your teeth at an abnormally fast rate. If you notice any teeth that look as if they are wearing too rapidly, it will benefit you to ask your dentist to help you get to the cause, especially if you happen to have soft teeth, since they will wear much faster given the same conditions. This normally is just a matter of checking out your habits, then finding and eliminating the culprit causing the damage.

These are the last teeth in your mouth, assuming you have not had any pulled. I have already talked about these somewhat but mostly as they relate to gum infection and the problems this infection can cause you. About 60% of the population should have their wisdom teeth checked, if not pulled, immediately. Here's why I say this about wisdom teeth.

a) They are softer and decay faster.

b) They are much harder to clean and thus decay faster — logical, huh?

c) They usually do not come all the way in and it is much easier to get gum infections around them.

d) They usually are of no value to you because they do not come in straight and thus cannot meet with the opposing tooth to allow you to use them chewing.

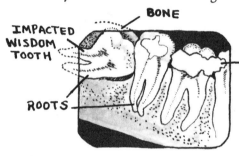

e) They can, when they come in at a bad angle (and they almost always do) move your other teeth and really make your teeth crooked. (This is very important for those of you who may have spent thousands of dollars on braces; if you do not have your wisdom teeth taken out, you may as well have flushed your money down the john! The wisdom teeth will move your other teeth in a short period of time. *Words of Wisdom:* I hope your orthodontist explained this to you.)

f) They can cause the back of the tooth in front of the wisdom tooth to rot.

g) The irregular positioning of the wisdom teeth can cause you to bite your cheek or tongue, and this is not only irritating, but painful.

h) They can — for all you lovers, particularly — cause very bad breath by allowing the grunge (food, spit and germs) a place to hide out and produce their foul odor.

i) They can mess your teeth up enough to cause your bite to change.

Is this list long enough to convice you to have your wisdom teeth pulled?

If you are not one of the 2% who were lucky enough to get good, sound, straight, healthy wisdom (ignorant) teeth, you'd better go see your oral surgeon about having them taken out.

13: GRINDING YOUR TEETH

The dentist will most likely insist on using the term *bruxism.* Anyway, when he says you *bruxate,* he means you are grinding your teeth too much. Most people who grind their teeth are not aware of it, for this usually takes place while they are asleep. So, unless you can talk someone into staying up all night and watching you, you will have to rely on other means of discovery. No matter how you find out, it is definitely not a good trip, and can cause a multitude of problems.

When you are not chewing, the teeth should not be touching, because after doing all of that chewing and biting all day, they need to rest. So, if you grind your teeth, knowingly or unknowingly, the teeth are not allowed to get the rest they require. It would be as if you worked twenty four hours a day, every day. That, you know, is not how it is meant to be and you couldn't do it very long without having some serious physical and psychological problems. Think about it — working one hundred sixty eight hours per week! Same goes for grinding your teeth all of the time, and here is a little taste of what happens:

a) The muscles you use to open and close your mouth will get *very, very, extremely* tired.

b) The teeth are held into the jaw bone by little fibers of gristle-like material (called periodontal ligaments) and when you keep pushing on the teeth, via constantly grinding, this gristle also gets very tired. The results being that your teeth and your jaw can become very sore. Unless this gets corrected, it gets worse.

Some of the suspected causes of grinding are:

a) A dental defect (bad filling) that can usually be quickly remedied.

b) Bad dreams. Since most grinding takes place while sleeping, it makes sense that some grinding may be your way of expressing fear and anger while dreaming.

Whatever the cause of it, it can turn into a nasty dental problem and can cause you to *wear* away your teeth, change your natural bite, loosen your teeth, and in extreme cases can cause much damage to the bone that holds your teeth in your jaw. So, look to see if the tops of the teeth are worn flat, ask yourself if your muscles are sore and if your teeth feel tired.

If you suspect such a problem it would be very wise to consult with your dentist and if you two cannot discover the cause of the problem in a reasonable amount of time, ask him to refer you to a "bite specialist." These guys are rare, but they are around. If you know that the grinding is caused by emotional conflicts, a visit to a psychiatrist may be of value to you.

14: PARTIAL PLATE OR PARTIAL DENTURE WEARERS

The best advice I can give you is to check to see whether your partial is ill-fitting or broken. Also, and very important, carefully check the teeth that hold your partial to see if they are loose or decayed, and if the gums around the teeth are diseased.

You will, of course, know if it is loose or broken, but if the other conditions I've mentioned also exist, you'd best get right in and have everything repaired and your partial remade.

Partials are designed to fit what existed when they were made and if your mouth conditions have changed, it must be remade. Check around and see if you can find a dentist who specializes in making partial dentures. Most dentists know very little about dentures, anyway.

15: FULL PLATES OR DENTURES

You will be a good judge of bad plates. If they are loose, sore, continually needing "relining," and are difficult to eat with, you need new ones.

Here again, most dentists don't know or don't take the time to make good dentures — and you are the one who suffers. So, going to a specialist is far and away the best thing you could do for your mouth and health. A specialist may charge a little more and take a little longer to make them, but the results, especially if you've suffered through lousy plates, more than make up for it. Until you've worn well-made dentures, you'll never know how much better they can be.

SUMMARY

Once you know how to recognize normal as well as abnormal conditions in your mouth, you can recognize any changes which might indicate disease. To put it another way, once you know what it all should look like when your mouth is healthy, you can then keep an eye out for anything that looks strange. Not only could this periodic peek save your teeth, but in certain cases it could save your life. So run this exam on yourself at least twice a year, more if it gets you high.

If it were possible to take every word in this book, program each one, and then run them through a computer to sort out the most important points, you would be left with these three items:

1) You must remove, as soon as possible, any and all food that goes into your mouth.

2) If you have dental problems now, it means that whatever you have been doing about taking care of your teeth is *not* working. (See the chapter on "Home Care" for more information.)

3) Take care of any existing problems as soon as they arise, and as soon as possible.

What I'm saying is this: *You are in control.* You can determine what the fate of your teeth will be. Good luck, and keep in mind that good things happen to those who help themselves.

4

GLANDS, ORGANS AND SPIT

MOUTH ORGAN
WHAT TO LOOK FOR
SIZE AND SHAPE
THE SPIT GLANDS
THE SPIT
WHAT SALIVA DOES

To complete your picture of the mouth, let's take a closer look at the following parts.

MOUTH ORGAN

In case you didn't already know it, the tongue is a very far out organ. It is highly efficient and powerful muscle. It is also a *very* sensual organ which allows us to perform a variety of activities, most of them enjoyable ones.

As a muscle, it is an invaluable aid to:
1) speech
2) chewing food
3) swallowing the food we chew
4) sensual excitation

As a sensual organ it ranks right up there with the best of our other sensory organs. Those of you who are into oral gratification can readily attest to that fact. But, as this is a dental book, I will not get into the tongue's various sensual applications. Use your own imagination for that.

In order to best study the tongue, you should get a small four by four inch piece of clean cloth. Stick your tongue out, fold the cloth over the tip of the tongue and gently pull it out to you. By holding it with the cloth you can keep the evasive little bugger from slipping out of your grasp. Some tongues may do this unaided, but the tongue doesn't always respond to command. You can try though; just tell it to come out and look around and that you won't bite it.

WHAT TO LOOK FOR

Taste Buds — these are found all over the top and sides of the tongue. Like their name indicates, they are the little characters that allow you to taste food and other things you place in your mouth. If you dry the tongue and look very closely (use the flashlight), you will see what looks like bunches of tiny strings, or soft, miniature, closely-bound brushes. Run your fingernail gently across the top of your tongue and you will better see what I mean.

While the tongue and the teeth are working together to chew and swallow the food, the taste buds are reaping the flavor rewards — assuming you are digging what you are eating. They do not get off on food that is too hot or too cold, so have a heart and think of them before scorching them with hot coffee or freezing them with a popsicle or ice cubes.

SIZE AND SHAPE

If you are doing this examination with a friend, you can compare tongues. The size and shape can vary and still be normal, as another unique feature of the tongue is that it has the ability to grow or shrink, depending on conditions. Like, if you lost all of your teeth and did not get them replaced, the tongue would grow larger and fill all the area available. The teeth keep the tongue in check — another good reason to keep your teeth around. It can also reverse itself and shrink in size, according to the area available. So, if you got false teeth after going around toothless for a few years, the tongue would eventually shrink to an appropriate size.

Don't let the difference in size and shape freak you out too much. You may have a flat, pointed tongue, and your partner may have a fuller, rounded tongue. (Anyone with a forked tongue?)

Another aspect of that slithering organ that you should be aware of is the coating on the top of your tongue. The color and thickness of this coating will vary from day to day. It is normally a whitish-grey color, and some days you may notice more of the coating covering a greater area than it did on the previous day you viewed it. It is the consensus today that this variation means nothing. However, it used to be thought of as an indication of your state of health. I personally feel that the change in the color of your tongue may indicate the condition of your body; it is just that this is a difficult thing to prove. If you happen to have some extra time and feel like doing some research you could check your tongue every day, note its color and texture and write this down. Along with this you could make note of how you feel that day and what changes you went through, if any. Who knows, maybe you could write a book. (The Tongue Trip!)

It used to be common practice to use the tongue as an indication of health. Today this thinking is not so prevalent, and many think it to be a very unscientific way of diagnosis. Maybe, or maybe not. But if you find anything on the tongue in your periodic examinations that you did not see before, you'd better get on downtown and have it checked out. And the earlier the better.

Some of the diseases whose signs can and do show up on the tongue are:

1) Tuberculosis lesions
2) Vitamin deficiency (particularly vitamin B deficiency)
3) Syphilis lesions
4) Anemias
5) Menopausal changes
6) Ulcers, related to tongue biting, burns or rashes
7) Certain types of cancerous lesions

Just remember, any bumps, open sores, ulcers, swellings, discolorations, or any pain or tenderness on or about the tongue is not normal.

THE SPIT GLANDS

There are three of them in your mouth. One is found under the tongue, directly behind the lower front teeth. You would be right on target if you stuck your index finger, of either hand, behind your lower front teeth and gently (always gently) lowered it downward until you touched skin. You would most likely be right on top of it.

The other two can be found in the cheeks, one on each side, opposite the upper last two teeth. These are harder to see, but if you notice two little

56

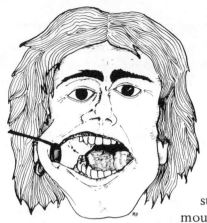

sack-like projections in that area you most likely have found them. It is nice to know you do not have to see them to know about them.

These glands are very important in helping you digest food, particularly carbohydrates and starches. They also help you fight decay by neutralizing the acid which germs produce when consuming the food you leave in your mouth. Other functions include keeping your mouth moist to help in speech, and to help you lubricate the food you eat, which makes it easy to swallow. It is almost impossible to swallow without the moisture produced by your spit glands.

The spit glands are very sensitive, and if bruised or damaged in any way, they can become very sore. When this happens it will feel like you have a piece of leather in your mouth around the area of the gland. This damage most often happens to the lower one. It is in these regions, particularly the lower one, that you must be careful when brushing or using the water pik.

Another possible problem you may face is when the spit glands get plugged up. This is usually caused by the formation of a stone-like object that grows because the minerals in the saliva combine and begin to grow in size. Eventually they reach such a size that they plug up the opening to the salivary glands. The result is that they prevent the spit from flowing and the gland swells up and becomes very painful. You will know this right away because of the location and the pain involved. At the first indication of the problem, see your dentist or preferably your oral surgeon at once — on an emergency basis.

THE SPIT

This brings us to another aspect of your mouth that is often overlooked and not appreciated — the spit.

As I have just stated, you have three salivary glands, and all three of them produce saliva and consequently moisten your mouth. The saliva or spit serves many vital functions and yet is only really appreciated when it is not there.

Each gland can produce different types of spit, the consistency of which can vary from person to person and from time to time. Yours could be thick and "ropey," medium or thin and runny. Any of these types can be considered normal, and the saliva can change if your system undergoes any changes; like when you are nervous or afraid.

Very few problems are associated with saliva; it is mostly working in our corner. However, as it contains many minerals, and can be somewhat sticky, it can aid in the formation of tartar which sticks to your teeth and cause dental disease. But this happens only if you do not brush.

The most serious problem with saliva is the lack of it. This condition, a total lack of saliva, is called *xerostomia* (another big fancy word you can throw around). If you have ever had a dry "cotton" mouth, you will understand what xerostomia is and how serious this condition can be. Imagine, if you can, having cotton-mouth for the rest of your life. Not many people suffer from this malady, but if you suspect it, you'd best get to the doc for confirmation and help.

– DIXIE COTTON MOUTH –

Because saliva does more good than harm, I will list some of the beneficial aspects of it; then you can better appreciate its importance.

WHAT SALIVA DOES

1) It lubricates your food and thus makes it possible to move the food around your mouth while it is being chewed.

2) It is absolutely necessary in allowing you to swallow your food.

3) It contains enzymes that help to pre-digest the starchy foods you eat, before they reach your stomach.

4) It acts as a buffer, meaning that is has the unique chemical ability to neutralize any foods that may be either acidic or basic. As both acids and bases can irritate and even burn the sensitive skin of your mouth, the spit helps protect you from harm of this nature.

5) It aids in the prevention of tooth decay by neutralizing the acid the germs in your mouth produce. This is the same acid that plays such a vital role in causing decay.

6) It is very helpful in disinfecting and healing wounds and cuts which at times occur in your mouth. The mouth contains about eighty different kinds of germs, many of which can cause serious infections anywhere else in the body. But in the mouth the medicinal action of the saliva fights the germs and the infection they can cause.

So, spit isn't that nasty old stuff you were conditioned to think it was. Remember, though, it does its good *inside* the mouth.

Above all else, the thing to always keep in mind, is just what a normal, healthy mouth is. You must firmly imprint on your mind the fact that only by knowing the normal can you recognize an abnormal or diseased state. After your self examination, you can take your concept of the normal to the dentist and confirm your findings with him. You could be right on, but it is always nice to confirm your findings.

5

MOUTH DISEASES TO
APPROACH WITH CAUTION

No doubt some people will say (mostly likely the bad dentist I constantly refer to) that there is more to evaluating your mouth than what I have taught you. They may also say that a little knowledge can be dangerous. However, that approach to knowledge only seems to be true in boxing and in making war. When we apply it to dentistry, we find that the facts (98% of the population suffering from dental disease) clearly show that little or no dental knowledge is not only dangerous, but is also extremely destructive, to *YOU*. So, don't be afraid of any knowledge, even if it's only a little; you have to start somewhere, and *anything* you know about dentistry will make you a healthier person.

You will be amazed at how much better your added knowledge will help you deal with the dentist, even if he is a bad one. Once he realizes how much you really know he will have no choice but to give you the service you pay for and deserve. It is true that you will only get what you ask for. Hopefully the new knowledge you have received will make you aware of what to ask for and what you should receive.

There are over four hundred known diseases of the mouth, just a few of these being; a) all types of vitamin deficiencies, b) tuberculosis, c) syphlis, d) anemia, e) diabetes, f) and about three hundred odd more.

I will describe some of the more common of the uncommon diseases. Please remember that if you are unsure about something you can check with your dentist or doctor. Don't let the fear of the unknown keep you from investigating any potentially serious problem. It may turn out to be unfounded or not serious. Whatever, the sooner you get after it, the better chance you have of eliminating it.

1) *Trench Mouth* – Most of you have heard of this one. Dentists like to be sophisticated, so they call it by other names: *St.*

Vincent's Infection, or (how about this one) *Necrotizing Ulcerative Gingivitis.* Trench mouth is much easier. It is actually a pretty common gum disease but I've included it here because there is so much false information circulating about it.

Trench mouth is *not* passed on by kissing someone who has the disease, no matter what your mom said! If you and your gums are healthy, the only thing that might happen to you by kissing a mouth that is "trenched" is that you might get turned off because people with trench mouth usually have bad breath. If you also have bad gums and get into a heavy kissing thing with someone who has trench mouth it probably won't help your case any. You have enough problems with your own disease. So, unless you dig bad breath and the rest of the bummers that go with trench mouth, you'd better get on your case. In fact, if the lover has it, pass on the information on how to cure it, which I'll give to you.

The symptoms of Trench Mouth are basically the same as other common gum diseases. You will have all the symptoms of gum disease previously listed in Chapter Five, Stage Three, plus:

1) The tips of the gums between the teeth are dead and instead of being V shaped they look like hollowed out craters (like gopher holes or a volcano).

2) The areas around these craters are covered with a gray, or grayish-yellow layer, which, when taken off (easily done and that's why they hurt), leave a bleeding infected surface. It's actually a serious open wound that has become heavily infected.

3) It may involve all or only some of the teeth.

4) Pain — mild to very severe.

5) Nasty smelling breath.

6) More serious cases can result in fever and a generally lousy feeling. It can also make any other problems you have much worse.

This is a *hot* one. If you let it go, you really can get more serious problems later. Call the dentist on an emergency basis and begin home care immediately. Here are some of the things you can do to cure it.

Immediately begin rinsing with the warmest salt water solution you can stand (one teaspoon of salt in full glass of water). Swish it around vigorously and try to suck it between your teeth. Make sure all gum surfaces get rinsed every two to three hours for at least three days. In between salt rinses, rinse with a two percent hydrogen peroxide solution, diluted with an equal amount of the warmest water you can stand. This is also done every two to three hours for three days.

Your diet during this period should consist solely of fresh vegetables (in salads or lightly steamed), fresh fruits and fresh fruit juices (all kinds). Also, drink lots of water, but no booze or soda pop. You should begin immediately with vitamin therapy: three to five miligrams of vitamin C, preferably from a natural source (most health food stores carry these). Also, start a one-a-day vitamin supplement, best from a natural source. (More on vitamins in the chapter called "Love Your Body and Feed It Right.") This vitamin C dosage should be continued for two to three weeks depending on how well you heal, but make sure you take the vitamin C with your meals, say around 1500 miligrams with meals three times a day. Don't forget this. It is also a must that you get *plenty* of rest (you are sick) and avoid any exposure to trauma, stress or strain. Just tell anyone who is bothering you that the Doc said to bug off and leave you alone.

2) *Periconitiis:* This is the infection you get around your wisdom teeth (last teeth in your mouth, both top and bottom jaws). It happens usually because the wisdom teeth have not completely grown in, giving food a chance to get stuck in between the tooth and the gum. This usually causes infection and other negative trips. It is a serious dental problem.

In doing your examination, check behind your last teeth and see if you can see the wisdom teeth growing in. They usually come in during the ages between sixteen and twenty-five. You may not get all four of them. They are on their way out of man's mouth and soon (in maybe one million years) we may not have them at all. Count your teeth. Normally, you should have twenty-eight regular ones and four wisdom teeth. So if you count up twenty-eight and haven't had any pulled, you may still have those nasty buggers around. Make sure you ask the dentist to check for them. Usually only an x-ray will show them up if they are under the skin.

Anyway, if you notice *any* tenderness, swelling, pain, pressure in the area back of your last teeth, see your dentist, especially if you are in this sixteen to twenty-five age group. Chances are good that if you have any pain or swelling, they are beginning to get infected. This infection around the wisdom teeth is more common than the cold; almost every person has already experienced it or will go through it. I did and so I speak from experience.

So don't wait. Tell the dentist to check your wisdom teeth and have him tell you straight out what his opinion is. If he feels they should come out (probably will), ask him to give you the name of the best *oral surgeon* in the area and go to him. It is a general rule of thumb that oral surgeons are much better trained and equipped to pull teeth, especially the more complicated teeth. The *good* oral surgeon pulls hundreds more teeth than the average dentist, and experience is what you want working for you. The oral surgeon may cost you a little extra money, but he can do the job for a lot less pain. So you actually end up getting your money's worth.

3) *Herpes:* Dentists do not have a home grown term for this one, but if you've had herpes before, you'll know what I'm talking about. These are little sores around the lips and inside the mouth. They seem to appear for no apparent reason and then go away shortly (seven to ten days), regardless of how you treat them.

Early features of this disease can be a fever and sore throat. Next you usually find tenderness and maybe some burning, followed by the appearance of what looks like little bubbles. Most often these little bubble-like areas break open and ulcers (open wounds) form. They can be found anywhere in the mouth and in the corners of the lips. No one is sure what causes them, but they do know that trauma, excitement, and worry don't help them any. Try not to irritate them, and alter your diet to eliminate foods that bother them. See your dentist; there is a salve that sometimes helps, and in fact, just about every dentist has something different for this. I suggest you eliminate all foods that irritate your mouth, such as vinegar, chewing on aspirins, etc.

4) *Torus Palatinus and Mandibuaris:* Another winner, but you don't have to know the name to find these guys. They are growths of bone found in certain areas of your mouth. One is commonly found in the roof of the mouth. You can feel this one with your tongue or finger. You can see it by using your dental mirror.

They can also be found on the lower jaw, on the inside, below the back four teeth, and usually on both sides. You can feel them with your tongue, or see them by moving your tongue out of the way and shining the light in that area. There is nothing bad about having these, as long as you keep your teeth. They become problems only if you have plates (false teeth) made. If you think you have these and were worrying about them, you can stop — but ask the Doc to make sure.

5) *Aspirin Burns:* These are very common, and as you've no doubt figured out, are caused by aspirins. Aspirin is a strong acid and it *burns* the skin. It will cause masses of *dead* skin to peel from the inside of your mouth. This can lead to ulcers, cause pain and more serious problems later if not stopped. Certain types of cancers are caused by constant irritation of this nature. With this type of burn the skin looks white and flaky.

Isn't it a crack-up; you wouldn't take an aspirin and chew it up unless something in your mouth was causing you pain. So now you take an aspirin and it causes more problems and eventually more pain!

Aspirins will never replace taking good care of your mouth, nor will they replace the dentist. Aspirin works from inside your body and you have to swallow them to make them work. Even when used as directed they still burn your stomach lining and cause you to lose five ml. of blood each time you take one! I don't dig them, period. It is always best to eliminate the problem and then keep it from happening again, thus you never need aspirin.

Pain is a warning from your body to you. Don't hide the warning too long with aspirin. See the dentist.

6) *Abnormal gums due to the drug Dilantin:* This drug is used to treat people suffering from epilepsy. Chances are that your doctor will have told you of this condition; the gums are generally very much enlarged (swollen).

It can be serious enough to cause the gums in the front teeth to swell up like little round balloons, almost covering the teeth. The color is reddish and they look like they may burst.

What you should know is that you can help by getting them checked and following good cleaning and home care procedures. Again, if they were in bad shape before the Dilantin treatment, the drug can only make it worse. Healthy gums react less negatively to the Dilantin. See your favorite dentist, but be sure you tell him you take Dilantin for epilepsy.

7) *Sore Gums of Expectant Mothers:* You may have thought you were taking pretty good care of your gums yet still find them to be swollen, sore and bleeding. Well, if you are pregnant, (no males here, please) there is a possibility that the stresses on, and resultant imbalance of your system during pregnancy may contribute to your gum problems. Usually, though, this only makes an already abnormal condition worse. Thus, if you already have a gum problem and then get pregnant, there is a good possibility your pregnancy will make it worse. The idea in pregnancy is to give the child as good a chance at life as you can. If you have gum disease, your unborn baby is going to suffer from it too. Your blood is his blood, your health is his health. You may not have known about it until now, but you should care, so get your gums checked and cleaned up for you and your baby.

Abnormalities We Haven't Even Talked About: If you feel you have detected any diseased conditions in your mouth, leave the final diagnosis to the dentist or the M.D. This could mean any lumps, swellings, sore areas, bumps, odd colored areas, bubbles, or anything else you think to be weird. If you are not satisfied with the first dentist or doctor's opinion, you can always go elsewhere and have his findings double-checked.

I cannot possibly cover everything in this book. My purpose is to provide you with enough information to recognize the normal so that you can detect the abnormal. It also allows you to better utilize the dentist as he should be used. So unless you think you've enough time to become a dentist, let him check things out for you. That is what you pay him for. Just make sure that he knows you want a *complete* examination; not just the teeth and gums, but the total mouth.

Then, when your mouth is healthy and together, enjoy it — you've earned it!

6

HOME CARE

HOW TO COMPELTELY PREVENT
TOOTH DECAY AND GUM DISEASE

In order to completely eliminate decay and infection from your mouth, you must:

   a) get your teeth repaired and your gums healthy
   b) remove all food from your mouth *immediately* after eating and drinking anything; carry toothbrush and toothpaste with you
   c) follow my instructions for brushing, using the water pick and disclosing dye (or plak lite) to make certain you brush well

66

d) check into a dentist's for full mouth x-ray and cleaning once a year.

This is the minimum. You will greatly improve your chances of maintaining healthy teeth and gums if, in addition, you:

a) assimilate the information in this book into a routine which includes periodic self-exams, thorough brushing and rinsing twice a day in addition to removing all food immediately after eating

b) remove all sugar from your diet and concentrate on natural, raw or lightly cooked foods; this means using natural fruit sugars or honey

c) stay *awake* when you go to a dentist's, insisting that he explain everything you don't understand, and using your knowledge from this book and your common sense (intuition) to make decisions while you're there

d) minimuze or eliminate "snacks" — even natural food snacks.

However, to do this stuff, you will have to make changes, *fairly major ones,* in some of your personal habits and routines. If you are willing, fine, start today — but go slow. You have a better chance of truely changing your tooth trip if you assimilate this new information at a gradual rate, rather than all at once. It is also much easier to go through this difficult period of change with friends, but you can do it alone. Remember, whatever you put your attention into you will manifest. So read on.

HOW TO DO IT AT HOME

I will assume that you have familiarized yourself with the tools which I have described in the chapter called "The Home Equipment Trip." Now I'll tell you exactly how to put them to use and about some methods which I have worked out in my search for ways to put an end to decay and to prevent gum disease. Since brushing is the most basic, let's start with that.

DOCTOR TOM'S BRUSHING DIRECTIONS

You should brush about two and one half minutes right after *every* meal, or about two and one half minutes at least two times a day when you do not eat (i.e., when you fast). That's a minimum of five minutes or a total of about seven and one half minutes worth of brushing each day. Time yourself the first three or four times until you can tell at least approximately what two and one half minutes of brushing feels like. Understand that there are two things you accomplish when you brush:

1) You get rid of food particles and other junk that causes tooth decay

2) You massage and stimulate your gums, making them healthier and thus more resistant to disease.

Just to make sure the whole brushing trip is covered, I'm going to pretend that you have just slipped on a banana peel, bumped your head and have completely forgotten everything you once knew about brushing your teeth. Okay? Try to get yourself into that head with me, and we'll be sure to get it on together. So let's make it happen.

PUT ON THE PASTE OR POWDER

Wet the brush with warm water and add the toothpaste or powder. If you use paste, apply enough to cover one half the length of the bristles. If you use powder, sprinkle enough on so as to lightly cover the bristles, or follow the directions printed on the particular powder package which you are using.

MAPPING OUT THE SURFACES TO BE BRUSHED

Every area of tooth, and the gums to about one half inch below or above the teeth, must be brushed. In order for you to get these areas clearly in mind, think of them as being in one of the four following groups:

1) Outer surfaces of all your teeth, upper and lower, and the inside surfaces of your back teeth, upper and lower

2) Inside surfaces of your front teeth, both upper and lower

3) Chewing surfaces of your upper and lower teeth

4) Backs of the last teeth, both left and right, upper and lower.

Okay, you've got that together. Right? Now I'll tell you exactly how I think each of these surfaces should be brushed.

Each of the four main tooth surfaces must be brushed in a slightly different way. Like, different strokes for different folks. Here they are:

1) Outer Surfaces of All Teeth and Inner Surfaces of Back Teeth:

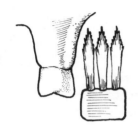

Here's how the brush is to be placed against the teeth and gums. Hold the brush firmly against the teeth. Brush the upper teeth downward toward the biting edge. Rotate your wrist and apply sufficient pressure so the bristles of

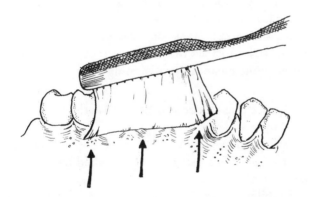

the brush travel across the gums, massaging them, and then passing over the teeth, polishing them on the way. Brush the lower teeth toward the biting edge and in the same manner as the upper teeth. Another way to put it is this: brush your teeth in the direction they grow — upper teeth grow downward, the lower teeth grow upward.

These directions cover the areas shown on the drawing of the upper and lower jaws. Brush each area ten times. If you have not been doing it the way I describe — and most people don't — practice until it becomes easy for you.

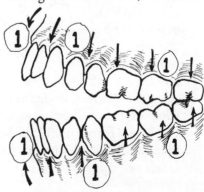

2) Inside Surfaces of Your Front Teeth, Both Upper and Lower:
The brush is positioned as
shown in the drawing.
Brush the insides of the
lower six teeth and
gums. Move the brush
from left to right, and
back again four separate
times, brushing up and
down as you move. Do
the same for the insides of the upper
six teeth, running back and forth four times,
brushing as you go. If your front teeth are
crooked or overlapped, the brush must be angled
in the same direction as the teeth are angled or overlapped.

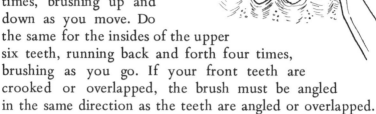

This area is the most difficult to brush, and for that reason is often the dirtiest area of the mouth. So it's worth spending some time learning how to clean it well.

One last note on this area: Make sure the gums get a good brushing and check out the insides of the front teeth, especially the lower, to see how your cleaning job is going. Use your little dental mirror.

3) Chewing Surfaces of Your Upper and Lower Teeth:
The grooves in the tops of the teeth run in all directions. If you're going to clean all those grooves, you're going to have to brush in all directions, too. This can be accomplished by placing the brush on the tops of
the back teeth, and while
firmly pressing the
bristles into
the grooves,
move the
brush in all direc-
tions. This *shimmy*
movement will allow you to
clean the grooves, no matter
what direction they groove in. While you are shimmying, move the brush forward and backward so that you clean every tooth. Shimmy forward and backward six times on each of the four areas: i.e., upper left, lower left, upper right, and lower right.

4) Backs of the Last Teeth:

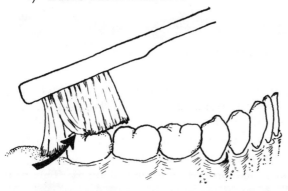

Because you are doing so well, you can begin on any back tooth you wish. Place the brush in the position shown and move your hand and thus the brush from left to right in short little strokes, just enough movement to clean the tooth. Ten strokes will do it — ten in each of the four areas, that is.

HOW TO HOLD THE BRUSH

Alot of people ask if there is any particular way to hold the brush. The answer is that there are many ways to hold the brush. Here are the two basic positions that I recommend. Check out the drawings, but keep in mind that you can and may need to adjust the way you grasp the toothbrush in order to brush properly. That's groovy, different strokes for different folks, as long as you get the job done.

Grasp #1: This grasp, (right-handed) adjusted where needed, will allow you to brush the lower teeth and all of the upper teeth except the left side.

Grasp #2: This grasp adjusted to fit your individual hand, will take care of the upper outer surfaces of the teeth on the left side.

Remember to change the angle of your wrist when shifting sides, and to change the grasp on the brush when brushing the outside surfaces of the left side.

In case you haven't yet figured it out, the idea is to hold the brush any way you want as long as the brush gets laid against the teeth and gums in the proper manner and you stroke the brush in the direction the teeth grow. So, experiment and practice, it'll soon be a breeze.

THE SHORTEST ROUTE THROUGH YOUR MOUTH

I suggest that you begin on the lower left side, outer surface of the back teeth and then brush the outer and inner surfaces of the lower jaw. When that's done, shift to the upper jaw, right side, and begin on the inside, changing the angle of your wrist as you go. Always brush in the direction that the teeth grow.

Remember, this particular order is just one of many. This order guarantees that you'll cover every area; it also happens to be the order in which I brush, so I know it works. The only secret to good brushing is really no secret. It amounts simply to brushing *every* surface of *every* tooth and also the gums that surround the teeth at least five minutes a day and in the proper direction. Best get started.

Footnote: Brushing the Tongue:

Some patients ask me about brushing the tongue. Personally, I think that a dirty tongue results from a combination of bad diet and poor home care, and by properly changing both of them, you will eliminate the cause of a dirty tongue and the need to brush it. I did try it though, and I gagged — besides, my tongue is clean, and I'm glad.

DOING IT WITH DENTAL FLOSS

Dental floss is a trip to use, but a good one. Until the creation of the water pick, flossing was the only way you could thoroughly clean below the gum margin, between the teeth, and along the edges of fillings.

Flossing is not the easiest thing to do. It will be awkward and feel unnatural, but like anything, practice makes perfect.

WHO SHOULD FLOSS

Everyone who:
1) does not brush regularly
2) eats a great deal of refined foods and processed foods
3) has previously had gum problems and who's gums have receded.

72

HOW OFTEN

You should floss once within every twenty-four hour period, and you should at least floss between the front six teeth, upper and lower. But, preferably, you should floss between every tooth.

FLOSSING AND FINGERS

The easiest way to floss is to use a long piece of waxed floss, about thirty inches worth. Wrap the floss around the middle finger of each hand, just below the first joint. About three times around will do it. You should now look like this.

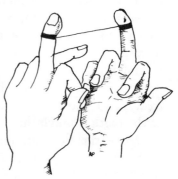

UPPER: To guide the floss while flossing the upper teeth, you can use the thumb of your right hand (lefties just the reverse) and the forefinger of the left hand. And you should now look like this. Easy, huh?

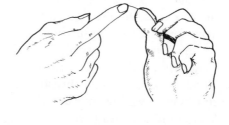

LOWER: The only difference in guiding the floss for flossing the lower teeth is your right index finger replaces your right thumb. Presto, you should look like this for flossing the lower teeth.

This has been easy so far, but don't relax your guard. I suggest that you practice flossing the front six teeth, upper and lower. Once you get this down, you can start flossing the rest. The basic principle is the same, but it is more awkward to floss the back teeth. Play with the floss until you get it down.

ACTUAL MECHANICS OF FLOSSING

Start on your *upper* front teeth and look in the mirror. Place the floss between your two front teeth. Do not force or jam the floss between your teeth, and if you find an area that is too tight, forget it. If floss won't get there, food won't. Once the floss is centered between the two teeth, gently slide the floss past the point where the two teeth contact each other. This is easier if you pull the floss toward one tooth or the other while you are gently but firmly forcing it down.

Once you've gotten by the contact point, the floss will move freely, and you're in the chips. The action of the floss on either side of the teeth is much the same as shining shoes.

Move the floss up and down and in and out each side of each tooth two or three times. Make sure you move the floss gently but firmly below the free margin of the gums (space between the gums and the teeth) until it stops. When you've finished both sides of each tooth, unravel the floss on the left hand and gently pull the floss through and out the space between the teeth. Continue on to the next two teeth and floss again. After finishing your uppers, move to your lowers. Take your time.

As I've said, flossing is a trip and some people say it takes too long. Well, it does take a long time, and in my opinion, you can avoid flossing only if you brush immediately after eating, rinse after drinking anything and use the water pick once a day. Which means you could get away without using it, but you've got to be good and you must get results. At least floss the lower front teeth once per day, at the bare minimum.

THE WATER PICK IS KING

Used properly, the water pick is the most far-out dental invention since the tooth brush. I have heard dentists say they don't like it, and others who say it harms the gums. Sure, anything can be harmful if abused, and the water pick is no exception.

HOW TO USE THE WATER PICK (DIRECTIONS FOR INSTALLATION COME WITH THE WATER PICK)

After you've brushed, etc., fill the water pick up with luke warm water (you can add mouthwash if you wish, but *no salt*). Place the

adjustable tip into your mouth and angle it
so it is barely touching the junction of the
tooth and gum. You can then begin at the
last tooth on the left side and follow the
teeth around, picking inside and out, upper
and lower and the backs
of the last teeth. Go
slow, and make at least
three complete cycles
around your mouth
— even more at the
lower pressures. Just
keep going around
until the water runs
out. (A good point
to remember here

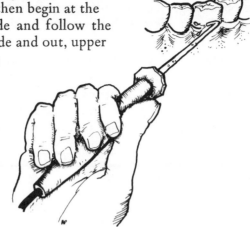

is to close your lips gently around the tip to keep the water from
splashing all over.)

You can guide the tip by keeping it lightly touching the junction
where the gum and tooth meet and by using the little adjustable
knob to change angles when needed.

I have seen the water pick clean up my mouth, and the mouths of
about 60% of my patients (everyone who got one and used it
correctly).

Use the water pick two times per day for the first three weeks,
with the pressure indicator dial set on two and one-half (on a scale of
ten) for the first week, five for the second week, seven and one-half
for the third week. After the third week, you can use the water pick
at a reading of nine and then use it once per day thereafter,
preferably in the evening and always after — not before — brushing
and flossing. The jet stream of water from the pick will rinse away
what the brush and floss have loosened and also very effectively
massage and stimulate the gums around and in between the teeth.

If you feel any pain or discomfort around any tooth or teeth at
any reading, turn the pressure down and work up more gradually in
that area. *Never* turn it on high when first using it — always work
your way up to higher pressures gradually.

Those of you whose gums are in bad shape may notice some
bleeding for a short while. All bleeding should be gone by the end of
the fourth week, if you've followed my advice. If it hasn't stopped
by then, your problem may be more serious than you thought and
you'd best check with a gum specialist.

DISCLOSING TABLETS

After brushing, flossing and water picking, chew up the tablets, mix the dissolved tablets with saliva and swish around and over the teeth for about thirty seconds. Rinse lightly with water and examine your teeth. Wherever the stain remains is where you didn't brush well, so get out your brush and paste and brush away the stain. The tablets thus act as a guide to proper brushing technique, showing you where you've missed and where you should be spending more time. Use them until you can brush without missing any areas and then you only need them to check out your teeth from time to time. Be sure to check the insides of your teeth as well, upper and lower. Use your little dental mirror.

PLAK LITE

The plak lite does the same thing as disclosing tablets, but much more dramatically. The plak lite system utilizes three main elements to perform its task.

1) A disclosing solution (fluorescein sodium) which is very safe and is often used as a diagnostic aid in medicine. The disclosing solution, when used as directed, stains the plaque (food debris) and allows it to be seen when

2) The optically filtered light-energy source, (the plak lite) is shown into the mouth. This light source activates the disclosing solution which has stained the plaque and makes it fluoresce brilliantly.

3) A filtered mirror which is mounted on the plak lite allows you to see what is glowing. It also contains a small mouth mirror for viewing the backs of your teeth.

Most dentists agree that plaque is the foundation upon which tartar (calculus) forms and that if it is not removed at least once per day, it will become so sticky that normal home care cannot remove it. In other words, plaque is the fuel that almost all dental disease feeds upon. But, you cannot effectively remove what you cannot see. The plak lite, or the disclosing tablets, will allow you to accurately check yourself on how well you are keeping your teeth clean. Disclosing tablets or a plak lite are also super good ways to motivate kids to practice good home dental care, since kids really trip on using them.

HOME CARE FOR YOUR SICK GUMS

If your gums bleed for *any* reason, or if you have discovered some form of gum disease in your mouth after doing your own evaluation (see chapter on "Evaluating Your Gums"), you will want to do the following:

a) Buy a jar of three percent Hydrogen Peroxide Solution, found in any drug store, or in most super markets.

b) Buy at least one bottle of vitamin C (Ascorbic Acid), preferably the five hundred-miligram size and in the oblong shape which is easier to swallow. I strongly recommend that you get "natural" vitamin C, as sold in most health food stores. Vitamin C from synthetic sources is not as effective, but it is better than nothing.

c) Buy a good supply of "One-A-Day Vitamins" — preferably the "natural" kind which most good health food stores carry. I recommend the "One Plan Vitamin."

d) Buy some salt, preferably sea salt as sold in health food stores. If you really can't get any of this, Leslie's will do.

It is a good idea to have all of these things on hand at all times. If you do, then you'll be able to stay on top of the problem of preventing or curing your sick mouth at the first signs of disease. To do this, you will, of course, have to be well aware of everything I've covered in the sections of this book called "Evaluating Your Gums," "Examining Your Teeth," and "Mouth Diseases."

HOME MEDICATION

Vitamin C: Take from two to three thousand miligrams of vitamin C every day for ten days if you have found some symptoms of gum disease in your mouth. Use two thousand miligrams per day if you think you are in disease Stages One or Two, and three thousand miligrams per day if you think you are in Stages Three or Four. (The different stages are covered in the chapter called "Evaluating Your Gums.") If you aren't sure, take three thousand miligrams per day. You need not take them all at once, but can divide up the dose and take a portion of it at every meal. It is important to remember that vitamin C is most effective when taken *with* meals.

After ten days of this routine, I recommend taking at least five hundred miligrams per day, every day thereafter. That would be just to keep things together in your mouth in the way of preventing gum disease on an every day basis.

I suggest purchasing the vitamin C in the five hundred miligram size because it is much easier to take six five hundred miligram tablets than it is to take thirty one hundred miligram tablets.

One-A-Day Vitamins: A good one-a-day vitamin should be taken every day. More about this is discussed in the chapter on "Diet."

RINSING TO CURE AND PREVENT DISEASE

Hydrogen Peroxide: Basically, the hydrogen peroxide is like liquid oxygen; the bubbling effervescent effect, though perhaps not very pleasant, really gets into the deepest areas of infection. It not only kills the excessive amounts of germs, but also provides the oxygen so necessary for healing in the presence of infection. Here's how to do it:

Rinse every four hours with hydrogen peroxide (four times per day) diluted with equal quantity of water as warm as you can stand. (Please test it — I wouldn't want you to burn yourself.) About one ounce of peroxide and one ounce of water is sufficient. You don't need a measuring cup — the two ounce total will be sufficient for two to three good mouth fulls (depending on the size of your mouth). Anyway, you swish and suck, trying to suck the solution between your teeth, making sure all areas of your gums get bathed. If you rinse three times, about fifteen to twenty seconds per rinse, you should cover it. Don't swallow the stuff. It might not kill you, but it's not meant to be swallowed (there are other ways to clean your stomach). This is to be done for three days if you are in gum disease Stages One or Two and five days if you are in Stages Three or Four or are not sure.

Salt Water: After completing the peroxide rinse, wait about five minutes and rinse with one half a glass of warm water, again as warm as you can stand it, to which you add and mix well one-half teaspoon salt. This should allow you at least three good rinses, maybe more, but however many, use the one-half glass (about six ounces) completely up — swishing and sucking and drawing and pumping, the same as you did with the peroxide rinse — fifteen to twenty second rinses is normally sufficient. Do this diligently for three days if you're in Stages One or Two and five days if you find yourself in Stages Three or Four.

The value of the salt water rinse is in its fantastic healing effect. Salt water on wounds has been an effective treatment for millions of people for as long as history has been recorded, and I bet for even longer. Just because they didn't have the time nor the inclination to write it down doesn't mean they (people) didn't utilize it. By now, you should fully realize that wounds, infection, pus, gum disease, bleeding gums, sore gums, bad breath, etc., are all one and the same animal, and whatever you can do to heal or cure it you should be doing as fast as you can.

Complain all you want about the peroxide and salt water treatment — as I'm sure you will — but thank whomever you pray to for their existence. You'd be in sad shape without them. If they sting or burn a little, grin and bear it. It only means you're probably in worse shape than you thought. But also keep in mind that your gums will soon stop hurting and get better.

It is also wise to keep in mind that if in your self-evaluation you found gaping holes in your teeth or if you've had prior toothaches (not gum aches), you might be in for some irritation. If, by chance, the rinsing unbearably hurts a tooth, call the doctor for an appointment and get some temporaries put in the caverns — when that has been handled, resume rinsing.

After three to five days of rinsing, and assuming you do everything else I recommend, you should no longer need to rinse with peroxide. (The exception being if for some reason your dentist feels you should continue.) I do believe, however, that you should rinse with the same concentration of warm water and salt three times a week, which amounts to rinsing every two days and balancing out the odd day. A half glass of water will be sufficient for each rinsing.

If rinsing happens to fall at the same time you would normally brush, including your three times per week salt water rinse, *always* repeat — *always* rinse *after* you've brushed, flossed and water picked. In keeping with the philosophy that I never tell you something without explaining why, I shall tell you why. The healing effect of salt water is only effective if it's left in the mouth for a reasonable amount of time, like say at least ten minutes. So, if you rinsed first and brushed later, you would lose the value of the rinsing. Make sense?

ALWAYS rinse your mouth with clear water after eating or drinking ANYTHING. Also, try to eat something at the end of your meal, like a carrot, that will help you massage your gums. If you can't find a carrot or an apple, your finger will do. Just massage your gums with your index finger in the same way I showed you how to do it with a tooth brush. If doing it with your finger embarrasses you while in the company of friends, go to the bathroom or go for a walk or a swim. Better to have all of your teeth and be a little embarrassed.

A SUMMARY

If you follow all of the above instructions, you will be very turned on by the results, especially if you presently have bad gums. The following will help you put together the various steps this chapter has covered:

1) Brush your teeth after every meal
2) Use dental floss
3) Use the water pick
4) Pay close attention to your vitamin intake
5) Use hydrogen peroxide rinses and salt water rinses at the first signs of dental disease
6) Rinse your mouth and massage your gums with your finger whenever you can't brush
7) Use disclosing tablets or a plak lite to discover dirty areas in your mouth and to improve your brushing technique.

You don't have to wait till you have gotten your teeth cleaned at the drill and fill office before you begin practicing home dental care on your own. Besides, the results you get will prove to you how much you can accomplish on your own. Start today.

As we go to press, I've just found out about a new Oral Hygiene Kit which might help you get your Home Care together. For the info, see page 233.

7

YOUR HOME EQUIPMENT TRIP

YOUR HOME EQUIPMENT TRIP
DESIRE
TIME
HANDS
GOOD DIET
TOOTHBRUSH
TOOTHPASTE
TOOTHPOWDERS
BAKING SODA
SALT
EARLY AMERICAN FOLK REMEDIES
SPECIAL PROBLEMS AND TOOTH CLEANSERS
A CLOSING NOTE
DENTAL FLOSS
HOMEMADE MOUTH MIRROR
DISCLOSING TABLETS
WATER PICK
STIMUDENTS
PLAK LITE
ELECTRIC TOOTHBRUSH

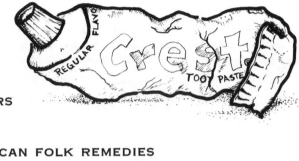

YOUR HOME EQUIPMENT TRIP

You will not be able to get your dental trip together by wishing or by hoping your problems will go away. You are going to have to get right in there and do the job. But to treat your teeth right, you will need the right tools. This chapter will give you the scoop on dental tools available to you. You may not need every one of them, depending on your individual condition, but it won't hurt to know about them all.

Here's a list of the tools I will discuss:

1) Desire   4) Good Diet
2) Time   5) Tooth Brush
3) Hands   6) Tooth Paste

81

7) Dental Floss	10) Water Pik
8) Mouth Mirror	11) Stimudents
9) Disclosing Tablets	12) Plak Lite
	13) Electric Toothbrush

Here's my rap about the tools:

DESIRE

None of the tools which I describe here will be of any use to you until you actually pick them up and use them. The tools have no inherent energy, and until the day of the toothbrush robot, you are going to have to supply your own energy and time. The point is obvious; you have to *want* to do something about your teeth.

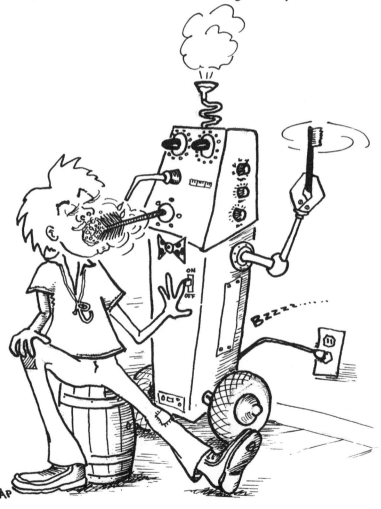

TIME

About five minutes every day. Preventing sick teeth and gums will require much less time than letting your mouth rot and then spending countless hours in the dentist's chair.

HANDS

You got them for free, and if you want to get rid of dental disease, you'll have to use them. At first this may be awkward, especially if you haven't been doing it right before. But in a few weeks you'll think you've been brushing my way (see page 67) all your life.

For those of you unfortunate enough to have lost your hands, a friend will hopefully assist you. If you have artificial limbs, an electric toothbrush and the water pik will work for you.

GOOD DIET

The only truly natural way to clean your teeth is through good diet, along with good home care. These will eliminate common dental diseases. See chapter on diet, page 126, for more information.

TOOTHBRUSH

There are many different kinds of toothbrushes available to you. What you want is one that will get the job done without causing any problems along the way. Here are the main points to consider:

1) Hard or soft bristle? For most people and most situations, a medium brush of any make is ideal. *Exception:* If while doing the self-evaluation of your mouth (see page 13) you found yourself in stage three or four of gum disease, you should then begin with a soft brush and work your way into the medium, using the soft one for about four weeks. Your dentist can help you on this, but the idea is that until you get your gums back to normal, you cannot do the things that would be okay to do in a healthy mouth.

2) Composition of bristle: If you can find them, a natural bristle brush, usually boarhair like a good hairbrush, is the best. But nylon bristles will do an adequate job, so don't worry too much if you can't find a natural bristle brush. If you are into the

natural trip, see page 95 for how to make your own dental tools the natural way.

3) Size:

For Grownups: The overall length should be about six inches; the handle about four and one half inches and the brush portion about one and one half inches. It should have between seven and thirteen rows of bristles the long way and three or more rows across.

For Kids: Small children will require a smaller brush. Make sure their brush is long enough to reach their back teeth but not so long that they will choke themselves with every stroke. Since there are so many sizes of kids and brushes, I will leave the measuring up to you. Also, until they are old enough to fully understand what is happening, make sure the brush is a soft one, and observe carefully that they are not abusing it — like make sure they are brushing with the right end. Children learn from you, so make sure you are doing your part right. If the kids just want to play, don't put toothpaste on the brush. Use paste with them only when they are brushing for real.

4) Shape: The straight, standard, average, old-fashioned shape toothbrush is just fine. Whatever the curved or angled brushes add, they are usually lacking just as much. The shape of the jaw is both curved 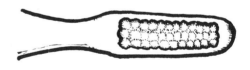 and straight, so while a curved brush might fit nicely into the curved areas, it is sorely lacking in the straight part of the jaw. The straight brush will bend nicely into any area and thus does all that is required. So stick by it.

5) Odd-Ball Brushes: You'll only need the odd-ball brush if you have:

    a) missing teeth
    b) crooked teeth
    c) severe gum disease

One of the odd-balls that I like is the one I call the shrunken headed odd-ball. It looks like this. This is a good brush for getting into those hard-to-reach areas behind the last tooth, for teeth next to where you have lost a tooth, for areas where you have lost a great deal of bone due to gum disease, and around and under fixed bridge work that replaces missing teeth. The number of odd-balls available are as numerous as the special mouth problems requiring them. If you do have a special problem and would like to know if there's a brush that would do the job better than the one you are presently using, I would recommend that you go rap with your dentist and get him to help you pick out the right tool for the job. The main thing you should understand is that *there are many brush designs available to you.*

6) Brand Names: Concern yourself with the above requirements rather than brand names. I feel that the manufacturers of the *Oral B* brush have a pretty good thing going. They have brushes for everyone. But whatever gets you high and does the job is fine. Just make sure that it is neither too big, too small, too hard nor too soft.

7) Color: Perhaps you have always wanted a bright orange toothbrush, or even a purple one, or whatever color makes you really feel good inside. If you are into Astrology, find out your astrological color and really get cosmic. Make it enjoyable!

Happy brush hunting, and in case you're interested, a few good places to get brushes and other dental tools would be your local discount houses and discount drugstores. They will give you the same thing as the more expensive stores, but for alot less. Another good place to hunt for a brush could be your local dentist's drill-and-fill office. Some care enough to keep a supply on hand, and a few will give you a brush for nothing. (Don't faint; some do!) But ask him if it's free, just to make sure it's not included in the bill.

TOOTHPASTE

Of the big brands, *Crest* and *Colgate* are the only ones that can legally advertise that they actually help fight tooth decay. Because of the claims made by Crest and Colgate, the American Dental Association (ADA) required that they undergo tests to make certain that they did fight tooth decay, and that they did it with no bad side effects. The fact is that Crest went through more tests than any other tooth cleaner I know of, and after studying over what the ADA reports have said, I am convinced that it works in helping to fight tooth decay. So it's my conclusion that both Crest and Colgate do a pretty good job of helping to fight decay without screwing up your teeth in the process.

You might want to know about the "glamour toothpastes"; these are the ones that advertise whiter, brighter teeth, kissing sweet breath, and all that trip. It has been my experience that these pastes are either too abrasive, too acidic, or both. This means that they can actually wear off too much of your tooth's enamel, too fast.

The enamel is the white part of your tooth, and even though it looks like it is a solid color, it is actually translucent (meaning you can see through it when it is thin enough). The dentin (see drawings of the teeth, pg. 145) that lies under the enamel is actually yellow in color, and it follows that if you wear off enough of the enamel, the yellow of the dentin will show through. Thus, in the long run, these toothpastes that advertise whiter, brighter, etc. teeth without saying they fight tooth decay and are approved by the ADA, can actually end up making your teeth yellow instead of white! At first you might think your teeth are whiter because the toothpaste, being so abrasive or acidic, will clean off the stains on your teeth. If you stopped there, that would be far out. But in people's continual search for beauty, they keep going for the movie star white teeth, not realizing they are wearing away the enamel and thus wearing away the white. Bad karma will surely come down on those manufacturers for that. If you happen to be born with yellow colored teeth, the glamour pastes (and you know which ones I mean) are misleading if they say they can make them whiter. Their total object is to be abrasive enough to remove the stains you may have built up due to smoking cigarettes, grass, drinking tea, etc. Aside from wearing off your enamel as I've explained, this also has the effect of keeping people from the dentist, making people think that if their teeth are white, they are alright. Don't fall for it. The harm these pastes can do far outweighs any good they might do. You just do not need them.

Nothing beats going to the dentist, getting a good cleaning and following it up with *fantastic far out* home care. (See page 66.) Once the teeth have been thoroughly cleaned, it becomes a simple job to keep them that way. It is always easier to prevent than to cure sick teeth. If you are not sure about a commercial toothpaste, go to Crest or Colgate, or check with your dentist.

Organic Natural Toothpastes

I like the idea of organic toothpastes best of all, although some may be a little too abrasive. Most of them do not make public the abrasive or acidic levels of their toothpastes. I have been experimenting with Shakley's Organic Tooth Paste, *New Concept,* and as of this printing, I think it's a very far out toothpaste. It seems to do the job and not abuse.

For those of you who do not wish to use anything commercially made and will use organic toothpastes, come hell or high water, there are a few things you should know. Take them for what they are worth, but at least I've told you.

1) If you happen to select an organic toothpaste that *is* too abrasive, the harm that it can do to your teeth by wearing them away too fast *may,* in my opinion, outweigh the value you receive by its being organic.

2) The more raw and natural your diet is, the more natural self-cleansing you receive from your diet and your need for an abrasive toothpaste decreases. This will all be covered later, but suffice to know that if you are going to take a chance on a toothpaste whose degree of abrasiveness is not known, you'd best be eating a good natural diet and know that you shouldn't be over brushing. Don't abuse it.

3) Many of you who are totally into natural things, are, of course, down on commercial pastes. For most commercial pastes, you are right on in your feelings. But as far as Crest and Colgate goes, you need not be so fearful. It is my opinion that the main fault with commercial toothpastes is that the sweeteners they contain will cause acid to enter your stomach. This is O.K., as long as there is food either in the stomach or on its way to it. Ideally, to prevent tooth decay, you should brush *immediately* after every meal. Thus, even if brushing with Crest or Colgate caused this acid to flow, you would have food in your stomach, and the

87

acid would not harm you, as it is needed to help digest the food. Besides, the idea is not to swallow the toothpaste, but rinse it out after brushing. Also, as far as preventing gum disease goes, you must brush (massage) your gums two or three times per day and to do this you do not need toothpaste, just the brush. So, say you're fasting and you realize that you must still brush your gums, but you know that when you use toothpaste and don't eat, it upsets your stomach. Well, if you don't eat, you don't need toothpaste, just use the brush — thus, no acid and all is groovy!

Ideally, diet should be the Number One tooth cleanser, (see chapter on "Diet," pg. 126) but, sadly, most of us either don't know what that ideal diet consists of, or if we do, we do not follow it.

In leaving organic pastes, it is important for you to realize that no matter what you do, it must get the job done, and with *no harmful side effects.* So, if your gums bleed, you still get decay, and your teeth are wearing away, whatever you are using and/or however you are using it is wrong and isn't working. It's definitely time for a change; immediately.

TOOTHPOWDERS

I realize many of you use powders, and before you start kicking, let me make it clear that if it is doing the job and not overly doing it, go right on, but again, the abrasiveness may be a little too much. Make sure you ask your dentist if your powder:
1) is doing what it should be doing — cleaning your teeth — and
2) is not doing things it shouldn't, like wearing off too much enamel.

BAKING SODA

This stuff works well for cleaning and scouring pots and pans, and I recommend it highly — for pots. But teeth are not pots or pans. I cannot advocate its use, for it is, as a dentrifice, much too abrasive to be used every day. Even though the teeth are the hardest part of your body, they can be worn down and baking soda will do that fast. Occasional use, say three or four times per week is ok, but no more.

SALT

I've looked everywhere and nowhere could I find anything or anybody that could prove to me that salt worked as a toothpaste. Ask your doctor about salt and heart attacks. Best to keep salt on the food and very little at that. When used properly and in certain cases, it is effective as a mouth wash in helping to cure gum disease. (See "Diet," pg. 126.)

EARLY AMERICAN FOLK REMEDIES

I'll show you how to make some of them (page 95). But for the record, I'm not advocating nor promoting their use. If you do use them, keep thinking about *results, good results,* and at least check with a dentist you trust to see how they are working.

SPECIAL PROBLEMS AND TOOTH CLEANSERS (Toothpastes for sensitive teeth due to abrasion, erosion, bone loss from gum disease.)

You should know that sensitive teeth can be the result of many things, and unless you eliminate what's causing the sensitivity, you are wasting your time on toothpastes that are supposed to cure the sensitivity. So, the best way to approach the problem of sensitivity is to first find out what is causing it. Three possible common causes are:

1) Decay
2) Sucking on lemons
3) Brushing the wrong way

You'll of course know if your teeth are sensitive, so until you can get to the dentist to make sure if the sensitivity was caused by decay, you can stop sucking lemons (if you do) and start brushing the right way (see "Home Care," page 66).

I recommend that you get a tube of either *Sensodyne* or *Thermodent* and use it until it's all gone. Hopefully, by then, you've corrected what caused the problem and you can go back to your regular toothpaste. Toothpastes that claim to help sensitive teeth act somewhat like an aspirin. They can relieve the symptom but do little for the cure.

I don't think it is groovy to continually take aspirin, nor do I think it necessary to continually need to use anti-sensitive toothpastes; they have their place, but if after using one tube you haven't solved the problem, you'd best ask the dentist for help. It just may be caused by other things than I've mentioned; maybe a fractured tooth, or gum infection. That means it's time to ask the Doc to help.

A CLOSING NOTE

Many things are fine if you don't abuse them. I'm emphasizing this because there is a good chance (especially if you're about 15 or 20) that you are going to have your teeth for a long time. (Even if you're 40 or 50, and follow my methods, you'll most likely have them around for a long time.) There is no logical sense in wearing them down any faster than you have to with toothpastes and powders that are too abrasive.

If the toothpaste you are using is either very rough or granular, or feels like it burns or stings your mouth, it's either too abrasive or too acidic. Also, if you think your teeth are getting yellow, and fast, (teeth get darker naturally with age, but not overnight) you'd best change brands. Crest and Colgate have been proven to be just abrasive enough to clean the teeth and yet not overly abrasive. They also have passed many of the other safety tests required by the ADA. No other dentifrice that I know of, including organic ones, can say that. By following the above guidelines when brushing, only use toothpaste when you've eaten anything, you also eliminate the only other possible side effect of using Crest or Colgate and still get all of their good advantages. Mind you, I am 100% for organic dentifrices, but I am also obligated to give you the whole scoop, and nothing but the scoop, and it just happens to be a fact that you can abuse some organic dentifrices, especially if they are too abrasive.

DENTAL FLOSS

This strong thread-like nylon substance is used to clean and polish between the teeth. It can remove food wedged between the teeth and if used daily can help prevent plaque from forming in these areas. It also has a slight massaging and cleaning effect on the edges of the gums in these areas between the teeth. Dental floss will help clean where the toothbrush cannot.

There are two types: floss and dental tape. The floss is easier to use and I prefer it to the tape. It can be purchased in any drugstore or supermarket. Ask for waxed floss, but unwaxed will also work. I will show you how to use it in the how-to-do-it section.

HOMEMADE MOUTH MIRROR

Get the inexpensive plastic-handled mirror from your dentist or drug store. You can also try to make your own. For more on mouth mirrors, see page 14.

DISCLOSING TABLETS

These are colored tablets that contain a vegetable dye, generally of a reddish color, that, when chewed and sloshed around in the mouth prior to brushing, will stain the food debris and plaque that is found around the teeth to a reddish-orange color. The tablets will not stain the teeth themselves, but only the food and junk left around the gums, on top of the teeth and in between them.

The beauty of these little guys is that they are excellent to test your brushing habits. They are harmless and inexpensive and can be found in most drug stores or at your dentist's. I'll tell you how to use them in the next chapter. The only side effect of these tablets is that they can stain clothes and fixtures (like sinks) if not used carefully.

WATER PICK

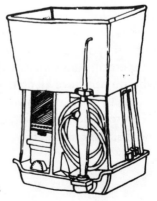

The water pick is one of the better inventions of man. Most of you will absolutely have to have the water pick to help you prevent the loss of your teeth. And it would be a good idea for all of you to have one. It is a must if you find yourself in Stages two, three or four of gum disease.

The idea behind water picks is to shoot a stream of water out a nozzle and under a pressure that can be adjusted to your individual needs. When turned on, it delivers a pulsating stream of water that, when directed properly, will allow you to clean areas of the teeth that the brush will not reach and massage the gums between the teeth, under fixed bridges, around and through orthodontic appliances (braces). The pulsating stream of water will lift out debris and massage the gums in the space between the tooth and gum.

It does not replace the brush, but helps it. The brush was designed to prevent decay and gum disease, but once you get disease, you change the natural design of your gums and teeth and this fact allows food to get into places that it normally would not. This is especially true if your gums have receeded, for now food can get into the areas that the gums once protected.

So, the brush will work well wherever it can reach and the water pick and dental floss will take care of the areas the brush won't get to.

The water pick fills the void the brush leaves and so, for most of you with advanced gum disease or recession, the water pick is the instrument that can save your teeth. Results always speak better than promises, and I assure you that if you follow my directions on how to use the water pick (see page 14) plus a good cleaning and home care, you will stop gum disease.

There are many kinds of water spray devices; I recommend the *Water Pik* brand. Whatever one you choose, make sure that it has a dial that will control the pressure of the water.

There are a few brands on the market that are not electrically operated; they attach to a faucet and are difficult to use. Most of these do not have a device to control the pressure and I'm against them. There is one type that attaches to the faucet, *Hydro Dent,* that has a knob at the faucet end of the hose which effectively regulates water pressure. No faucet model water spray is suitable if you have a sink with separate hot and cold taps, because you cannot regulate the water temperature. Usually most water coming from the cold water taps is too cold for your teeth, and of course the hot water is too hot. If you do have a single level faucet, you can balance the temperature and all is well. The faucet type is good for those of you who do not have electricity.

As to price, the *Hydro Dent* is around $12, and the *Water Pik* can be purchased through your dentist from between $15 to $18, or in the discount stores for around $20 to $25 (1972 prices).

STIMUDENTS

These have been around a long time and are designed to clean the teeth and massage the gums in between the teeth. They work like a toothpick, but are much more effective and non-abrasive. They are designed to conform to the shape of the spaces between your teeth.

Made out of balsa-like wood, they are just compressible enough to form to the shape of your teeth and gums, which allows them to contact all surfaces. They are soft enough to massage the gum and yet not injure it. The stimudent is also firm enough to polish the areas between the teeth without being too abrasive. They are also nicely flavored and the packages are small enough to carry with you. Most drug stores carry them.

PLAK LITE

The plak lite does the same thing as disclosing tablets do — show up the food particles you leave in your mouth, but does this more dramatically but is also more expensive — like about $25.00 in drugstores. Your dentist could order you one for about $18.00. You'll need electricity, also.

ELECTRIC TOOTHBRUSH

Except in cases where someone has been unfortunate enough to have lost their hands, you could call the electric toothbrush the Lazy Toothbrush.

As you can probably tell, I'm not sold on them, but you should know their good and bad points and then decide for yourself. The good part first:

They are good for massaging most areas of your gums because you'll get in many more "strokes" per unit of time. This is only true in the areas that will be brushed in an up-down direction. Because of its design, there will be some areas of your teeth that simply cannot be properly brushed with the electric toothbrush; like the backs of the front teeth, upper and lower. Borrow a friend's and try it for yourself. You'll soon see what I mean.

The bad points result because an electric brush is not 100% effective in brushing every area of the mouth.

I would never recommend the electric toothbrush unless you supplement it by brushing at least once a day with the more flexible hand method. Your hand can more effectively get into more areas than *any* electric brush ever could.

So, it's up to you, but to brush right, you can't escape from the time-proven hand brushing method. For the record, I don't recommend electric toothbrushes.

8

THE NATURAL HOMEMADE DENTAL KIT

THE BASIC NATURAL TOOTHBRUSHER
MAKING BRUSH BRISTLES FROM VEGETABLE MATTER
THE NO-TOOTHBRUSH-GOOD-TEETH ROUTINE
MAKING YOUR OWN TOOTH CLEANER
NATURAL PAIN KILLERS
NATURAL BREATH SWEETENERS

Here are a few recipes and instructions for making your own natural toothbrushes, dentifrices, toothache remedies, and breath sweeteners. A great deal of the information which this section contains came from a.book called *The Herbalist,* by Joseph E. Meyer. It can be found in many health food stores, and it costs $3.95. Aside from its knowledge of early dental cleansers, it contains information on almost every known herb and its uses. If you can't find the book, you can order it from: Indiana Botanic Gardens, Hammond, Indiana, 46325.

THE BASIC NATURAL TOOTHBRUSHER

A fairly serviceable natural toothbrush can be constructed in the following manner:

Use a dried twig, preferably applewood, or other fruit wood, for the handle. It should be about six inches long, smooth and round, and about one fourth of an inch in diameter. Carve one end flat on one side, like this:

Then make notches on each side of this flattened part to hold the bristles from slipping back and forth. Like this:

Divide the bundles of natural bristles, which you have already prepared (more on that later), and fold them over the handle, working the bristles into the notches.

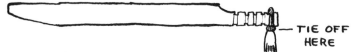

— TIE OFF HERE

Using strong thread, tie the bristles off close to the handle. Tie them as tightly as possible, having someone help you to hold them as you tie. Proceed in this same manner until you have secured all five sets of bristles. Then wrap the bristles with strong thread to prevent them from twisting around the handle.

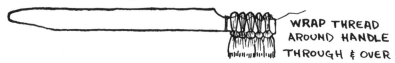

WRAP THREAD AROUND HANDLE THROUGH & OVER

When you've done all this, trim the bristles off evenly with a sharp knife or scissors.

FINISHED

MAKING BRUSH BRISTLES FROM VEGETABLE MATTER

There are three kinds of vegetables which make fairly good bristles, and which are also readily available in most sections of the United States and Canada. I will describe each one separately, and tell you how to prepare each of them, below:

A. *Marshmallow Roots* (Althea Officinalis, Mallow family) The common names for this are sweet weed, wymote and marshmallow. It is a perennial, which grows to a height of two to four feet. Its leaves are serrated, one to three inches long. Flowers are purple in color and about two inches in diameter. See if this drawing helps you to identify it. *To make the brush:* Take the straight and rather large roots. Cut them into lengths about five inches long. Unravel, or peel, the two ends, sort of like you would untwist a rope. Boil these with a few sticks of cinnamon to sweeten them. When tender, withdraw them carefully to avoid breaking, and soak them for 24 hours in brandy to dry and strengthen them. After this, dry the roots in a warm oven or a warm room. After drying, you can arrange and tie them in bundles, attach to the handle and trim to size. When they are to be used, run them under warm water for a few seconds until they're flexible. Then add your powder or paste and brush your teeth.

B. *Alfalfa Root* (Medicago Sativa, common names are lucern and alfalfa)
This nutritious plant is found throughout most of the United States and Canada. It is from one to one and one-half feet high and it flowers from June to August. The leaflets are obouate — oblong racemes pod, several seeded, linear, and coiled about two turns. The flowers are violet, purple, or bluish.
To make the brush: (Save the leaves for tea.) Take only those roots which are fairly large in diameter, and strip off the outer skin or bark, then dry them slowly at room temperature. When the roots are well dried, cut them into small pieces about three to five inches in length. Strike each end lightly with a hammer, thus detaching the fibers and forming a brush. Beat it only enough to create a bristle. You can then fold the roots in half, bundle them up and attach them to your handle. Remember to soak your brush in warm water before using.

C. *Licorice Root* (Glycyrrhiza Glabra, common name is sweet wood)
Licorice is a perennial herb, two to five feet high; leaflets in pairs of

four to seven are ovate and smooth. They are glutinous beneath a dark green color. The flowers are yellowish-white or purplish, with pulse-shaped racemes, the fruit legumes being about one inch long of brownish color, ovate and flat, one to six seeded. The root is grayish brown or dark brown, wrinkled lengthwise, internally yellow with a sweetish taste.

The only useable portion is the root. Aside from making a nice natural toothbrush, a teaspoon of the dried root in a cup of boiling water will act as a demulcent and a laxative.

To make the brush (which is a good one for delicate and tender gums): Select roots that are sound and straight. Divide each root into lengths of three to five inches and after drying them naturally by mild heat, rasp off the outer skin at each end. Again, fold over and bind together. The number of roots needed for all natural root brushes vary, depending on the size of the root.

Some people do not tie the bristles to a handle, but just hold the bristle bundles in the fingers to brush their teeth. However you do it, the idea is to clean the garbage off your teeth. Bear in mind that whether you use a natural root brush or a nylon one, you must brush immediately after eating to be effective. Also, remember that all types of natural toothbrushes must be soaked for a few minutes in warm water prior to their use.

THE NO-TOOTHBRUSH-GOOD-TEETH ROUTINE

The following six points describe how to keep your teeth healthy without brushing. It looks like an especially good plan for people traveling light, or for when you're caught at your friend's place with no toothbrush of your own and you don't want to use theirs. Here's how it works:

1) Completely avoid all refined and processed foods.

2) Finish every meal with a fibrous, raw vegetable, such as a carrot, celery, apple, etc.

3) This is followed by a thorough rinsing of the mouth with water, and a massage of the gums with your finger for at least one or two minutes after each meal. This finger massage should be done at least two times a day, even if you don't eat that often.

4) If your meal consists of nuts, or fruits such as raisins, dates, figs, etc., a more thorough and prolonged rinsing is necessary in order to remove these stickier food particles from your teeth and gums.

5) You must rinse with water right after drinking any other liquid.

6) Rinse once a day with a salt water solution; i.e., a tablespoon of salt, well mixed in a glass of water. While rinsing, attempt to suck the salt water between your teeth.

This natural cleansing method will not only be good for your teeth, save you dough on pastes and brushes, but it will also be good for the rest of your body too. Even if you can't do it this way, and you are into natural foods, your children can at least benefit from it. Strange, how difficult the above natural tooth cleaning method sounds to us, yet for about 200 million years man used this very method to naturally clean his teeth and massage his gums. NOTE: This 100% natural method predisposes the fact that you have all of your natural teeth and no existing dental problems or poor fillings.

MAKING YOUR OWN TOOTH CLEANER

When using powders or pastes to clean your teeth, it should be understood that if your diet is mostly raw, natural and preferably organic, you may only have to use the dentifrice once a day, prior to retiring at night. If you are eating a lot of refined and processed foods, especially of the sticky variety (breads, sweets, etc.) you must brush with a dentifrice after every meal· or snack. Many things, natural and synthetic, can work for you, and you can tell if they are working by checking your gums and teeth regularly. If the gums stay healthy, and you do not harm them in any way, and the dentist does not find any new tooth decay when he checks you out, whatever you are doing is working! If it ain't working, you'd better re-evaluate what you're doing and study the "Home Care" section of this book again.

Here are two dentifrice recipes from the 1800's. If they seem to fit your trip, give them a try. Remember, whatever works . . . .

1) a) Mix a small quantity of powdered *sage* with about one ounce of *myrrh*. All should be ground into a fine powder.

   b) Mix the following ingredients carefully:
   1 pound powdered arrow root
   3 ounces powdered orris root
   20 drops oil of lemon
   10 drops oil of cloves
   12 drops oil of bergamot
   Simply rub the oils with the powders until thoroughly mixed, and then brush with ecstacy.

2) Combine ingredients and mix until you have a paste of the consistency that you desire.
   ½ ounce powdered chalk
   3 ounces powdered orris root
   4 teaspoons tincture of vanilla
   15 drops of oil of rose gerranium
   Honey — enough to get the desired consistency

This can be kept in a small, airtight container and scooped onto the brush with a small stick kept in the jar for that purpose.

Psychologically, going back to nature should get you off. Enjoy, enjoy and enjoy, and you can do this much better with a healthy mouth.

NATURAL PAIN KILLERS (TOOTHACHE REMEDIES)

Again, attempting to cover it all, I will assume that some of you have or may have an unexpected emergency or you may know a friend who does. Here are a few ways of relieving the pain of an emergency naturally. Just remember that these methods are only designed to give you *temporary* relief — enough relief to get you to the dentist. Don't abuse them; pain is a warning, your condition ain't going to get better.

a) The best of the lot is *Oil of Cloves,* obtainable at most pharmacies or drug stores. It certainly is the most popular natural home remedy. Oil of Cloves is also easy to apply. The oil is put on a piece of cotton, (saturate it) then place the cotton into the cavity left by decay. If possible, you can take a safety pin bent at a 90% angle at the end and attempt to remove any food that may be stuck in the hole. Gently, gently — if it hurts, stop. If you can clean it out, place the cotton pellet in afterwards. If it's too painful, place it in immediately, without probing around. Next, get thee to the phone and start dialing for help.

b) The "old timer's" recipe of chewing the root of bull nettle, on the tooth that is hurting, has been highly spoken of.

c) There also happens to be a tree, the Prickly Ash, whose common name is the "toothache tree." It was named, of course, because chewing on its leaves is supposed to relieve a toothache.

d) If you get your toothache in the West Indies, the natives there alleviate the pain of toothache by chewing ginger root.

All of these remedies work to varying degrees. The very best toothache medicine is prevention. So get your mouth checked before it happens.

NATURAL BREATH SWEETENERS

The *only* causes of bad breath are rotten teeth or gums — the smell you get when something is eating away at your body — and the odor of stomach gases from an upset stomach. Both are diet-oriented, and though you may mask your smelly breath with so-called breath fresheners, the only permanent way to end bad breath is to eliminate the cause of it: disease of your mouth, or bad eating habits. Once you do that, you might just want to add the extra mellow touch to your now naturally sweet breath. Far out.

a) If your bad breath is due to bad eating habits, try drinking a cup of warm chamomile tea. Then find out what it is that you're eating to cause your stomach to get messed up. (See the section on "Diet.")

b) From the people of the Middle Ages, we learn: "Anise seeds chewed in the mouth ... maketh a sweete mouth and easie breath and amendeth the stench of the mouth." For some reason, that impresses me.

c) Cardamon Seed is much used in the Orient as a breath sweetener. Today it is most often seen in Europe — as I'm told — in fancy eating places and in cocktail lounges. If you see a seed in a dish, ask the proprietors if it's the Cardamon seed, and if it is, take a chew. This seed is now becoming available in many natural foods stores in the United States.

d) Also from the Orient, a small piece of sweet flavored Star Anise is nibbled, the same as you might nibble our sugar-containing after-dinner mints. It gives you star-like breath.

102

e) Whole cloves have been chewed to sweeten the breath for more than four thousand years. Some people claim that cloves have "antiseptic powers and are valuable preservatives."

Well, you can top this off with a good belt of warm salt water rinse and you'll now have a pretty good idea of what people did before they were "saved" by the industrial revolution and Madison Avenue money makers. I'll leave the natural trip with the reminder that hundreds of different ways may be available to clean your teeth and massage your gums. The few I've mentioned are not meant to indicate they are the only ones. Whatever you use, it should fulfill the time tested requirements for a healthy mouth:

1) Do what it is intended to do and have no harmful side effects
2) Be practical and readily available
3) Be used in conjunction with a good, sound, healthy and natural diet.

My trip is prevention and preventing is a thousand times easier than curing. I know no better way of preventing tooth and gum disease than a natural diet and supplementary brushing.

9

YOUR KID'S TOOTH TRIP

ORIENTATION

To begin with, you should examine your child's mouth in the same manner as you would examine yours, both teeth and gums. The difference here is that you will be doing the examination and the child will be "patiently" letting you examine him or her. As the parent, you will often have more control or influence on your child than will the dentist, and you can be of invaluable assistance to both your child and the dentist that treats him or her.

I will discuss your child's "Tooth Trip" in as logical and chronological order as I can. There may be some deviations which are necessary to fully discuss a subject, but I will include all you need to know. You should read through the chapter completely and then begin your examination. This chapter is intended to let you follow your child's mouth development from the pre-natal stage to the age he loses his last baby (primary) tooth. As you can see, this chapter is written to grow with your child. Don't lose it. It can help make your children's Tooth Trip a much better one than yours most likely was. Okay, here we go.

PRENATAL CARE

The first three months of pregnancy are the most critical for the child. It is during this period that the fetus is most sensitive to drugs and other substances that enter your body, and it is during this time that most birth defects occur.

The first development of the mouth begins when the fetus is about three weeks old, perhaps before you know you are pregnant. The first signs of teeth occur at about six weeks. Between four and five months, the crowns of some of the baby teeth have formed. By the time of your baby's birth (nine months), the crowns (parts of the teeth that will eventually be above the gums) of all twenty baby teeth will have formed.

The first three months of pregnancy are the time to watch your diet very carefully and to avoid *all* drugs — even the ones that haven't been proven to specifically cause birth defects. First, the diet . . .

DIET AND PRE-BABY

While you are pregnant, you will be feeding two people, you and your baby. Whether you care about your diet or not, you have the obligation and responsibility of another life and until the child is old enough to make decisions on his or her own, you owe it to the child to give it the best care and food you can.

I can only speak for myself and my old lady, but I would eliminate all unhealthy and harmful foods from my diet (See "Diet," page 126), and at least during pregnancy eat as many raw vegetables and fruits as possible, whole grains and rice, little meat (and make sure it's organic), raw milk, plenty of liquids and juices of all kinds, take a complete array of natural vitamins daily (from your health food store), get plenty of rest and exercise and don't get fat. Of course, it would be best to do all of it this way before you decide to make babies. You are what you eat, and so is your baby. Also, avoid stress, as this puts a strain on you and a strain on you is a strain on your baby. Give him a good shot at life; that's what it's all about.

DRUGS AND OTHER HARMFUL THINGS

Almost every drug you take will, in my mind, have a negative effect on your child, especially if taken in the first three months of pregnancy. During these months, the child not only needs good food, but also is more susceptible to changes in your system. While the child is forming, you should avoid:

1) alcohol
2) tobacco
3) white sugar
4) preservatives
5) caffein
6) diet pills (speed)
7) cocaine
8) LSD
9) heroine
10) downers—
    barbituates and sleeping pills
11) grass
12) all other artificial food trips

It has been conclusively shown that if you are strung out on something, there is a good change you child will be born addicted to the same thing. Best not to lay your hangups on your baby too soon.

If your diet is natural and balanced and you take vitamins, I do not recommend taking fluoride pills, for the reasons stated in the chapter on flouride (page 218).

ERUPTION OF THE TEETH

Your normal child will eventually have twenty baby teeth. I will enclose a chart that will give you the approximate eruption and shedding ages and names of the baby ones and the approximate eruption ages of the permanent ones. A drawing will show you where they are located. Remember, these ages are average and your child's teeth can still be considered normal if the ages shown vary from as much as six months to one year. Any longer deviation and you should check with your dentist.

NAMES AND AGES OF PRIMARY TEETH	AGE AT ERUPTION	AGE AT LOSS
Four Central Incisors	5th to 10th month	6 to 7 years
Four Lateral Incisors	6th to 11th month	7 to 8 years
Four First Molars	11th to 15th month	9 to 11 years
Four Cuspids	15th to 21st month	10 to 13 years
Four Second Molars	19th to 26th month	9 to 12 years

NAMES AND AGES OF PERMANENT CHOPPERS	AGE AT ERUPTION	HOPEFULLY NEVER LOST
Four Six-Year Molars	5½ to 6½ years	
Four Central Incisors	6 to 7 years	
Four Lateral Incisors	7 to 8 years	
Four First Bicuspids	10 to 11 years	
Four Second Bicuspids	11 to 12 years	
Four Cuspids	10 to 12 years	
Four Second Molars	12 to 13 years	
Four Third Molars	16 to 24 years	

Please note that matching upper and lower teeth carry the same name, so the drawing applies to both.

As the chart shows, your baby's first teeth can erupt as early as six months; some have even been known to erupt at or shortly after birth. This may be a little hard on your breasts, but hopefully it will not interfere with nursing.

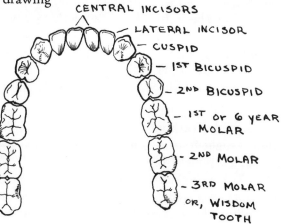

CENTRAL INCISORS
— LATERAL INCISOR
— CUSPID
— 1ST BICUSPID
— 2ND BICUSPID
— 1ST or 6 YEAR MOLAR
— 2ND MOLAR
— 3RD MOLAR OR, WISDOM TOOTH

The eruption (teething) of baby teeth in the child is a normal part of its development and growth. Some children have a harder time of it than others, and as I've said, the child's age of eruption may safely vary. There is no need to panic over slight variations; besides, there are some things, as I'll explain shortly, you can do to help your child through their teething trip. Also, if your child gets his or her teeth a little later than the average, don't listen to those who will tell you this will mean he or she will be a slow developer. There is no basis for that — it's nothing but an old wive's tale. In fact, it just might mean the child may just be a little mellower and not in a hurry, and that's good.

Anyway, a good time to start your examination of your baby's mouth would be at about six months old. It wouldn't hurt to start taking a peek before then. Babies are interesting little critters and you will no doubt be so proud and happy to have him or her that you'll want to thoroughly look the little dude over.

If your observations of your baby's actions (irritable, slight fever, excessive crying for no apparent reason) make you think the little beauty is having eruption problems, you should check his mouth out thoroughly. The area around soon-to-be front teeth is where you should look first.

If the gums in this area look red and angry and you see the tip of a tooth breaking in, you can pretty much assume your child is hurting. There really isn't alot you can do to help the child through one of its first traumas, but here are some things to try:

1) Mix about one ounce of 3% hydrogen peroxide and one ounce of warm water; mix well and apply this solution to the areas affected with a cotton swab.

2) Let the baby chew on teething toys at a very early age — before six months if he or she so desires. *Avoid hard and sharp objects* — meaning, don't let him or her chew on ashtrays or knives, etc. It is said that allowing babies to use teething toys early reduces the trauma of teeth eruption. It's definitely worth a try.

Difficult teething can cause pain and discomfort. It may even cause a slight fever. It should be noted that if your child suffers from nausea, extremely high fever, congestion, etc., you should consult a baby doctor (pediatrician) for these symptoms may indicate other problems, especially if you do not see evidence of a tooth erupting.

Follow the ages on the chart and you'll usually find the baby is more irritable at eruption time. Apply this medication when needed.

All of the baby teeth should be in by two and one-half years of age, and as the first permanent tooth will not erupt until about six years of age, your baby will be free of teething problems until then.

Breast and bottle feeding also play a role in the eruption and formulation of your baby's teeth. Many doctors feel that the longer you breast-feed your baby, the more healthy, teeth and otherwise, your child will be. This I believe is true — if your diet is good. Scientists have proven that there is no food that is as complete as a healthy mother's milk.

This is best understood when you realize that a baby that is breast-fed for two years requires no other source of food. This means that mother's milk supplies everything the child needs to grow. No other food can make that claim. So, it is ideal to breast-feed your baby until all the primary teeth are in, about two to two and one-half years, at the latest. If, for some reason you cannot or do not wish to breast-feed your baby, then make sure you take the child off the bottle at two to two and one-half years. The reason the child should not be allowed to use the teat or bottle past this age is that once all of the baby teeth are in, the child's swallowing pattern changes as the tongue adapts to the shape of the teeth. Thus, if the child is still allowed the bottle or the teat after the baby teeth are in, he puts unnatural pressures on his teeth with both his tongue and lips, which can lead to deformities. Nature gave the child his teeth to eat with and since eating the proper foods is one of the child's few ways of self-cleansing the teeth, you deprive the child by keeping him on the bottle or breast. Chewing at this age is also important in strengthening the bone that holds the teeth in place; the more they are used, the stronger the bone will be. Just keep in mind that bottles and pablems are new, and for millions of years the child was eating his/her own food as soon as it stopped nursing.

It has also been shown that overuse of the bottle often leads to pacifiers and then thumbsucking. Nature's way of aiding survival is to allow the child to get on its own as soon as possible. Don't resist nature's way by allowing your child to become dependent on unnatural things.

Another problem closely related to this is tongue-thrusting. This is also caused by keeping the child on the teat, bottle or pacifier so long that he/she isn't allowed to develop an adult swallowing pattern. This pattern comes naturally to the child as soon as all of his baby teeth come in. When the baby is allowed to suck, which thrusts the tongue forward, it consequently pushes the front teeth out, and presto! buck teeth.

The growth and development of the child's face (muscles and bones) demands you help him or her avoid habits that place unnatural pressures on the teeth or face. A child's bones are very pliable and can become deformed very easily — even by continual sleeping with the hands under the face. So, keep an eye on your child's sleeping habits.

Remember not to leave a bottle of milk in your baby's crib with him at night in order to "pacify" him. When he's hungry, feed him, but then take the bottle away. Otherwise, the acid in the milk will remain on his teeth all night and rot them pronto. Use water instead.

Decay moves so fast in baby teeth that periodic exams are necessary. You can do your part by keeping your eye on his or her home care and examining his or her mouth. It's a good idea to write down the dates you examine your child — every three months is a good average number. Writing eliminates forgetfulness.

At about the age of six, two things may happen:

1) Your child's four first permanent molars will erupt. This may be uneventful or it may be sore and painful. The top of each molar is very broad and has a hard time breaking the skin. It slowly breaks through the gum tissue, often leaving a flap of tissue overhanging the tooth. Food sometimes gets jammed under this flap and the irritation and toxins released by the germs eating the impacted food may cause the gums to become sore and infected. It is possible this may even turn into an abcess, causing swelling, pain and even fever. If you let it go this far, it

will need treatment at the dental office. At first indication of this, have your child rinse a few times with one ounce 3% hydrogen peroxide mixed with one ounce very warm water. If it gets worse, make an appointment. The dentist can often cut this troublesome tissue away and eruption proceeds normally.

2)   Your child may start losing his baby teeth (check chart). You can do one of three things:

    a)   Let them fall out on their own. If it seems to be taking an inordinate amount of time and the permanent tooth seems to be hung up, you can

    b)   pull it yourself. You do-it-yourself buffs should dig this.

    c)   Make an appointment and have the dentist pull it.

PULLING LOOSE PRIMARY TEETH

If the tooth or teeth are very loose (can be easily wiggled), *you* can be the dentist. Often the tooth is loose yet painful, and you can't get in touch with the dentist. This adds up to doing it at home.

Get a two foot long piece of dental floss or nylon string and wrap it around the tooth, going between the teeth on either side. Tie a square knot so the tie is at the gum line. When this is secured, pull with an outward and slightly upward movement — be firm. If the tooth is painful prior to pulling it, you can give a child's dose of aspirin about one half hour before pulling.

Once you get it out, you can control the bleeding by placing a tea bag soaked in cold water into the space where the tooth once lived. Have him or her bite down to hold it in place with slight pressure. Do this for at least thirty to sixty minutes. Bleeding should have stopped by then, but if not, continue with the tea bag until it does. If the bleeding persists and is still present twenty-four hours later, make an appointment and have the doc check it.

When bleeding stops, put your kid on soft foods for a few days. The day after you pull the tooth, have your child rinse with one-half teaspoon salt in one-half glass of warm water about three times per day. Have him or her swish well and do this for two days.

CHECKING FOR PRIMARY MOLARS

With your previous knowledge, perhaps some insight can be gained about the importance of the first permanent molar (six-year molar) which actually can erupt as early as five years of age. It is most important for you to make sure that all of the primary molars are in place before the six-year molar pops into view.

These baby molars stick around until about ages nine to eleven, at which time they are replaced by the permanent bicuspids. The importance of the healthy primary teeth being present in a normal position is more easily understood when you realize that their position greatly determines the position of the six-year molar, because they act as guiding planes for the permanent teeth. As the six-year molar is the key to the placement of the permanent teeth, it is imperative that the primary molars be right so that the permanent molars can come in right. If the six-year molar comes in okay, the chances are excellent that all the other permanent teeth will do the same. You watch for this and check with your orthodontist if you need help.

If this happens, far out; it'll be a breeze from here on in. There may be some discomfort caused by the loss of the remaining baby teeth, but that should be minor.

THE PEDODONTIST

If your kid's diet has not been excessively sugared, his or her primary teeth should not begin to show any signs of decay before the age of four or four and one-half. This is a good time to take him or her in for that first check-up. I recommend you go to a dentist who specializes in children's teeth. These guys are called *pedodontists* and are usually listed in the phone book as such.

I will mention some of the things you can watch for that will help tell you if the pedodontist is good or not:

1) Unless it is an emergency, explain to him that you'd appreciate it if he would avoid doing anything that might hurt or frighten your child. If he's good, he'll do this anyway. If you've paved the way and helped prepare your kid, he will probably enjoy his first visit. At four or four and one-half, kids are super intent on learning and are also receptive to the truth.

2) If the dentist does not want you in the room, heed his wishes. The child may try and use you as a crutch, show off, or try to pit you against the dentist. Be patient and caring, but stand firm. Give your pedodontist his chance alone with your kid.

3) If your child suffers from decay in his primary teeth, make sure they are filled. If this is not done:

a) he or she could run the risk of losing a tooth or teeth, and the other teeth could shift, resulting in the permanent teeth not having room to come in.

b) If decay occurs between the teeth, it can cause the teeth to move closer together. This can screw up incoming permanent teeth also, for if enough decay is present, a significant amount of space can be lost.

The above mentioned conditions can screw up your child's bite because, by natural laws of gravity and force, the teeth, jaws and their muscles are in a constant dynamic equilibrium. If any of these balancing forces are reduced (decay) or eliminated (lost teeth), teeth will move either forward, downward (for example, if a lower tooth is lost, the upper one will grow downward into the space), or both. This explains the importance of filling children's primary teeth or using a device called a space maintainer to fill the gap caused by premature loss of a tooth. The teeth are in essence always trying to move, and as long as there is a tooth next to or above or below it, a tooth cannot move and will maintain the healthy relationship needed to allow the permanent teeth to come in properly.

This dynamic equilibrium is necessary and natural, for as the tops of the teeth wear down (especially the soft baby teeth of the child), the top and bottom jaws would, in theory, get closer to each other. The more the wear, the closer they'd get. If this happened and nothing was done to prevent it, many kids would go around looking like their lower jaws were trying to touch their noses.

Nature designed your jaws, jaw muscles and teeth in such a way that you get the maximum force just prior to closing your jaws. If the teeth were allowed to wear down, it would mean you would now close down past the mid-point of maximum strength and efficiency and wouldn't be able to chew as hard. If they wore down far enough, you'd barely have enough strength left in your jaws to chew your food up.

Well, because the teeth are always trying to move, in all directions, they erupt a fraction more each day and thus replace the distance that was lost by wear. This couldn't happen if the teeth were closed twenty-four hours a day, so nature allowed for the jaws to remain open long enough each day to let the teeth erupt the necessary distance. This happens because the teeth are slightly separated at all times, except during eating and talking. You can check this out — swallow and then let your jaws relax; you'll find that they don't close. Anytime you think of it, stop and see if your teeth are touching. They won't be.

A good pedodontist understands these principles and will either
1) fill a decayed primary tooth or
2) pull it if the permanent tooth is due in shortly.

Have him identify the tooth and check your chart (page 106) yourself before making this decision. A good point to keep in mind is to always make sure any decision has been fully discussed.

If the tooth is filled, amalgam (silver) should be used, unless the tooth is badly decayed or broken, in which case the stainless steel crown is best. But remember, the tooth is a primary and need only last until your chart shows the permanent one due to erupt. You don't need gold fillings in primary teeth.

Many times, because decay moves so fast in soft baby teeth, the nerves of the teeth get infected and must be removed. The nerve can be removed and the tooth capped with a stainless steel crown. This is an invaluable aid in saving the tooth and preventing the loss of its space. But again, this work is valuable only if the primary tooth must hold its space for a considerable time. Otherwise, save your money and ask the guy to pull it.

BRUSHING

Sometime around the age of three or four, your child is co-ordinated enough to begin to be able to use a toothbrush. When that time comes, when you "feel" he or she is ready, go get a small, very soft brush and introduce it by brushing *with* your child. Put paste (or powder) on your brush and demonstrate, then put paste on his or hers and let 'em go. Make sure their brushing is gentle and they pretty much stay on the teeth. Once they get the hang of it, brush with them regularly. That's the way to transfer your *Tooth Trip* to them.

PREMEDICATION

Many of you will be interested in what can be done to relieve your child's fear, pain and anxiety while at the dentist.

If you go to a good pedodontist, he will be well prepared for this situation. Many kids just don't dig going to the dentist. Without going into the many possible reasons why this is so, I still feel it is important to minimize the negative aspects of your kid's dental visits. Since one way of relieving a child's fears is premedication, I want to familiarize you with what's available.

First, observe the situation. If you feel your child is upset because of the actions or the "feeling" in a pedodontist's office (with good reason) seek another pedodontist. Far better to politely leave the office than to become emotionally involved with the pedodontist or your child, which only reinforces the child's fears and doesn't alter the situation.

Second, realize a situation frequently exists wherein the cause of the kid's upset is not the pedondontist, but rather is due to factors not accessible to the dentist, such as something in the child's past, or his or her relationship with the parent. In these situations, the pedodontist will want to advise premedication in order to calm your child so he can work. I am not in favor of the use of chemicals as "tranquilizers" but there may be times you or the pedodontist feels there just isn't another choice. However, be sure to check with your doctor about possible allergies or other side effects from the drug before you allow the pedodontist to administer them.

Choice of drugs:
a) Nitrous Oxide
b) Demerol or Nisintil
c) Quaalude

Nitrous Oxide (laughing gas, magic air) is the safest drug used in children's dentistry. It produces a mellow and relaxing state of mind that makes the child very receptive to whatever is taking place. This state has even been described as euphoric and offers the following advantages:

a) It increases the pain threshold so your child won't even feel the shot. Guaranteed. Works on adults, too.

b) It has an amnesiatic effect. The appointment will seem short and the child remembers little, greatly reducing future apprehension.

c) It has an euphoria effect. Your child may experience a great deal of pleasure.

d) It is extremely safe. There are only a few contraindications for its use: if your child's respiratory track is congested by a cold or sinus trouble or by genetic defect, which your physician should know about; or if your child is an asthmatic. Nausea is the only known side-effect. Make sure your child doesn't eat at least six hours prior to the appointment.

e) It acts for a short duration only, and your child returns to a normal state within five minutes. This allows your kid to leave the office alert and in good spirits.

Demerol and Nisintil are both stronger drugs than nitrous oxide and, while safe, should be used only if you feel strong medication is justified by the situation. Do not let the doc talk you into this stuff (or anything else) against your judgement or intuition. Always attempt to work things out before using these forms of medication.

Another drug which is very effective is a non-narcotic drug called Quaalude. It has proven itself both as a sedative and as a reliever of fears and anxiety. It is also good because it has few side effects — except perhaps occasional nausea.

The use of *tranquilizers* is, in our opinion, neither wise nor effective on children or adults. These barbituates should be discouraged. Their side effects are more severe than the above drugs, yet they are not more effective.

ORTHODONTICS

A short rap on orthodontics and children should effectively close out this chapter.

First, remember to ask your kid's dentist when the best time would be to see an orthodontist (brace man) for a check-up. Today, orthodontists deal mostly with prevention and interception of the problem. This attitude saves you money, for less work has to be done, and the experience is definitely less traumatic for the child.

If the orthodontist has a chance to examine your child at an early age, say five or six, he can often predict, by taking measurements of tooth sizes and their rates of growth, if your child will need braces in the future. If he feels this is the case, he can perform what is called selective serial extractions and in some cases, this will be all that is needed to do the job.

I feel that orthodontics is one of the most positive aspects of modern dentistry (oral surgery and preventive dentistry being the others) since it is very important that one's teeth be straight and one's bite good. Straight teeth are much easier to keep clean, while correct bite will let you avoid the trauma and future pain that often results from bad occlusion (bite), which is much more difficult if not impossible to correct later on. Mom, you owe it to your kid to check his orthodontic needs early. It will most likely be easier on your wallet, too.

The only aspect of orthodontics I can't recommend is cosmetic orthodontics. The straightening of a single tooth simply for cosmetic reasons — but it's your money, and it's up to you.

Getting into the technical side a little further, here are a few things you should know.

All facial contours, boney growths, and teeth sizes and shapes are hereditary. So, the orthodontist will want to talk to you about tooth-size and jaw-length relationships. It can be seen and measured that if a child inherits his mom's small jaw and his old man's large teeth an imbalance may result and the end product (your child) may have teeth too big for his small jaw. So, if your old lady is small and you are huge, you can expect your children to have ortho problems, and it would be wise and kind to get them to an orthodontist at a young age. To have teeth too large for the mouth is a drag. Among the negative trips it can cause is preventing some teeth from erupting and crowding or impacting others. (An impacted tooth is one that is buried in the jaw.) This situation also results in an abnormal bite, called malocclusion. It is like gears that should join in harmony but, due to irregular size and positioning, are jammed up and do not function well, or at all. This causes excessive trauma and stress in the mouth dynamics, which makes the teeth extremely difficult to keep clean. Also, as the person gets older, malocclusion can result in gum disease, bone loss, and loss of teeth.

Other forms of malocclusion involve facial deformities related not to teeth but to profile. On one extreme there's the "Bucky Beaver" profile. This is a jaw to jaw mismatch in which the upper jaw sticks out further than the lower and "Bucky" appears.Or the reverse condition may result. This is the classic "Andy Gump" profile, with the lower jaw sticking out much further than the upper. In both instances, teeth need to be extracted and the orthodontist has to realign the teeth and jaw to regain a normal relationship. Sometimes chin straps and headgear (straps with elastic positioned around the neck) are used to correct this situation. Every trip is different, so don't worry till you find out where your child stands. Remember, the *earlier* you get your kid started, the easier and cheaper it will be.

Some orthodontists attempt to use removeable appliances to straighten teeth. This is not good, and a warning is in order. You should definitely avoid the removeable appliances, and perhaps the orthodontist who advocates them as well. All removeable appliances do is tilt the teeth — without repositioning the bone. Relapses and failures often result from this form of treatment and it's a waste of your time and money and is a trauma for your child.

TEEN-AGERS

I hope you've gotten my point about prevention and home care being the best treatment. If you didn't, your child will pay a heavy price during his or her teen-age years, when heavy emotional trips and growing social responses coupled with a poor diet and parental rebellion can add up to hard times. The best thing for you is to cultivate the desire for good health in your child before the teen-age years.

Good luck!

10

EMERGENCIES

HOW TO TELL WHEN YOU HAVE ONE
PAIN
WISDOM TEETH
DECAY
GUM DISEASE
FRACTURED OR BROKEN TEETH OR FILLINGS
BITES AND FIGHTS
LIP AND CHEEK BITING
BURNS
HERPES SIMPLEX
WHAT ELSE?

HOW TO TELL WHEN YOU HAVE ONE

In general, an emergency is any situation which you or somebody else judges
needs immediate attention. However,
I've had lots of experience dealing with
emergencies of all kinds and have
generally come to the conclusion
that most people do not
really know what consti-
tutes a true dental
emergency. As a re-
sult, they overreact
(usually with an
excess of fear and
haste) and end up
paying an emer-
gency fee to the dentist when the condition wasn't all that RED, or
they underreact, calmly ignoring the symptoms of real emergency,
and end up losing teeth and spending money which could have easily
been avoided.

Much of the responsibility for this waste of human effort, energy, money and teeth must lie with the dental profession itself, for this profession has not exactly distinguished itself for its efforts to educate you on the subject of dental emergencies. Nevertheless, you are the one who suffers for this lack of knowledge, so you are the one who must supply what the dental profession has not. This chapter should help fill the gap.

First, I'll discuss the concept of the dental emergency, in an attempt to show you how to distinguish a true emergency from a false one. Then, I'll cover most kinds of possible emergencies and show you what you can do at home yourself. Okay? Here we go.

PAIN

Basically, there are two kinds of emergencies:

1) a condition which threatens the vitality of the organism and which left unattended will result in the (immediate) further deterioration of that organism. Example: severe or recurrent bleeding, or, less obviously, advanced gum disease.

2) severe recurrent pain which doesn't seem to be relieved by aspirin or oil of cloves. This is a psyche emergency (it really bends your head, causing fear, anxiety, tension) and is NOT NECESSARILY a true indicator of an emergency condition in your body. This is not to say, of course, that the pain is not real, nor important to eliminate.

It is not always true, of course, that a situation will be distinguishable into emergency number one or number two, but these are useful general distinctions. An emergency number one is usually the result of an unforseen event, such as an accident, or other sudden occurrence. An emergency number two is more likely the accumulated result of poor dental care or body inattention on your part. Like, not keeping your Tooth Trip together.

Of course, in either case, you're going to feel that you want immediate relief from the pain, the bleeding, or whatever. So would I. But here's the general guideline to use. When you judge, after trying to get yourself somewhat calm and together, that unless you act immediately your present condition will deteriorate further, then you're in an emergency number one and it's best to go straight to the phone and call the Doc. If, on the other hand, you decide that really you have an emergency number two, then you should take a look at my suggested home remedies, which I'll go into in a minute. Most of the time you probably won't be able to tell which situation you are in, and maybe you'll have some of both most of the time. But remember, an emergency number one is likely to occur at most any hour, often when the dentist (or doctor) is off work and will therefore charge you AT EMERGENCY RATES, which are considerably higher than standard office rates. If it turns out that your emergency is a number two, you might be able to wait it out until regular office hours (with the help of my home remedies) and thus save yourself some dough. So, the key to distinguishing the one situation from the other may be PAIN, which after all is the body's built-in warning system — to let you know something is going on that needs attention. However, in most cases, pain is just a symptom and therefore the relief of pain does not mean the *cause* of the pain has been remedied. And in general, pain is more often associated with emergency two than emergency one.

One last word about pain. In the remedies listed below, primary attention is focused on relieving pain. This means that the remedies below may help you deal with an emergency number two, but only TEMPORARILY. Do not think that because your toothache has "quit hurting" the tooth is repaired. All that has happened is that you may have won a temporary respite — designed to give you time to make that appointment.

As a parting shot may I say that emergency number twos are all situations indicative of the fact that you haven't got your tooth trip together.

WISDOM TEETH

Wisdom teeth are the number one cause of dental emergencies. They are the most difficult teeth to keep clean, they are the hardest to see and to brush and they often only partially erupt in your mouth. All this means they are prime candidates for decay. When your gum back along the jawbone or at the jaw hinge feels sensitive or dully aches, I suggest you rinse well with a hydrogen peroxide solution (3% H.P. diluted with an equal part water) then follow this with a salt water rinse (one-half glass salt water and one-half teaspoon salt). If you are into pain killers (chemicals) you can swallow one. Best call your Doc and get those teeth x-rayed.

If you let this situation go until it gets extremely painful, what can I say? Try a few aspirins, rinse every hour and in between call the Doc until you get an appointment. This situation is a true number two emergency, which you could have prevented by getting that tooth checked out maybe several months ago when it first began bothering you.

After the tooth is extracted, follow the dentist's instructions. Usually, these are:

1) ice pack 15 minutes an hour for the first two hours
2) take the pain killers or antibiotics he gives you
3) stay in bed the first 24 hours
4) begin rinsing twenty-four hours after extraction with warm salt water, gently, and about every four hours for two days
5) eat only soft foods for the first several days
6) call your doc if there is any sudden change in your mouth condition.

The space where the tooth was will take about six weeks to heal and does so from the inside out — do not be alarmed if a hole is there. If you notice any pain beginning about two days or so after the extraction, call your dentist at once. You may have what is called a *dry socket* — meaning the blood didn't clot well and the bone and its nerve endings are exposed. Your dentist can treat this. These things sometimes happen and are not necessarily the dentist's fault.

Immediately after extraction, the dentist, or surgeon, will have you bite down on a piece of gauze for about two hours. Do this and don't talk; it is to allow the bleeding to clot. If the bleeding seems to continue after you take out the gauze, it's O.K. As long as it is not gushing, that is. You can put a moistened tea bag in place of the gauze if the socket still bleeds. If you're concerned, call him.

DECAY

The best treatment is prevention, but when you have the pain of toothache, the best home remedy is OIL OF CLOVES. You can get it at just about any drug store. The only time I recommend using it is as a temporary measure. No matter how big or little the cavity is, OIL OF CLOVES will not cure it. You must get an appointment with the dentist as soon as possible. You can do a few other things along with the OIL OF CLOVES:

1) Saturate a cotton ball or small piece of cloth with Oil of Cloves and place it directly on the painful area.
2) Take a pain pill, aspirin or whatever, but swallow it. *Do not ever* place an aspirin in your mouth without swallowing it.
3) Do not chew anything hard or sticky until the tooth is fixed.

4) Do not eat anything with *sugar* in it — it'll be like stepping on the tooth's nerve.

5) Do not eat or drink anything too *hot* or too *cold.*

GUM DISEASE

All you need to know to care for your gums has been thoroughly covered in the section on "Home Care."

FRACTURED OR BROKEN TEETH OR FILLINGS

Most fractures are more frightening than painful. If you break a tooth or a filling and it hurts, the chances are you either have decay under it or you've exposed or come close to exposing a nerve. In either case, it is a full fledged emergency number one, and you can:

1) Apply Oil of Cloves on a piece of cotton or cloth and place directly on the painful area. Leave it on until the pain goes away. You may need to resaturate the cotton periodically.

2) Take a pain pill and follow my directions for decay, above.

3) If the tooth in question does not hurt, even when eating or brushing, you generally will have more time and therefore less emergency. Any fracture is a potential source of future trauma, so don't let the lack of pain keep you from making that appointment. The fracture can get worse. The gum can overgrow the area of the fracture and cause pain, or food can get stuck in the area of the fracture and eventually decay the tooth. If the tooth doesn't hurt, keep it clean (brush and water pick it).

BITES AND FIGHTS

Any human tooth-inflicted bite is potentially very serious, especially if the person who bit you had bad gums. You may not get a chance to ask the person who bit you or to check his or her mouth out to see how clean it was. Most bite wounds result from fighting; wounds from a fist hitting the teeth are especially serious.

Regardless, the treatment should begin immediately. You should:

1) Clean the wound with something sterile and antibacterial — hydrogen peroxide, iodine, etc. Just plain water is better than nothing, if that's all you have.

2) Call a doctor if the wound is in any area of your body other

than the facial area. An oral surgeon should be called if the wound is in the facial area. Your regular dentist may have to be seen if no oral surgeon is available. Also, if you really got wacked, there may be damage to your teeth, so have the dentist check that out.

3) If the wound is painful, you can take a pain pill, if you wish.

4) The wound should be closed up if it is large (stitched) and if the Doc doesn't prescribe a broad spectrum antibiotic, you should ask him why. It is possible that because the wound is small, you may not need antibiotic therapy, but have him explain this.

Don't wait to get attention for bite wounds. You may be interested to know that the most serious of all bite wounds are caused by humans and this is because we have the filthiest mouths. In dental school, we were taught that other animals who inflict serious bite wounds are:

1) Cats
2) Monkeys
3) Camels (!)

The dog is pretty far down on the list and makes me wonder if it isn't better to be licked by a clean dog than frenched by a dirty chick.

LIP AND CHEEK BITING

This type of biting is mostly found in kids and young grown-ups and can be caused by many things.

1) Nervousness, asleep or awake
2) Trauma from an accident
3) Bad fillings rubbing on cheek or tongue
4) Bad bite in which cheek is bitten every time you chew
5) Wisdom teeth becoming "sensitive."

Generally, this is discovered because the mouth wound is either painful, bleeding or both. The treatment is partly your responsibility and partly the dentist's. He can correct the problem if it is caused by an accident, bad fillings, bad bite or wisdom teeth. If the problem is caused by nervous chewing, either while asleep or awake, you're going to have to work on your head, find out why you think it's happening (source) and stop doing what's causing it. Like, maybe your girl friend or your boss is hassling you. You could just be sleeping in an awkward position. As for the immediate pain or trauma, you can rinse with hydrogen peroxide, salt water or both. Just please make sure you eliminate the real cause of the problem.

BURNS

Burns of the mouth can be caused by numerous things; some of these are more serious than others, but if the agent causing the burn is removed or diluted, the wound usually heals without further incidence.

The most common causes are:

1) Burns from hot foods. Most people aren't always aware of the cause since the pain may not develop until the skin sloughs off. Rinsing with a mild mouthwash usually helps relieve the tenderness. If the wound is very painful, call the dentist; he may either have you come down or prescribe a drug, possibly a dental ointment such as 4% butyn and 1.1500 metaphen.

2) Aspirin burns. Usually caused by placing aspirins (especially if it's crushed) or toothache drops or toothache gum in the mouth and leaving it there long enough to burn the gums or cheeks. Only way to stop this is to stop chewing or placing the aspirin in your mouth. Even a bad dentist is almost better than aspirin burn! Again, a mild mouthwash will help.

3) As I've said, many substances can cause burns, especially those which should never have gone in the mouth in the first place. Either follow the directions on the label for the antidote or rinse with neutral (temperate) water at least five to ten times until the symptoms stop. If you're not sure of the damage, get in touch with the Doc.

With almost any burn, the pain is minimal until the skin that was burned sloughs off. This allows the exposed skin to come in contact with anything put in the mouth. Also, when you swallow or speak, you can irritate a burn if it's near the areas of movement. Watch the acidity and temperature of your foods until the burn heals; stop smoking until it heals. If the burn doesn't go away in ten to fourteen days, you'd best check with the doc.

HERPES SIMPLEX

These cold sores or fever blisters are covered in the chapter "Mouth Diseases To Approach With Caution." Principally, there's not much you can do except wait them out; they usually clear up in seven to ten days. If not, call the Doc. In the meantime, try our mouth rinse home remedy, eliminate all spicy and hot foods from your diet, and try taking lots of natural vitamin B..

WHAT ELSE?

Any emergency situation not covered in these pages is either a good emergency number one or directly in the province of "Mouth Diseases To Approach With Caution." In either case, the telephone is what you head for first and the dentist or doctor second. Please, please don't wait my friend; waiting will only make it worse.

11

LOVE YOUR BODY AND FEED IT RIGHT

EAT RIGHT AND SAVE YOUR TEETH
GETTING YOUR FOOD TRIP TOGETHER
FAKE AND NATURAL VITAMINS
VITAMIN E
DOSING UP
THE GARBAGE DIET
YOU AND THE COWS
THE HUNZA
BOOKLIST

Someone once said, "The best way to eat a lot is to eat good food and little of it; that way you'll live long enough to be able to eat a lot." Who was that?

Diet is directly or indirectly the cause of almost all human ailments, including the most prevalent of all human diseases, tooth decay.

I believe that at one time man ate a beautifully balanced and natural diet, and most likely died of accidents, predators and old age, but not of the diseases we all suffer from today. The facts speak for themselves. Had early man suffered from the diseases we now suffer from, without any of the medical aid we now have, he just wouldn't have made it. The same facts tell us that most people today either do not know or care about proper diet.

If you do not happen to be concerned about finding out what diet is all about, you are welcome to skip ahead, for (at least dentally speaking) you can prevent tooth and gum disease and still eat what you are presently consuming if you follow exactly and rigidly the "Home Care" plan I've explained. You have little margin for error, though, as the toothbrush and other devices are only meant to be a replacement for a healthy natural diet.

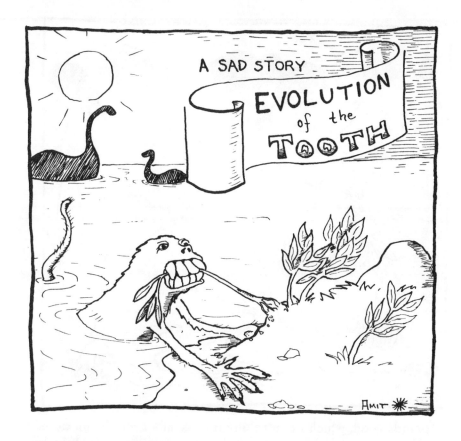

EAT RIGHT AND SAVE YOUR TEETH

I believe the best diet to be the diet that early man ate, beginning two hundred million years ago and lasting up until man began to refine and process foods.

This diet varied from place to place and from time to time, but basically it consisted of mostly raw fruits and vegetables and a minimum of cooked foods and a minimum of meat. Contrary to many people's beliefs, especially the meat industry, man was a vegetarian for countless millions of years and he got along very well, as do most people today who eat little or no meat.

So, I believe the ideal diet (guaranteed not to cause decay) consists of raw vegetables and fruits (some steamed) and a small amount of meat. If you do eat meat, get it from an organic source, which means it's the same meat as the other, but without the antibiotics, various types of speed and hormones that commercial meat and fowl are shot up with. The commercial guys do this to grow bigger animals faster and to keep more of them alive. Even if

this sounds good, which I don't think it does, all of the chemicals are passed on to you in your meat and they will screw you up. I doubt that you'd voluntarily take antibiotics, speed and hormones all the time on your own. No medical person of any stature would recommend continually taking these three drugs, and yet if you eat meat, three times a day, that's what you're doing! Same goes for getting your vegetables organically grown. You eliminate the pesticides that non-organic vegetables are grown with. Remember, pesticides have been in use less than 100 years; they are designed to kill, and are harmful enough to man that they have finally gotten around to banning DDT, the most widely used one. It may not always be possible to get organically grown vegetables and fruits, but you'll be better off when you do.

The more people, the more difficult it is to feed them, and the commercial types originally hoped that through the use of pesticides, more food could be grown. It is true that more food can be grown, but it is also true that pesticides have proven harmful. It is time to control the population through positive birth control measures instead of resorting to the use of pesticides.

Anyway, the second most important thing to do with a natural diet is to balance it so you are sure you get all the vitamins and minerals and protein you need for sound health. If you decide to get into the natural trip, please read up on the books I recommend in order to find out what nutrients do and how much you need. The space I have to cover this aspect of the diet would not allow me to tell it as it should be told. So, if you are really interested, the books are there and the results await you.

I know it will not be possible nor practical for many of you to change your diet radically. The next best thing is to alter it in as many ways as possible, for whatever you do toward improving your diet, you will be just that much better off.

GETTING YOUR FOOD TRIP TOGETHER

The basic principle of the diet I recommend is to increase the quantity of natural foods in your diet and decrease the refined and processed foods which you eat. Here's why:

1) Raw fruits and vegetables are excellent natural cleansers of teeth and excellent massagers of gums. Man used this method successfully for nearly two hundred million years, during which time he had neither the dentist nor the Tooth Trip to aid him. The abrasiveness and fibrous nature of raw food is the reason that it cleans and massages. This, in essence, aids in the prevention of tooth disease. The fact that raw fruits and vegetables do not cause decay also adds to their preventive character. This value is lost if the fruits and vegetables are excessively cooked or canned; the sugar and preservatives that are usually added destroy the naturally cleansing effect and add the stuff that can cause decay. If a fruit or vegetable is excessively cooked, it loses its fibrous nature. Compare the difference between cooked and raw cauliflower, and thus their beneficial massaging action.

2) Even the natural raw sugars found in many fruits are not harmful to the teeth, as the size of the natural sugar molecule is still much too large for the decay-causing germs to eat. The fact

is that natural raw sugars need to be left in the mouth for days before the enzymes of the mouth can break them down to a size small enough for the germs to digest. Honey is a natural sugar and its molecules are too large for the germ to eat without help from the mouth's enzymes. Of course, brushing your teeth, you never will leave anything in your mouth long enough to do damage.

3) Salad should be eaten at the *end* of the meal; or at least one-half of it at the end and one-half at the beginning. There are two reasons for this:

a) the salad (a mixed vegetable salad, not the restaurant salad of just lettuce) acts as a cleanser for the teeth and

b) as a source of bulk for the stomach and intestines. This is important, since the intestines rely on bulk to move the food along at a normal rate. Most refined and processed foods, or cooked vegetables and fruits, are either so broken down and/or dehydrated that they have no bulk. This means that under any form of pressure, this type of food loses its form and in essence, collapses. You can readily see this and test it by feeling the difference in bulk and texture between a raw carrot and cooked, canned or mashed ones.

Every plant, fruit or vegetable is composed of millions of cells. Each cell's membrane or covering is called *cellulose*, and raw cellulose cannot be digested by man's stomach juices. It is this fact that allows raw vegetables and fruits to maintain their bulk and shape under pressure. When plants are cooked or processed or refined, this cellulose is either softened by the cooking or broken down by the refining or processing procedures. When you chew raw plants or vegetables and you swallow them, they enter the stomach to begin the digestive processes. Then the food enters the intestine, and the intestine enlarges to accommodate the size of food that enters it. The intestine will accommodate just about any amount of food, as many of you may know, but once inside, the opening closes down and the muscles that surround the intestine contract behind and around the food mass. When the muscles contract on the food, they exert a great deal of pressure. If the bulk of the food is raw, it will not collapse under all of this force. The trick here is that the rate at which the food is moved along the intestine is dependent upon, to a limit, of course, the amount the intestine is distended. The intestine is circular, and if the food that is pushed into it (raw) maintains its bulk, it will be moved through at a constant rate. Normally, this takes about four to six hours and is more than enough time to allow all the good things in the food to be assimilated into your body. This means that you should be going to the bathroom about twice a day.

If your diet does not consist of raw foods, especially at the end of a meal, all the same things happen, except that when the muscles of the intestine close down on the overly cooked or processed and refined foods, it has no bulk to stop the muscles from squashing down on the food. Thus, when this happens, the size to which the intestine can open is much less than the size the intestine opens if the bulk of the food is natural and raw. The fact that the refined food collapses under muscle pressure and has no bulk means that the food is moved along in the intestines at a much slower rate. Thus, instead of taking four to six hours to pass through your body, it now may take twenty-four or forty-eight hours. This means that every bit of water, which probably isn't much with processed and refined foods, is taken up by the body. This, of course, further dehydrates the already dehydrated food and means that by the time you get ready to defecate, you'll have to pop your little eyeballs to get it out. What I've been telling you is exactly what causes constipation, hemorrhoids, colitis, and many other painful man-made diseases. It is also the reason why Americans spend millions and millions of dollars on laxatives and enemas that will, hopefully, allow them to flush the food out of their intestines. Diet, brother, diet! If you want to go regularly to the bathroom, raw fruit and vegetables will do a better job than the artificial stuff in the pharmacy. Also, the fibrous nature of the raw plants acts like a broom for your intestines — in effect — and very efficiently cleans your intestines. This is important when you consider how much oil and grease the normal American diet consists of. This grease, lard, oil, etc., coats your stomach and prevents the proper assimilation of food into your body. If you've ever tried to clean grease from a pan, you'll know what I mean. It ain't easy. And you can't use Dutch Cleanser and steel wool in your gut.

Another value of raw and natural plants is in the food value they release. Plants are living things just as animals are. They contain their own digestive enzymes and more food value than most meats. Of course, much of this fantastic value is destroyed when plants are cooked, but when they are raw and chewed up by the teeth, the cellulose is broken down and the nutritious contents of the plants' cells are released. Thus, you not only get the cleansing value for your teeth and intestines, but you also get the food value and bulk which your body and intestines need to work well. Can't beat that.

I didn't invent these principles. This is the way man's system naturally evolved. It is why we have and need teeth. They evolved to allow man to chew up the only food available to him for millions of years. Early man, at this time, didn't have fire to cook his food, didn't have seeds to plant and cultivate, didn't have knives and machines to chop and grind his food, and for certain he didn't have huge machinery to process, refine and preserve his food. Nor, I might add, did he have supermarkets to sell him food in cans.

Everything that enters your mouth, starting with the milk from your mother's breast, affects both your mental and physical well-being and health. You are what you eat, and if you don't eat well, you will lose not only your teeth, but the rest of your health too.

FAKE AND NATURAL VITAMINS

Most commercial foods are vitamin enriched (meaning that vitamins are artificially injected) because in the act of refining and processing most foods, the vitamins and many minerals are destroyed, and we must add synthetic vitamins to the food or we'd all die of malnutrition and vitamin deficiency.

Man did not invent vitamins. We only discovered their existence and how they affect the quality of our lives. The need for vitamins was not even recognized until about four hundred years ago when ships began to travel long distances, putting man in an environment separated from land. What happened to enlighten us as to the need for vitamins (which, of course, they didn't know existed) was that sailors would die of *scurvy* before these first voyages were over. More than concerned, the British recognized the need for finding out what caused scurvy and went to work on the task immediately. The results were that they figured out that a lack of fresh fruits and vegetables caused scurvy. They still didn't know that it was vitamin C that caused this, for in the 1500's and 1600's, man hadn't reached such "high" levels of intelligence as he has today. Anyway, this experience proved that a lack of fresh fruit or vegetables over an extended period of time (3-6 months in some cases) resulted in *death*. Yep, people died from a lack of vitamin C and they called it scurvy. Once the British figured that out, they stocked their ships with limes, (limes happen to be an excellent source of vitamin C), and lo and behold, the British Navy stayed healthy and came to be called "Limeys."

When we "opened" China during the Boxer rebellion (only a few hundred years ago), we came steaming into a country that had one of the longest recorded histories known to man; we proceeded to tell them it was not civilized to husk their rice and showed them how to make nice fluffy white rice. Millions of Chinese died as a result, for in husking their rice, they destroyed the natural vitamin B that was stored in the husks of the natural rice. Instantly, we created a new disease (after all, we had to make up a name for the disease the Chinese were dying from) which we called beri-beri. Later we proved what caused it, and we decided it was best that the Chinese did not husk their rice any more. For those who insisted on husked rice, the answer was vitamin B complex pills. How civil of us!

Vitamins C and B are soluble in water and are thus not stored in our bodies. We need them daily to survive. Such is not the case with the non-water soluble (fat soluble) vitamins, as I shall mention shortly.

Because the C and B vitamins are not stored and because they, especially C, are destroyed rapidly when they come in contact with the air (oxidized), we suffer. If they aren't taken on a regular basis, we eventually die of scurvy, but in between the two states (ideal amount of vitamin C and total lack of C) and over an extended period of time there can be found other stages of disease such as:

1) Malaise (run down feeling)
2) Decreased resistance to colds and infection
3) Slow healing rate
4) Bleeding and painful gums
5) Headaches and pains in joint
6) Nausea and vomiting
7) Loss of teeth
8) Death

Recognize any of these stages? You should, most of you have some of them, and in essence, are on the road to scurvy. Whether you finally get there or not has nothing to do with how much you can suffer along the road. Look at this list again. Don't depend on "chemical" vitamins. Be sure you get them from a natural source. (That's where they came from in the beginning and that's where you should get them.) Almost all health food stores sell vitamins from natural sources. Read the label. A synthetic ("chemical") vitamin is not a vitamin, no matter how much cheaper it is. Isn't your health worth a few extra cents? Think.

VITAMIN E

In my research, I found that heart attacks were almost non-existent prior to 1900. There were strokes, which are much different and more infrequent than heart attacks, and mostly caused by stresses and hereditary defects, but almost no heart attacks. In looking further, I discovered that the rate of heart attacks increased dramatically about the turn of the century, shortly after the machine that made white flour from whole wheat was invented. Other research showed me that two of the foods that were eliminated in the making of white flour were vitamin E and lecithin. It so happens that these two *foods* were what kept excess cholesterol from forming in the arteries. It is this excess cholesterol that is now thought to be a major cause of heart attacks. How's that grab you? If you are one of the millions who've eaten white bread all your life, I'd run (walk, be calm) to the health food store and get me some E and lecithin, some C and D and A and B and find out in what proportion they should be taken. Always remember to take vitamins right before, during or immediately after meals.

As far as taking too many vitamins, I really don't think you need worry. I have yet to see concrete evidence that proves anyone has taken too much of a vitamin, but I've seen thousands of cases where people haven't gotten enough. I doubt if a heart attack or scurvy or beri-beri is worth finding out that you haven't been taking enough.

If you are still a little skeptical about vitamins, this ought to cinch it. Tests have shown that one group of mice (and mice are often used to show what would happen if you gave the same thing to humans; like they use mice to test drugs and other things and most medical people consider the tests valid) who were fed only white bread and water died, and another group who were fed whole natural wheat and water lived. Same length of time and same amounts.

DOSING UP

I recommend at least five hundred miligrams per day of vitamin C from a natural source and a good natural one-a-day vitamin. Take your vitamins when you eat, of course. You may need more than one or more vitamins, depending on your particular diet and metabolism — like extra vitamin E for example. Go through some of the books I recommend and find out in detail about vitamins. A few hints may help, though:

1) If you like to drink alcoholic beverages, get a good B complex vitamin (natural) and take it preferrably before boozing it. It even helps if you take one before retiring. Some say it helps the next day, but I'm not so sure.

2) If you smoke grass or cigarettes, you should double the amount of vitamin C you take every day. Cigarettes especially take a heavy toll of vitamin C, supposedly twice as much.

3) If you start to get a cold, increase the amount of vitamin C you normally take. At the start of one, I'd recommend at least 2500 miligrams a day until it gets better, with plenty of rest and liquids. Spread the dosage out through the day — say five hundred miligrams every three hours. C is far out, but it needs help.

4) If you live in a heavily polluted area and lots of you now do, I'd increase my vitamin C level to 1000 miligrams per day with meals. You've nothing to lose.

There are some "chicken littles" who run around saying too many vitamins are bad for you, etc. No proof and empty words, or perhaps they've never had scurvy or beri-beri. These people remind me of the doctors who treat their patients for heart problems and die of heart disease themselves.

The only warning I might give about overdosing yourself on vitamins would be that some research has shown that vitamin A, under certain conditions, can be toxic. But a person must be seriously malnourished — extremely low on vitamins and minerals — before he could take enough vitamin A to harm him. If you are skinny, depressed, unhealthy, have a runny nose and runny bowels, plus general weakness, then I'd say don't take vitamin A supplements. But I'd also suggest that if you're in that bad shape, you'd better get yourself in to see the doctor right away. Just in case you're interested, the first symptoms of vitamin A overdosing come in the form of losing your body hair — it happens over a period of many months, during which time you'd have to be gobbling down a whole big bunch of vitamin A and very little of anything else. After a few months or years of this, you'd begin to lose your sight and your liver would become enlarged. So if you're eating okay, and you are pretty healthy, I'd recommend keeping your vitamin A supplement at no more than 10,000 usp units per day. I know a lot of people taking five times that much with no apparent ill effects, but I wouldn't support them in their habit. Like I'm always saying — everything can be abused.

If you're a super holy dude living on brown rice alone, I'd avoid the vitamin supplements. Vitamin C would be okay, but nothing else. Like you might be holier than I, brother, but your body is still undernourished if you're making it exclusively on brown rice. It might be noted here that Zen monasteries like Tasajara in California pay strict attention to diet and they avoid "holy visions" induced by malnutrition.

I'm not so stuck on vitamin supplements that I don't believe you can still get them from natural sources, but it is getting increasingly difficult to get enough vitamin C out of raw oranges and lemons and impossible to get it from canned or bottled foods. For example, an average lemon, which, by the way, happens to be a good source of C, is said to contain only about 50 miligrams of C per lemon. That's ten lemons to get 500 milligrams. As I said, you can just about forget about the C from a canned or bottled orange, even if it says fortified. By law, the packers only have to prove they put the C in. They don't have to prove you get it when you open the can. A fresh pure glass of orange juice loses its vitamin C in about fifteen to twenty minutes if left undrunk. So, by the time you open the can or bottle of OJ, you can be pretty certain that the vitamin C has been oxidized. It is very stable in pill form if the pill was made from natural sources. Don't be half-safe.

One more thing: our dark-aged medical profession is finally coming around to recognizing stress as a causative factor in many diseases. And boy, do many of us suffer from stress. Some advanced thought is that stress also causes vitamins to be used up more rapidly. This means that if you are under a lot of stress, you'd first better try to eliminate it, and at least make sure you're fully covered with vitamins.

THE GARBAGE DIET

OK, into junk and garbage foods and what you can replace them with. Here's the worst of it:

1) White Sugar — in any form, plain or mixed with anything. You should use honey in place of white sugar. Brown sugar ain't much better, for it contains about 87% white sugar, stained with molasses. I know it sounds better than white sugar, but it mostly *is* white sugar.

2) Candy — Stay away from all candy unless it's made with honey; you can find this kind in health food stores.

3) Soft Drinks — Most twelve-ounce bottles of soft drink contain about four and one-half teaspoons of white sugar. Plus phosphoric acid — both bummers. Drink fresh juices and water — always rinse with water after drinking anything else.

4) White Bread — (or anything made from white flour). You already know about what white flour has done to increase the incidence of heart attacks. Don't be fooled by some brown breads — read the labels of everything you buy and see what you're getting. You want bread made with *whole grains*. This means avoid pastries, cakes, etc.

5) Preservatives — Most canned and packaged goods are full of preservatives; some more than others. Check the labels. Remember, too much of anything can damage you, and preservatives can be stored in your body and cause problems you haven't even heard of yet.

6) Salt — Most things are already salted enough, and doctors tell every heart patient to cut out salt. If you use salt, use sea salt. Also, even sea salt in moderation, even though sea salt is better than regular commercial salt. Commercial salts have a bunch of chemicals added to keep them nice and free flowing, and these

chemicals are not good for you. Sea salt may clog up occasionally, but it is much better for you.

7) White Rice — It is of little or no value to you except as a source of carbohydrates: no vitamins. Remember, don't go getting sucked into this "Vitamin Enriched" claim. Get the food the way it was naturally made before they stripped it of all the goodies. Always use brown rice.

8) Too Much Meat — Most commercial meats not only are shot full of the drugs I spoke of earlier, but they are also high in cholesterol. So, it is simply a bad risk to eat meat three times a day. Pork is especially bad for you. If you need to eat it, use it no more than three times a week. You can get as good a source of protein from nuts and natural cheeses and it's less harmful, especially from the excessive drug standpoint.

9) Too Much Milk — I'm speaking of the pasturized and homogenized white water they pass off for milk nowadays. In the first place, we happen to be the only animals who give milk to their off-spring after they are weaned. So, although I'm not hassling you about breast feeding your baby, I am saying that at the super market you're wasting your money. Milk in the carton has been cooked and filtered so much that almost everything of value has been taken out — again, they work it over so badly that they have to "enrich" the depleted milk to make it even tolerable. It is said that more than 30% of the U.S. population is allergic to milk. You don't need lots of it, but whenever you do drink milk, it should be certified *raw* milk.

10) Dry Packaged Cereals — There is now good evidence to show that the packaged cereals you feed your kid so readily are of very little value to him. The government has begun to crack down on the false advertising the cereal manufacturers have been putting out. Most of them are also coated with white sugar. So, not only is it not very good for you, but it has extra junk food added to it. Feed the kids hot whole wheat cereal or "granola."

11) Wine Vinegar and Anything It's Found In — Wine vinegar is a major cause of stomach disorders. Many people in Italy, where lots of wine vinegar is consumed, suffer from stomach ulcers. Try not to buy and eat things with wine vinegar in them, like catsup. Use only whole, unfiltered, pure apple cider vinegar. Whereas wine vinegar contains the acetic acid so bad for your stomach, apple cider vinegar contains malic acid which is good for your digestion.

12) Spices — Too many spices aren't good for you, especially if

139

you feel lousy after eating them. Your body is telling you something — and your head should listen.

13) Heavily-Salted Butter — You'll get too much cholesterol and salt if you eat too much. Health food stores carry lightly, as well as unsalted, butter.

14) Almost all margarines have now been proven to be somewhat harmful for you — most containing the same type stuff they make plastics out of. Again, health food stores carry the only good margarine out.

15) Eggs — Ones that are from chickens shot full of drugs are *bad*. Get organic eggs, but don't eat too many. The white is the worst part. It's a good idea to trim most of it off after you cook them. And never eat *raw* egg whites.

I know it sounds like there is nothing left for you to eat, and this, of course, is not true, for as I've already told you, fresh fruit and vegetables, nuts, juices, whole wheat and rice, raw milk and cheeses made from raw milk, honey, organic fertilized eggs, and occasionally some organic meat (if you still dig meat) will not only keep you healthy and happy, as it did billions of people for millions of years, but will also allow you to live longer and more free of disease.

Just take a visit to your local health food store. You'll find everything you like, but without the health-robbing garbage that is put into commercial foods. You don't have to take my word for it — go see for yourself.

YOU AND THE COWS

For those of you who might scoff at the possibility that vegetables, nuts and fruits are all that are needed, let me ask you a few questions and see what you think after dwelling on them.

A cow is a vegetarian, eating only grasses like alfalfa, hays and grains. Yet, he grows up to be the 2500 pound hunk of meat that you love so well. I doubt whether or not you can say cows are unhealthy or weak. Same goes for race horses, who, after they are weaned from mom, eat nothing but carrots and grass. Yet, here is another example of a vegetarian who is strong, fast and large.

So, even when you eat a piece of meat from a cow, you are just eating what the cow ate and formed into meat. The secret here is that plants (vegetables) are made up of amino acids and when these amino acids are added together they can form, among other things, meat (protein). Amino acids from plants are very easily digestible after you chew up the cellulose to get to them. When it becomes protein, the amino acids are bound together so strongly and their molecules (protein) are so much larger than molecules of amino acids, that they are very difficult for our weak stomachs to digest. What I'm saying is that if plants contain everything necessary for life and in a form that is much easier to digest and assimilate, there isn't much reason to get the same things from meats which are truly much more difficult to digest. More to the point, if you eliminated everything from your plate at every meal except meat, you would die. If your meals were balanced with vegetables and fruits and then you eliminated meats every day, you'd live.

For those of you whose teeth are in such bad shape that you have a hard time chewing vegetables, you can "juice" them, using a blender or electric juicer, and you can also grate the vegetables up to make them easier to digest.

THE HUNZA

For those of you who wish more concrete proof that diet can prevent tooth disease and most other diseases as well, I'll offer you some quotes from Renee Taylor's *Hunza Health Secrets*. The book tells the story of the Hunza people who were more or less isolated for over 2,000 years. Free of so-called "progress," these Hunza people offer conclusive evidence of the advantages to us all of a natural diet with no preservatives or white sugar. This is a fantastic book and should be read by all who wish to further their knowledge about good healthy foods and diet as a way of life.

Today, Hunza is a part of West Pakistan, but it functions as an independent kingdom. For most of 2,000 years, very few outsiders ever saw this little country of Hunza, but those that did were in total agreement as to what they saw.

"In Hunza, people manage to live to over 100 years of age in perfect mental and physical health; men father children at ninety. But their greatest achievement is the fact that sickness is rare, that cancer, heart disease, heart attacks, high or low blood pressure and childhood diseases are virtually unknown."

More specifically, Dr. Robert C. McCarrison, a British surgeon who spent seven years with the Hunza people, believed that the superior chemical free diet of the Hunza and the fact that the baby is breast-fed undoubtedly gave the Hunza children a magnificent start in life. The diet of the mother will always be reflected in the health of the child, and in Hunza, the mortality rate of infants is almost non-existent.

The teeth of the Hunza children more than proves my belief that good diet not only aids in the formation of good strong teeth, but also keeps them that way.

"The baby teeth are forming while the foetus is in the mother's womb and are erupted shortly after birth. All Hunza children have perfect teeth and healthy gums and yet they have neither tooth powders, toothpastes, nor toothbrushes. They clean their teeth with little twigs which they chew on until one end resembles a brush and with this they clean in and around the teeth and massage the gums. This cleaning is aided by the natural diet."

Hunza children don't eat sweets, ice cream or drink soft drinks. They do eat lots of fresh fruit or chew on dried fruits as well as on such self-cleansing vegetables as raw carrots. They drink natural, pure water, rich in all the minerals needed for normal health.

Strange, dental disease is non-existant in Hunza, and they have no dentists and no fluoride treatment. Yet, in the U.S. where we have nearly 100,000 dentists and pay them $4 billion a year to help fight dental disease, 24 out of 25 American children suffer the plagues of dental disease before they are six years old.

Diet and teeth, teeth and diet — twins, and if you change your diet, your teeth suffer. At the very least, its something to think about.

BOOKLIST

Hunza Health Secrets, Renee Taylor, Award Books. $.95
Diet and Salad Suggestions, N. W. Walker, Norwalk Press, $2.00
Food Is Your Best Medicine, Henry Bieler, M.D., Random House, $5.95
Raw Vegetable Juices, N. W. Walker, Norwalk Press, $3.00

12

A MANUAL FOR
SURVIVAL IN THE DENTAL OFFICE

PRELIMINARIES
YOUR OWN PRIMER ON READING X-RAYS
GUIDELINES TO THE DENTAL OFFICE
THE FIRST CONTACT
THE DOLLARS AND SENSE OF THE FIRST VISIT
MAKING THE APPOINTMENT
YOUR DENTIST AND YOUR MONEY
THE FIRST APPOINTMENT: CLEANING YOUR TEETH
THINGS TO WATCH FOR
THINGS TO CONSIDER ABOUT X-RAYS
X-RAY PRECAUTIONS
X-RAYS AND OCCUPATIONAL HAZARDS
HOW OFTEN SHOULD I ASK TO BE OR
    ALLOW MYSELF TO BE X-RAYED?
YOUR FIRST ENCOUNTER WITH CHIEF WHITE COAT
PROFESSIONAL DEFENSES
COMBATIVE TECHNIQUES
MAKE A CONTACT WITH YOUR DENTIST
SHOOTING UP WITH PAIN KILLERS
GETTING DOWN TO BUSINESS
TYPES OF FILLINGS
GOLD CAPS (CROWNS), PORCELAIN JACKETS (CAPS),
    BRIDGES AND MISSING TEETH
GOLD
PORCELAIN CAPS
SOME THINGS TO CONSIDER WHEN
    GETTING FILLINGS, CAPS, ETC.
WHAT FILLINGS ARE BEST
REMOVEABLE PLATES
NO TEETH LEFT, OR FALSE TEETH,
    DENTURES, AND PLATES.

SOME THINGS TO REMEMBER WHEN GETTING DENTURES
THE CARE AND FEEDING OF FALSE TEETH
ROOT CANALS
WISDOM TEETH
DENTAL EMERGENCIES
MONEY — THE BIG BITE TO REPAIR YOUR BITE
HOW TO CHOOSE A GOOD DENTIST
WOMEN IN DENTISTRY
THE BAD DENTIST

PRELIMINARIES

Even before you have made your first appointment you should know how to read a dental x-ray. Here's why:

1) The dentist will take x-rays of your teeth to determine what work will need to be done.

2) Since he bases all his work on what these x-rays reveal, you should — if you've done your homework — be able to understand what these x-rays are saying, so you will be able to double check what the dentist decides should be done about your mouth. You would probably not allow a mechanic to repair your car before you had some evidence of the need for repair. Likewise with the dentist. Your knowledge of x-rays will provide you with real evidence of what does or doesn't need repairing.

3) You will be able to judge, from reading the x-rays, what work should be done first in your mouth, and what work can wait.

4) Your knowledge of x-rays will greatly increase your overall understanding of your teeth.

Once you grasp the rudiments of reading x-rays, don't ever again let the dentist do any work in your mouth before he has verified to you, on the x-rays, why that work should be done.

YOUR OWN PRIMER ON READING X-RAYS

Basically, reading x-rays to find decay is not too difficult. A few principles will help you understand the theory, and the x-rays and drawings I'll enclose will fill in the gaps. With this knowledge you can easily identify the teeth that are decayed, those that are abcessed, impacted wisdom teeth and advanced gum disease on any dental x-ray.

144

A healthy tooth shows three degrees of density on an x-ray — the enamel is the most dense, followed by the dentin and then the nerve, in that order. On an x-ray the enamel appears lighter, because it blocks off more x-rays from printing on the film. The dentin prints grey in color and the nerve prints nearly black. Parts of the tooth which are hollow allow more x-rays to penetrate, exposing more film and making a darker print. Spaces between the teeth print black. When a tooth is decayed, that part of the tooth has in effect been dissolved; x-rays can penetrate the dissolved areas easily, which will therefore show up as a "dark" line or area on the film. An abcess that dissolves the bone around the root tip also shows up as a darkened area. A filling shows up very white.

The examples I've enclosed will allow you to understand how to look for decay. Just make sure the Doc points out to you every place he feels decay has occurred. Likewise you question him about every place it looks to you like decay might be. Working together in this way, you're more likely to get a better job on your teeth.

1) This first x-ray shows normal, healthy teeth and gums.

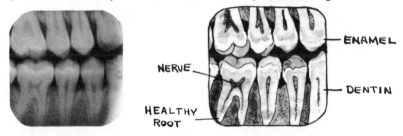

Look on the x-ray for the details noted on the drawing.

2) Bone loss due to gum disease and resulting decay. The white portions of the teeth are fillings.

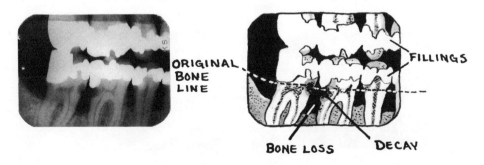

3) Here you can see decay under a filling, a tooth missing and a rotted tooth.

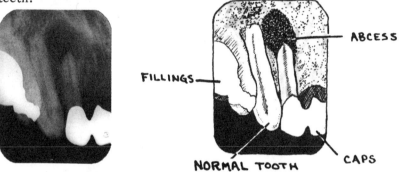

4) In this example, you see an abcess at the base of the tooth due to extreme decay, a normal tooth and caps on neighboring teeth.

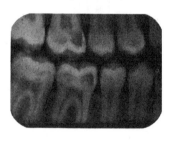

5) Examples of decay in unfilled teeth.

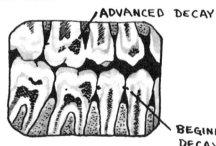

6) This last x-ray shows an impacted wisdom tooth.

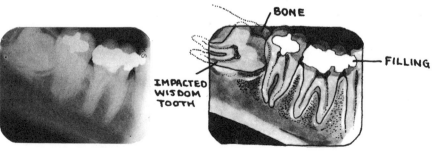

GUIDELINES TO THE DENTAL OFFICE

The remaining pages of this chapter will show you how to handle your first visits to the dentist. They will cover you from the opening phone call or visit for your appointment through and including major repairs. From your home examination you can estimate the repairs your mouth will need, and from this chapter learn what to expect in the chair.

THE FIRST CONTACT

Most of you will have your first contact with the dentist via Ma Bell's telephone service. The rest of you will have your first contact either

on an emergency basis, or by going down to the office to make your appointment. I recommend going down to the office to make your appointment, especially if you are choosing your dentist from random rather than through the recommendation of someone that you trust. Here's why I say this:

1) The personal visit will give you the opportunity to see what kind of office the dentist has; i.e., the chances are that if the place turns you off aesthetically, the people running it probably will too.

2) You may be able to find out what kind of equipment they have, new or old. You should ask if they have the following (see "Dental Equipment," page 184):

a) High speed drill (if they only have the old fashioned low speed rig, I'd recommend going elsewhere).

b) Cavitron (special cleaning tool).

c) Rubber dams (makes fillings much more comfortable for patient).

d) Outside services (if you need bridgework, caps, etc., you will want to know if your dentist has these services available — most do not make their own).

3) It is also wise to check out the office help; if they are friendly, polite and helpful, the chances are that their boss (the dentist) will be a pretty good guy too.

In general, open yourself to the vibrations of the whole scene. If they turn you off, it's best to find another dentist whose vibrations please you more.

THE DOLLARS AND SENSE OF THE FIRST VISIT

You will want to ask the receptionist how much the dentist will charge for:

a) a *full mouth* set of x-rays

b) a cleaning

c) an examination

All this should run about $35.00 (1972 prices). If you require more than one cleaning, because you have not been careful about cleaning your teeth at home, you can expect this to go up to $45.00 or $50.00. If you start the home care plan which I describe in this book about three weeks prior to your cleaning appointment, the first cleaning will probably be less expensive and less uncomfortable for you.

Once the receptionist quotes you a figure, and it is around $35.00 (remember, that is a 1972 price), tell her you would like to make an appointment, and that you understand that the first appointment will include the following:

1) A full mouth set of x-rays (that includes 18 x-rays of your mouth)

2) A complete oral examination (to include teeth, gums, roof of mouth, insides of cheeks, spit glands, tongue, etc.).

3) A treatment plan (consists of a written description of what is wrong, what is the best way to treat it, how much it costs, and how you can pay it off).

4) A home care instruction plan (two parts: a) what specific follow-up instructions the dentist has in regard to work he has done; and b) his equivalent of what I call "Home Care" in this book. (You might even take him this book to read and ask if he has any additions to my chapter on home care.)

All of what you've just asked for should be included in the first price quoted you. If the receptionist tells you that all this will cost more, tell her that all insurance companies' price schedules include what you've asked for in their basic fee, and it is not supposed to cost extra. Most good dentists include what you have asked for in the first fee quoted, and if yours doesn't tell the receptionist that you are:

a) going to another dentist, and
b) going to report them to the American Dental Association.

Do it, too. The Association's address is:

American Dental Association
211 E. Chicago Avenue
Chicago, Illinois 60611

In fact, you should report any dental practice you think to be unethical to them. They can assert a great deal of power over the dentists who belong to the Association.

MAKING THE APPOINTMENT

OK, if you got through the above part, you'll now have to actually make an appointment. Chances are good that the work you've requested will be done in at least two visits, maybe three. Some dentists do it in one visit. It matters not how many appointments it takes so long as everything you're paying for is included. Assuming that it isn't an emergency, feel free to pick your own appointment time. Tell the receptionist what day and time would be best for you. You may have to wait a little longer for the appointment, but go for it. Like, if you ask for an afternoon appointment on a certain day and are told they have only a morning one, ask when you can get an afternoon appointment. Try to get the appointment when it is most convenient for your work, baby sitters, weather, traffic, or whatever. When you reach an agreement, ask the receptionist to call you the day before each appointment to remind you, or to send you a card if you have no phone. Some dentists will charge for a broken appointment, so protect yourself. You also have an obligation to him, so if you can't make the appointment, you should cancel it at least one day in advance. Most dentists will understand if you neglect an appointment and really do have a valid excuse, but if you don't, chances are good that he won't want to see you again. And I can't blame him.

YOUR DENTIST AND YOUR MONEY

Expect to pay the charge for the cleaning, exam, etc. the day they are done. If done on separate days, pay the balance on the day the services are performed. If you do not have the $35.00 or whatever, don't make the appointment until you save it up. Everyone will be happier and you'll save a lot of hassles.

Dentists get ripped off a lot, and because of this, most of them are paranoid about the money trip. Also, I don't know many dentists who will do any further work on you if you haven't paid for services already rendered. Faith and trust work both ways, and if you show him you intend to pay for his services, the possibilities are excellent that you two can work out a financial arrangement suitable to both of you.

THE FIRST APPOINTMENT: CLEANING YOUR TEETH

The first appointment is a breeze — nothing to lose sleep over, anyway. Whether it be x-rays and exam or cleaning and instruction. Hopefully, you'll be on time; that really gets them off, even if they are not ready for you. Next, announce to the receptionist that you have arrived. You may get rushed right in, which lightens the apprehension that waiting increases. Or, it is possible you may have to wait for several minutes.

The cleaning will be the first physical contact you'll have with the dentist or hygienist, and if you've followed the "Home Care" instructions, it should be painless.

THINGS TO WATCH FOR

1) The cleaning, regardless if it is done by the dentist or hygienist, should always include the following operations:
    a) The hand scraping or mechanical removal (by a far-out machine called the Cavitron that vibrates like a tuning fork, see "Dental Equipment," page 184) of the hardened calculus, the soft junk around your teeth, and the cleaning of the

grooves on top of your teeth. Nothing else will effectively remove calculus, so don't let them skip this phase, even if whoever is cleaning your teeth says you don't need it. Just say you'd like to experience it anyway and as you've already paid for it, why not?

b) The polishing of the teeth, including the tops, with an abrasive material called *pumice*. Feels a little strange, but effectively does the job. Some dentists use flavored pumice; it does the same job and is less objectionable to your taste buds. The polishing is absolutely necessary to effectively remove anything the scraping leaves, and to smooth the surfaces of the teeth so food cannot stick to them.

c) Dental floss is used in between the teeth to remove the junk found there and also to polish these spaces; nothing else gets between the teeth like dental floss.

All these steps should be done, and all are necessary if you are to receive the cleaning you need and have *paid for*. If for $some$ reason your hygienist missed one of these phases, politely ask them to complete the part or parts they left out and also ask why it was left out. If you get hassled here and do not get a satisfactory answer — and no answer can justify not doing what should be done and what you have paid for — you can be pretty sure you're going to be short-changed in everything else they'll be doing. If you do not feel you've been satisfied, go find another dentist and report the negligent one to the American Dental Association. (Word to the Wise: Be sure to tell your friends not to go to a dentist who cannot satisfactorily explain to you any phase of dentistry you'd like to know about, or who does not perform the services you are paying for. The success of most dentists hinges upon word of mouth — your word. Do not promote a bad dentist; but do tell all about the good one.)

2) Some bad dentists will have their hygienists do the examination on you. This is not good for you; it is profitable for them. If the hygienist does start to do the examination, poking around your teeth and writing things down in their special code, ask her if the dentist will also examine you. If she says no, I'd get my fanny on out of there. It is the dentist's responsibility to do the examination, and if he isn't conscientious enough to do it, he isn't conscientious enough to do anything else that may need doing in your mouth. Spread the word about this character.

3) If the hygienist tells you she just makes note of the more serious decay so the dentist will know which teeth should be taken care of immediately, and that he will perform a complete examination on you, you can rest assured. Chances are the dentist will be good.

4) If the hygienist cleans your teeth, you may not get to see the dentist for at least another month. If she sees some decay that will need treatment before your appointment with him, she will be able to get you in on an emergency basis, possibly saving your teeth — and that's what it is all about. Of course, if you see some decay during your home examination and you are not sure as to the seriousness of it, ask the hygienist. If she isn't sure, ask her to please set up an emergency appointment to have the decay cleaned out and a temporary filling put in its place. (The old story that if you've waited this long you can wait a little longer does not hold true with your teeth. That extra week or month may just cost you an extra $200.00 or $300.00.)

5) If the dentist is the one who does the cleaning, you're covered as far as emergencies go. But point out anything you are suspicious of at this time and inform him you'd like to have any emergency work that he feels is necessary done at this time — just in case he may have forgotten.

OK people, this information should help you get through the cleaning, no matter who does it. Also, you should know more about the type of dentist you are going to be dealing with. Pay close attention to the vibrations in the office, but make sure yours are good and high so as not to interfere with theirs.

THINGS TO CONSIDER ABOUT X-RAYS

If you got through the cleaning alright, you may now find yourself seated in the x-ray chair. Hopefully everything is going well and you're not nervous and apprehensive. If you happen to be concerned about x-rays, the following information should answer your questions and eliminate your concern.

Without x-rays it would be impossible for a dentist to completely diagnose your mouth. The holes caused by decay in a tooth are very small on the outside, but if not treated will rapidly grow. X-rays will reveal decay which would go undetected by the naked eye. As 98% of all Americans will have or get decay, the x-ray can be invaluable.

So insist on a full mouth set of x-rays. The actual taking and diagnosing of the x-rays should run about $20.00 (in 1972).

But what about the harm which x-rays are reputed to cause? Well, the potentially harmful aspects of x-rays is in the form of *excess radiation.* Nowadays everyone is freaked out about radiation, and rightfully so, but it is not just any radiation you should be concerned about — but excessive amounts of radiation. It is true that certain substances exist that can give off tremendous amounts of radiation, but the dental x-ray isn't one of them.

You receive much more radiation naturally than you'll ever get from a set of dental x-rays. You can find such "natural" radiation all around you, the main source being the sun. In the form of "cosmic" radiation, we can receive from the sun enough radiation to equal many hundreds of sets of dental x-rays. When you add the radiation you receive from the illuminated dial of your wrist watch and the radiation found in elements contained in the food you eat daily, you can be certain you are being radiated daily — a great deal more if you're a sun freak.

Because radiation can accumulate in your body, the less you receive the better off you are, but until you get your dental health trip together, you are going to require x-rays. So, although you shouldn't jump up and down about getting x-rayed, you don't have to freak out, either.

X-RAY PRECAUTIONS

There are precautions you can take to minimize the amount of radiation you receive while being x-rayed. There are also certain areas of your body where some concern is justified. These precautions include:

1) Checking with the person x-raying you to make sure the machine is a new one with an electronic timer. This would be a good question to ask before you schedule an appointment. An electronic timer, used with *fast* film, allows x-rays to be accurately taken and with less exposure time than the old-fashioned mechanical timer. Less exposure time means that you'll receive less radiation and that is what we want. Also, the fact that the dentist has a new x-ray machine means he may have other new equipment and also might be more concerned about your health and safety.

2) The areas of your body that are more susceptible to radiation are women's ovaries and men's testicles. Contrary to some people's belief, the testicles are more susceptible to radiation than ovaries because they are outside the body and the x-rays do not have to travel as far to reach them. The reason for the potential danger in these regions lies in the fact that excessive radiation can cause genetic mutations, and although some mutations can be beneficial, most are harmful. You certainly wouldn't want to pass on harmful genetic mutations to your kids. Don't worry, though. In order to protect yourself from this possibility, ask the one x-raying you (if they don't do it on their own) to give you a lead apron to cover these most delicate and sensitive areas. If they can't provide you with a lead apron or similar device, there are other dental offices which will.

X-RAYS AND OCCUPATIONAL HAZARDS

There are some people whose occupations require them to be exposed to radiation in excess of that which is considered normal. These would include x-ray technicians, radiation laboratory employees, dentists, medical technicians, and anybody else exposed to radiation other than the sun and wrist watches. For those of you who fall into this category, I advise you first, before getting x-rayed, to have yourself checked out for how much radiation you have stored up. Next, get your mouth cleaned up through "Home Care" so you don't have to get x-rayed any more than is absolutely necessary.

HOW OFTEN SHOULD I ASK TO BE OR ALLOW MYSELF TO BE X-RAYED?

Full Mouth X-Rays: If you get your mouth together and know you are taking good care of it, I'd recommend a full set of x-rays about every five to seven years. Once you get it together, you shouldn't have any more new decay, so the full mouth set would be used to check for tumors and abcesses. Make sure you tell the dentist that the five to seven year set of rays should be thoroughly checked for the above-mentioned items.

Bite-wing X-Rays: (the ones with the little tabs attached that you bite on to hold in place). These should be taken every six months for about a year and a half. This is for your own protection

— to insure that your home care is working. The bite-wing series consists normally of four x-rays; two on each side. Some dentists may use only one on each side, the x-ray being longer to make up the necessary difference. I personally like two on each side, but one on each side works okay. If, after three checkups you have no new decay, I suggest you skip the bite-wing series and assuming again that you are still taking excellent care of your mouth, have the bite-wings taken every five to seven years also.

Warning Word: If you start fouling up and not taking care of your teeth you should get back on the regular six month visits. You'll need them!

YOUR FIRST ENCOUNTER WITH CHIEF WHITE COAT

Before he begins his examination, tell the dentist that you would like him to include an examination of your entire mouth — including the tongue, cheeks, and the roof and floor of your mouth. Let him know before the exam begins so it will be fresh on his mind. He could be looking but not seeing, and unless you remind him, he may forget. Also, make certain he tells you if everything is okay or if it is not. You can hold him to this if he misses something he shouldn't have. Remember, be nice about it; you want him working for you, and you can ask him anything odd you may have discovered during your home evaluation. This is the time to verify what you thought the normal healthy mouth looks like.

Following whatever questions and discovery period you and the dentist may go through, you might just ask him if the x-rays or his examination turned up any decay or infection that will need emergency or immediate treatment — at least before your next scheduled appointment with him. If you do have problems which call for immediate attention, you should be prepared to pay for that work just as it is completed. (For more on finances, see "Money — the Big Bite to Repair Your Bite" later in this chapter.)

Anyway, if you do not require any emergency work, you'll just about be finished with this trip. It is now that you ask the dentist if he won't please make out a total treatment plan (what he proposes to do). Make a point to tell him you'd like this to be the best treatment plan available and you'd also like an alternate treatment plan (second choice). I strongly suggest you do this, as I've come in contact with dentists who, because they think you can't pay, or feel that if they were to offer you the best treatment plan available, you'd freak out at the expense. In essence, this means that if you don't ask for it, you may be getting second or third best and not know it, regardless if you could pay for it or not. Even if you think you can't afford it, you still have paid for the right to find out what the best available is. It is always sound to get the best. So, you've gotten it all out and now you'll most likely get a month or more to wonder how bad it's going to be, financially. You can worry if you want, but it'll just be a waste of energy . . . Don't think about it until it happens. What you can be getting together is:

1) The dough you owe him.
2) Keeping your mouth clean.

These are about the only two ways the dentist can tell if you are serious. Show him you are — if you are.

PROFESSIONAL DEFENSES

Many dentists become bitter and pessimistic about their patients. To some degree they are justified in this. For whatever reasons, patients tend to neglect their teeth through improper brushing, and by letting dental problems go too far before doing anything about them. Because of this, many dentists eventually develop "professional defenses" through which they put off patients who want to discuss their dental work. Here are some ways that a dentist might do this:

a) Bulldozing: By telling you too quickly, and too curtly what he plans to do with your teeth; at the same time, he may project to you a feeling that your questions are interrupting a very heavy work schedule.

b) Technologizing: By using highly technical language to describe what he plans to do with your mouth. This often makes you feel that you are too stupid to understand, and that he is both the guru and higher authority in the matter, to whom you must bow and submit.

c) Drilling while Rapping: By explaining things to you while he is working on your teeth, and while it's impossible for you to respond intelligently. This technique is one of the more successful ways the dentist has to prevent you from asking questions.

d) Pamphleteering: By handing you pamphlets and other written materials for you to take home and read. He knows that nine out of ten patients will never read this stuff, but it will serve to put an end to the questions — the answers to which the dentist does not believe you are interested in anyway.

156

Here are some ways to deal with these "professional defenses." It is important for you to learn them. If you do, you and your dentist will become allies in doing the right thing by your teeth. Thus:

COMBATIVE TECHNIQUES

a) Bulldozing: Tell the dentist simply but clearly that he is going too fast for you. Then, as he slows down, try to establish eye contact with him, and respond to each of the points he brings up, either by telling him that you understand or by asking questions of him about whatever you don't understand. If you can't slow him down, go and find yourself a dentist who will take the time to explain things to you.

b) Technologizing: Dentists, like most professionals, have their own jargon. You should not be expected to understand their language, but there is no reason that they can't put whatever they have to say in language which you can understand. If your dentist technologizes, tell him: "I don't know the terms that you're using. Is there a way you could tell me in language I can understand?" Don't feel embarrassed to do this. And if your dentist does not respond positively, go find yourself a dentist who will.

c) Drilling While Rapping: If your dentist does this to you in excess, and if you really are interested in what he has to say, wait until he has stopped drilling. Tell him that you were interested in what he said, and ask him to tell you more. Most dentists will be flattered, and will probably respond positively to this approach. If your dentist continues to talk while drilling, hold up your hand as a signal for him to stop, and then tell him that it is hard for you to concentrate on what he is saying as he drills. If the guy is negative ... well, go find a dentist who wants to communicate with you.

d) Pamphleteering: If your dentist pulls this one on you, thank him and take the stuff home. Now read it. When you go back the next time, tell your dentist, "I read the stuff you gave me, and I still have some questions to ask you." It would have to be a very cold dentist not to respond to this sort of sincere approach on your part. And if he is cold about it, I would highly recommend that you start looking around for a new dentist.

If you know that you will not be seeing your dentist again for another month or more, then you've got a different problem;

tell him that you will read the pamphlets which he has given you, but ask if in the meantime he can give you a short answer to the question you have just asked. Another way would be to read the pamphlets that night, and telephone the dentist the following day to thank him for giving you the pamphlets, and to ask for further clarification of stuff you've read in the pamphlets. Your purpose in this is twofold: to get information and to establish workable communications between you and your dentist.

All these above suggestions are designed to get the idea across to your dentist that you really are interested in taking care of your teeth. Let him know that you have read this book (carry it in under your arm if necessary), and that you are also doing your best to really take care of your teeth. Tell him that you would also like to hear his ideas about keeping any new work which he might do in good shape. Ask him if he has any special advice for taking care of the work he has done. This will help to establish his faith in you. Look at it this way: He is much more likely to do his best work in a mouth which he knows will be properly cared for.

Think of your dentist as a craftsman. Like all craftsmen, he really gets it off by having his work appreciated and well cared for. If he suspects that his work will be neglected, he may well adapt an "Aw, what the hell?" attitude and may end up doing no more than a passably good job. So be sensitive to him. Remember, even dentists have feelings.

MAKE A CONTACT WITH YOUR DENTIST

You are not expected to become a full fledged dentist by reading this book. But among other things you should be able to help make your dentist a better one. One of the best ways to accomplish this is to make sure you make him explain to you exactly:

a)   what he is doing,
b)   why he is doing it, and
c)   what results you can expect.

It is also essential that you ask him
d)   how long he thinks anything he does should last (assuming of course, that you are going to take very good care of your mouth).

Thus, if you do not get the results he promised you, he certainly has not done what he has said or what you have paid for, and you have legal recourse.

Many will no doubt try to avoid committing themselves, like saying there is no way they could say exactly how long their work should last. If they lay that trip on you, ask them *why* he cannot tell you. It is the dentist's responsibility to tell you how to repair your mouth to the very best of his ability, which also means the longest lasting way. Hound him about this.

Remember, though, the only way you will be able to hold him responsible is by:

a) having him commit himself, and

b) by you keeping your mouth clean.

There is an old saying about, "If you expect to bitch about someone else's trip, you had better make sure your own trip is together."

SHOOTING UP WITH PAIN KILLERS

To do his best work, the good dentist must feel secure that the work he is doing is not causing you unusual pain. For this reason, he will shoot you up with an anesthetic solution which will deaden the nerves around and in the tooth or teeth that he's working on. The shot is administered with a hypodermic needle near the left or right "jaw hinges," or into the gum in the general area of the affected tooth itself.

Most dentists now use a local anesthetic prior to giving you the shot so that you will not be able to feel the needle when he finally administers the stronger solution. If you are particularly sensitive about getting shots, you may want to ask your prospective dentist if he uses this local anesthetic. This *local* is sometimes sprayed on, and sometimes swabbed on with a Q-tip; if this is done properly, there is absolutely no pain involved.

If your dentist starts drilling before your teeth are numbed by the anesthetic, ask him to stop. There is *no* reason in the world that you should have to experience any pain or unusual discomfort in modern dentistry. Often after administering a shot, you will have to wait longer than usual to feel the benefit of the shot. And sometimes, too, the first shot has no effect, in which case a second one should be given. The good dentist will press on your tooth and ask you if it is numb before he starts drilling.

Following your dental visit, your mouth may remain numb for a few or even several hours, depending on how much work was done, and how much anesthetic was used. During this period of time you should take care not to bite the sides of your mouth or your tongue (if that's numb too). Dentists often fail to warn their patients about this, and later they return with infections caused by biting their cheeks or tongues during the time they were numb.

GETTING DOWN TO BUSINESS

Every dentist has his own way of getting into the rap about how much work needs to be done, and how many dollars it will cost you. But before you make any decisions about what work or how much money is going to pass between you, make absolutely positive that you fully understand what services will be performed. The information on the next few pages will assist you in making your decisions:

a) *No Work Needed* (about 2-5% of the people who come to my office):

Even if the dentist has nothing to do past the examination of your mouth, you will still have to pay for the cleaning and examination. But before you rush home to celebrate, ask the dentist or the hygienist if they think you could wait a year or longer between cleanings. It may turn out that you can if you continue to do as well as you apparently have with your *home care* plan. Many of my patients can wait at least a year, and some go much longer than that, depending on how diligent they are about home care. However, it is possible to not have any decay and still have gum disease. Only the dentist can treat and correct decay and missing teeth. Except in rare cases (see the chapter on rare gum diseases) only you can correct, treat and prevent gum disease.

b) *Simple Fillings Only* (No missing teeth, and no gold work needed):

This could conceivable run from as little as $10.00 to several hundreds of dollars, depending on how many fillings are involved. Whatever the cost, the best way to have your work done is to get as many filled in one sitting as possible, both for you and the dentist, and if one sitting won't do, get the remaining work done as soon as possible. If you have the money, there is a good chance the dentist will complete the work in one sitting.

If the dentist has performed his homework well, he will know exactly what should be done, and the approximate cost may vary only slightly once he gets to drilling. He can also tell you what work should be done first and how much time you can wait before you have the rest of the work completed.

If you have studied the section of this chapter which shows you how to read x-rays, you should have some basis for judging which work should come first, which next, etc. You should ask the dentist to go over your x-rays with you, so that your own eyes and knowledge can confirm which teeth need filling, why they need them, and when the work should be done. If your dentist refuses to show you the x-rays, get out of there as quick as you can.

If you find that you need work immediately but cannot afford to have regular fillings, explain this to him and tell him you'd like to have temporary fillings placed in the teeth that need relatively immediate work, say those that will need repair within six months. Ask him how much time you have on the remaining work and inform him that as soon as you get the money together, you'll come in and have it done. Right now you must get any immediate emergencies taken care of. (If you just wait, and do not have the temporaries done, the decay may grow so large that you would at best end up paying more in the long run, and at worst you may lose teeth.)

Whatever, make sure you get the teeth needing immediate care fixed up *now*. The fillings needed in this group consist of either silver ones (amalgam fillings) or the new quartz type fillings best suited for the front teeth.

TYPES OF FILLINGS

There are really only a few kinds of fillings and even the best ones aren't as good as your natural teeth. Nature still makes better teeth than man, but until we can get it together enough to take proper care of our teeth, fillings are the next best thing. These are:

1) Silver — Amalgam Fillings: You most likely know this as a silver filling. In reality, it is a mixture of silver, mercury, copper, zinc and tin. This has been the most popular of all dental fillings. When first mixed it is soft and easily compressed into the cavity. It hardens in minutes and reaches maximum hardness in about twenty-four hours. The silver filling is certainly not the best filling substance; it is just that research has not found any better

one to take its place. The quartz filling is close, but is not good for larger cavities. Gold is superior to silver but, as I will explain, is much more expensive.

The best thing I can say about Amalgam is that it is easy to use. The other side of the Amalgam coin points out its many disadvantages, like:

a) Should only be used in small cavities where it can be supported by healthy tooth structure and the adjacent teeth.

b) Contains mercury, which we all know now is not the best thing to have in your system. Some doctors in Europe have cured people of previously untreatable diseases by removing and replacing silver fillings with gold. This indicates some people are so sensitive to mercury that it can poison their systems by being used in their fillings!

c) They erode in the fluids of the mouth and need replacing.

d) They fracture fairly easily.

e) They stain the teeth because the filling darkens with age.

f) Amalgam also conducts hot and cold better than the natural tooth and often causes the tooth to be sensitive to temperature changes, particularly cold.

2) Quartz or glass: This type of filling is for the front teeth and very small fillings in the back teeth. The best of these is called *adaptic*. So far (1972) I've found no better type. This filling can closely match the color of the teeth and, being that it is quartz, it resists stain and normal wear very well.

Ask your dentist if he uses adaptic or a similar quartz filling. If he doesn't, I'd go elsewhere, for if he doesn't that means he'll use a plastic or silicate type filling. Many of the older dentists still use them, but I cannot find one good reason for it and many reasons for *not* using them, like:

a) They are harmful to the tooth.

b) They are very difficult to match to the color of the tooth.

c) They stain more readily than the quartz-type filling.

d) They "wash out" much faster than quartz and thus need replacing more often (more $$$).

Remember, this is just another sign of a bad dentist; if he tells you he uses plastic or silicate fillings, you can bet he is doing other second-rate work. Find another dentist.

GOLD CAPS (CROWNS), PORCELAIN JACKETS (CAPS), BRIDGES AND MISSING TEETH

You will find yourself in this group if:
1) You broke off all or part of a tooth or teeth.
2) You have teeth so decayed that a silver filling won't be strong enough.
3) The fillings in your front teeth are so large that a new filling might weaken the tooth and cause it to fracture.
4) You have missing teeth and you still have a tooth or teeth left on one or both sides of the space.

The trip here is that all of the above mentioned happenings and any variations of them are going to involve some sort of a cap or a bridge to restore or replace rotted or missing teeth and get your mouth together. If the cap or bridge is needed, the dentist must spend more time working on you than he would if a simple filling was required, and he must use more supplies. Along with this, the cap or bridge must be sent to the laboratory to be constructed. This also costs more money.

Gold fillings start at $60.00 and rapidly rise skyward. If you are in this group, your bill could easily run (excluding exam fees) to thousands of dollars. If you are a Hollywood star or public celebrity, it could easily cost you tens of thousands ($). You should be getting the idea.

GOLD

Gold is the most compatible filling with the fluids of the mouth, and the strongest. Gold work lasts up to a lifetime if done right. If you can afford it, and have to have cavities filled, I think gold is the very best filling for the back teeth.

Gold crowns are absolutely necessary when:
1) Part of the tooth fractures
2) The cavity is too large for silver
3) If a tooth needs to be built up (because it is weak or worn down)
4) A tooth that will have a partial denture clasp attached to it needs a different shape, or a stronger base to fasten the bridge to.

Again, the better the dentist, the better will be the work; if you have to have any gold work done, make sure you've picked a good dentist.

Aside from the cost, the only negative side of gold crowns is that they too conduct heat and cold better than natural teeth and so you may experience some sensitivity to temperature change.

PORCELAIN CAPS

These fillings can be used on any tooth, but they are most often used on the front teeth. A porcelain cap consists of porcelain baked onto a high-fusing gold alloy. The result is a durable and beautiful restoration job; its only drawback is its cost (1972 figures put it at $140-$160). The gold crown is just as functional as the porcelain cap, but some people do not like the way gold looks. I suggest using gold when esthetics is not a problem and porcelain when it is.

Never settle for a porcelain cap that does not match your other teeth to your satisfaction. If the dental profession was not so egotistical, there would be no problem with color matching. The dental lab that makes the tooth for you and the dentist has only a number to assist him in matching the color of your teeth. This is a very subjective trip, for the dentist tries to match up your teeth with a bunch of different colored shade guides, each having a number. He holds them up to your tooth and attempts to select one that will match. (He could be color blind.) He then sends that number to the lab, who has a similar shade guide and they try to match it up.

Some dentists, I for one, send the patient to the dental lab so the laboratory technician can mix the shade that matches on the spot. This is almost 100% effective, yet the arrogant dentist doesn't want to admit that he can't do it all himself.

So, if it were my mouth and I was having some front teeth capped, I'd ask the dentist what lab he used and go get the shade matched in person. This will only work if your town has a dental laboratory, but it's worth finding out.

In place of this, the next best thing is to never accept the tooth, nor pay the remainder of your bill, unless the tooth shade is correct. Do not listen to any excuses. For $150.00, you more than deserve a tooth that matches. Just make him send the poor work back.

When dealing with porcelain caps, you should also tell the dentist that you want the margins of the tooth to go under the gumline. If he's good, he can do it, so don't forget to ask.

SOME THINGS TO CONSIDER WHEN
GETTING FILLINGS, CAPS, ETC.

Read the following points carefully, and make certain that you understand them all before letting a dentist go ahead with any work in your mouth:

1) Getting the right bite: It is important with any filling you have done that the bite is correct. This means that when you close down in a normal position, your teeth should be hitting evenly. The dentist has ways of checking for this, but they are not infallible, and you can assist him. If, when he has finished putting the filling in, it still feels like you are not biting right, ask him to recheck it. If the bite is not checked and is off, you can either:

   a) Crack the tooth
   b) Crack the filling
   c) Kill the nerve
   d) Cause continuous discomfort

It ain't worth it, so make sure it feels good. You are in the best position to check this, so speak out or forever hold your peace.

2) Warning — Bad Quality Fillings, Etc: Some dim-witted bad dentists still use the older and inferior fillings that were used before there was anything better. One is plastic over gold. Another is porcelain without a high-fusing gold alloy backing for support. And a third is the gold foil filling. The plastic one wears, stains, chips and changes color, and also costs almost as much as the porcelain baked to metal. The plain porcelain cap is too weak and breaks and fractures very easily; it also costs almost as much as the porcelain baked to metal. The gold foil filling kills about 50% of the teeth they are done on. Don't let a bad dentist talk you into one of these three restoratives. You'll end up having it redone and the total cost will be far more than having it done correctly the first time.

3) Pre-Payment of Gold Work: I don't know of a dentist who will start a case that involves gold or porcelain without at least 50% of the total fee as a down-payment. Almost any gold work a dentist does will cost him 50% of the fee charged (out of his pocket), or more, depending on the laboratory and work involved, just to have it constructed. This includes materials used in the office, the gold and the laboratory charges. You can call him greedy for the profit he charges, but not for the first 50%.

4) Stainless Steel Caps: Stainless steel is sometimes used in place of gold for caps, crowns and other dental work. Stainless steel is, of course, somewhat less expensive than gold. But it is not that much less expensive. Remember, you are paying for a very intricate series of procedures when you get a crown: fitting, molding, and installing. You may as well pay a few dollars more per cap or crown and have the best material available installed. Consider, too, that gold surpasses stainless steel in that it is more compatible with the chemistry of your mouth. However, stainless is often used to cap children's teeth when it is known that these repairs will 'only be temporary. The material itself is quite serviceable.

5) Cavity Liners and Insulators: Ask your dentist if he would please place a base (insulator) into any deep cavities before filling them. If the filling is not deep, ask him to place a cavity liner in the cavity prior to filling it. This cavity liner also insulates the tooth.

WHAT FILLINGS ARE BEST

Ideally, it is best to have either "adaptic," where possible, or gold if you can afford it. If you can't get either, you'll have to go with the silver.

Many times dentists place silver fillings into cavities that are too large for the weak silver. This means you run the risk of having either the tooth or the filling fracture and then you'll have to have a gold cap put in, which now means you've paid for the silver filling and also the gold. You can save yourself this trouble and double charge if you make sure you have him tell you if the cavity is too large for a silver filling. A good way to check the Doc on this is to ask him how long the silver filling should last if you take good care of your mouth. If the filling is done right and the cavity isn't too large, they can easily last 15-20 years and longer.

The silver filling *can* be sensitive to hot or cold for up to eight weeks. Even though it may not seem like it to you, this is considered normal, but only if the sensitivity is caused by:

a) Hot
b) Cold (don't chew on ice)
c) Biting hard on something

Any time you have a sharp pain in *any* of your teeth, and it appears to be for no apparent reason, you should have it checked out.

The only valid reason for having removeable plates (partial dentures) is if you have lost all of your back teeth (one or both sides), upper or lower or both. This means that you do not have any teeth left in the back of your mouth to connect a fixed permanent bridge to and so must attach the plate by the use of spring-like clasps to whatever would now be the last tooth. This means the plate will be removeable and this, unless made perfectly, is a drag. Even when done right, removeable plates are difficult to clean and most are very hard on the teeth they attach to.

You must keep in mind that once you are this far along the disease trail, the condition of your mouth will worsen at a much faster rate than if you'd lost no teeth. Even though partial plates are not as good as fixed bridges or your natural teeth, they are a lot better than nothing at all. For example, say you are missing the last four teeth on the bottom right side. (This example will hold true for all cases — only the area and number of teeth lost may vary.) This means you not only have lost the function (chewing) of these teeth, but of the upper four as well, for now the upper teeth do not have the lowers to help them, and as far as function goes, you might as well not have the upper four teeth either. It also means the upper four teeth do not have their opposing lower teeth to help hold them in place and the upper teeth can then grow downward. Many times I've seen the upper teeth grow down so far they touch the bottom (toothless) jaw bone when the mouth is closed! This makes matters worse.

Another problem is created because now you must do all of your chewing on the opposite side. Nature only meant for you to do half your chewing on each side. The new situation puts twice as much wear and tear on the remaining teeth. This is especially bad if you have gum problems. Gum disease most likely caused you to lose those teeth in the first place, and now chewing on one side means it will be more difficult to keep these teeth and gums clean and thus more difficult for you to prevent their eventual loss.

If you are in this group, you must follow my instructions on "Home Care" 100% and you must get the missing teeth replaced. You have experienced the realities of dental disease and unless you eliminate what caused your condition to happen in the first place, prepare yourself for false teeth, because that's what will happen to you next. It is very important that you find a GOOD dentist to help you. As I've said, partial, removeable plates are difficult enough for a good dentist to do well, and in the hands of a bad dentist, you can really get messed up.

I have some recommendations for those of you who find yourself in this situation:

1) First of all, find the good dentist I speak of, page 175.

2) Ask him if he feels qualified to make your partial denture or dentures.

3) If he says he is not, ask him to refer you to a dentist who does specialize in partial dentures, or

4) Write or call your local dental association's president and ask him to recommend a dentist who specializes in partial dentures.

5) As research and techniques continually improve, new younger dentists usually are better qualified in this field. If any older dentist can prove to you that he has kept up to date, then you'll be in good hands. Ask him if he's taken post-graduate refresher courses in partial plates.

6) Call one of the dental laboratories and ask them for the name of a dentist who does good work. The dental laboratories are the only places qualified to judge a dentists' work.

As a final check and sometimes the most effective one, make sure that prior to paying any money and prior to having any work done you receive from the dentist a verbal or written statement as to how long he feels your partial plates will last. (Of course, you must tell him you will follow your home care program diligently or no dentist can be held responsible.) Under normal conditions, and if the partial is made properly and you do your share, it should last you from ten to fifteen years, and even longer. So, if he tells you he does not know or says maybe two or three years, you can bet he's either not sure or doesn't know what he is doing.

The important thing here is that once you've made him commit himself, and you take care of your mouth, you will have legal recourse if the partial plates are failures. But no lawyer or court will handle the case unless you do these things:

1) Take care of your mouth so an examining dentist can attest to your oral hygiene.

2) Swear to the dentist's verbal statement (try and get it in writing — it's always best).

3) Get testimony from another dentist who will state the partials were poorly made.

NO TEETH LEFT, OR FALSE TEETH, DENTURES AND PLATES.

Never let your dentist pull your teeth to make plates until you've had an opportunity to practice the home care plan discussed in this book. Just tell him you want to save every tooth you can, even if you have to go to the gum doctor (Periodontist). If he insists on pulling them without conclusively proving to you that none can be saved, then try another dentist. Even one tooth is better than none! Often the thing that decides whether you can save your teeth or not is how well you can take care of them.

If you must have plates made, make sure that you get good ones. This is just as hard as getting any other good dental work done, and there are some things you should know before getting false teeth made or replaced.

1) The credit dentists may be less expensive at first, but I don't believe anyone can make a good denture in one day, as most of them claim to be able to do. You'll end up paying a much bigger price later on if the plates are not made right. Ill-fitting plates are not only painful and often impossible to chew with (or wear) but they can also cause bone in your jaw to be destroyed. Once your jaw bone wears away too much, no one will be able to construct useable plates for you.

2) Even a regular dentist can make ill-fitting plates, and in fact most of them do. Most dentists have been so poorly trained in the field of dentures that it is a wonder there are any decent plates made today. In dental school we are told that if it were not for the fact that people adjust to plates so well, no denture wearer would be satisfied. This simply means that most dentists rely on the fact that you will adjust to a bad denture. A well-made set of dentures will require about seven office visits. If yours took only two or three, you may very well be in trouble. There are dentists who do nothing but make plates and partials and if I were ever to need one, I'd go to them. Here's how to go about finding a dentist who will make good plates for you:

a) Call your local dental association; if it is not in the phone book, any dentist will give you the number or address. Ask them who they recommend that is good and specializes in dentures – called a prothodontist.

b) You can also write or call the nearest dental school and ask them to recommend a dentist.

c) Call an oral surgeon in your area and ask him to recommend a good dentist who makes false teeth. The oral surgeon often works closely with the dentist who makes plates.

d) If you live in a city that has a dental school and you have the time, you can get better plates made at the school than at 90% of the private dentists' offices.

e) If you take pot luck, make sure that you get some form of a commitment from the guy for making the plates to your satisfaction. You don't want to pay all that money and then not be able to wear them. You must follow his advice, of course. It is very common to have a few sore spots with a new set of plates, but he should be able to adjust them.

Once you've selected your man ask him how many visits it will take. A good set of false teeth cannot be made in less than seven normal visits.

SOME THINGS TO REMEMBER WHEN GETTING DENTURES

You should be satisfied with the way your false teeth look and feel. If you are dissatisfied, you should demand satisfaction from your dentist. For example,

1) If your dentures are properly made, you should have a hard time getting them out of your mouth, especially the uppers. They should not, of course, slip or fall out while eating or talking.

2) Your dentures should be pleasing to look at, and should be "characterized." Very few people have naturally perfect teeth. The easiest way to spot someone who wears dentures is to look for a sixty-five year old person with perfectly white teeth which are so straight they look like piano keys. Tell the dentist that you want the color of your teeth to fit your age, and that you want to "characterize" the arrangement of the teeth (that means making a few of them crooked, the way natural teeth usually are.)

Demand satisfaction. Remember, your dentist may have to add an extra hour or two to making your teeth look and feel right. But you are the one who will have to wear them — for the rest of your life.

THE CARE AND FEEDING OF FALSE TEETH

Here are some things to remember after you start wearing your dentures:

a) False teeth must be cleaned just like natural teeth. You can't get tooth decay, but tartar and food can stick to your plates, causing stains and unpleasant breath. You should rinse them after eating and brush them thoroughly at least once a day. A regular tooth brush will do and so will regular tooth paste. Most of the commercial false teeth cleansers will work — take your pick.

b) It is best to take your teeth out at night and put them in water. This keeps them from drying out and distorting. Your mouth needs a rest too.

c) Don't use your front teeth to chew or tear. Do this with the side teeth.

d) Always cut your food into small pieces and chew equal and small amounts of food on both sides. If this is your first set of dentures, you will probably have to adjust your eating habits.

e) In some instances, loose dentures can be utilized longer by having them relined. This process adds new acrylic to the old denture, which fills in the voids left when your gums and bone recede. This procedure is often only temporary, and will never correct a poorly-made set of dentures. Remember, a bad set of false teeth will irritate the jaw bone and cause it to dissolve. If the problem is not corrected, it will only get worse. No amount of commercial false teeth "glue" will help. If the dentures are properly made, they will stick better than any glue or adhesive will ever do. So, if you have to resort to glue, you need new plates, and no amount of rationalization will change that fact.

f) The average person should have their dentures *remade* about every three to five years. The better the dentures are made, and the better you take care of them, the longer you can go without having them remade.

A good set of dentures will cost you from $300.00 up (for the teeth themselves), depending on the dentist and the difficulty involved in making them. Some are easy to make and others are very difficult. Just make sure you find out if your dentist thinks he can handle your particular case, and if not, have him direct you to one who can.

ROOT CANALS

Many times decay reaches the nerve and the germs infect it and may cause its death. It can die gently with little pain, or not so gently, abcessing and causing lots of pain. For a long time there was nothing that could be done except to have the affected tooth pulled. This is no longer the case and you should know this, for now you can save a tooth that at one time you would have lost.

So, that's what "endodontics" (root canal) is all about — saving your teeth. In essence, the endodontist cleans out the nerve tissue, drills open the nerve canals so all the infection is out, sterilizes the canals and fills the now empty canal with material (either silver points or a rubbery-like material called guita percha). By sealing the canals, germs cannot travel down them to the bone. This is a very tedious task, and I suggest that if possible you go to an endodontist to have it done. They have the equipment and more experience in this area of dentistry than the average dentist. Here are some things to know about root canals:

1) Once the tooth has fully formed, the nerve is not needed for the tooth's survival. That is very far out, for it means the tooth will not die if the nerve does.

2) The tooth becomes drier without the nerve, and more brittle. Because of this, almost every tooth needing a root canal should be capped with either gold or porcelain to metal.

3) When a cap is to be made on a tooth with a root canal, a post should be drilled into the root. This gives the tooth more support and prevents it from breaking. The idea is much like that of making a fence and digging post holes. The deeper the hole, the stronger the post. Insist that the dentist making the crown or cap do this.

4) Root canals are not cheap, ranging from perhaps $60.00 for front teeth to $200.00 for back teeth. But it will still be cheaper in the long run to have one done, than to lose the tooth.

Say a bottom tooth became abcessed and you asked the dentist what could be done. Well, if he's good, he'll tell you that to have it pulled will cost about $35.00, and then to have a fixed bridge put in to replace the now missing tooth will cost about another $300.00 or so. So, you'd have a false tooth and two other possibly good teeth capped and you'd have spent at least $335.00. Now, if you had had a root canal done, it would cost you say $150.00 (for a molar) and another say $90.00 for a crown. This way, you keep your tooth, save two others from being capped, and save about $95.00. So, do not let a bad dentist talk you into pulling a tooth just because $35.00 sounds cheap. If you did have it pulled and didn't get a bridge, you would most likely foul up your bite.

WISDOM TEETH

In most cases you will want to have them pulled. But, before you make any decisions about this, read my rap about wisdom teeth in the chapters on "Home Care" and "Dental Emergencies."

DENTAL EMERGENCIES

The basic principles of getting emergency work done are the same as in the other groups. So, for those of you who cannot immediately afford to have all of the work done, ask the dentist how much time you'll have to raise the money before your condition gets worse. Also, see if anything can be done temporarily to prevent your situation from deteriorating until you can fix it. Bear in mind that regardless of the cost, the work must be done to restore you to normal dental health.

MONEY – THE BIG BITE TO REPAIR YOUR BITE

I've been ripped off enough to make me business minded, if not a little paranoid, and I'm sure that most other dentists have been too. It is bad karma to rip off anyone – even the dentist with his outrageous prices. The following suggests some alternatives which we can all live with:

1) Cash Payoffs: This is the hardest of all for most patients, but as you might suspect, it's the way the dentist most prefers being paid. I'm not even going to attempt to tell you how to get your money together, but it will have to be done – before, during or after the dentist is doing the work.

2) Insurance: *Any* insurance that will help you pay *any* part of your dental bill is a good one. There are many different kinds of insurance, and I will only be able to generalize about them.

a) Many insurance salesmen do not tell you the full story, and in order to make their policy sound more attractive, they sometimes avoid the up front facts. Most dental insurance plans say they will pay a certain percentage, say 80%, of your dental costs. That sounds good, but in fine print it says 80% of the insurance company's fees, always much lower than the dentist's. So, instead of 80%, it might be only 50% of the dentist's actual fees. Keep this in mind when you go to the dentist. Always wait until the insurance has been sent in and figured out before you jump up and down. And who knows, it may just pay 80% of the dentist's real charges.

b) Most dental plans have a yearly limit that they'll pay. For some, it's $500.00, for others it's $1,000.00, etc. Again, wait until it is sent in and the money returned before you celebrate.

c) If you are covered, make sure you utilize the insurance. Get all of your work done and ask for the best. Even if you have to pay 50%, it's still a good deal.

3) Credit: If you establish credit, some dentists will carry you; you pay a certain amount down and so much per month, depending on the size of your bill. This in itself is a good enough reason for paying your initial exam and other costs. Having paid, you will stand a much better chance of getting the credit. Such a payment plan as this is carried by the dentist if your bill isn't too high and no gold work is involved.

4) Welfare: Most welfare systems allow the dentist to do only minimum service on a welfare patient, and the state pays the dentist less than what he normally gets from "paying customers." The result is that most dentists won't even work on a welfare patient and the ones that do usually don't take time to educate the welfare patient on how to prevent dental disease. So, not having the proper care, no education, the average welfare patient usually ends up having all his teeth pulled. This bum situation needs a social overhaul.

5) Emergency — But No Bread: If you've paid your way so far, the chances are super good that the dentist will let you put emergency work on your bill. If you haven't paid anything yet, he still make take care of your "emergency work" (assuming he considers it an immediate emergency), but you probably won't get any further work done by him until you cough up the dough.

6) Breaking the Faith: The dentist may, if you've shaken his faith by not paying, inform you that any further work will be on a cash basis. I feel he is justified in doing this, especially if you've made no effort to pay him.

There *are* good dentists around. A few. The difficulty lies in finding them. You should also recognize that the bad dentist is often bad only because your lack of knowledge about dentistry allows him to get away with his evil ways. By knowing a good dentist from a bad one you can help to make the bad dentist a good one; by knowing the right ways that things would be done you can often make the bad dentist do what he would.

Here are some ways to choose a good dentist:

a) Vibrational Level:

   1) What does his office feel like? Are the vibes good?

   2) Do you pick up on feelings of confidence? Fear? Conflict?

   3) Do the people working with him seem happy and content?

   4) How about the pace — do you feel he is rushed? Too rushed can mean sloppy work.

   5) When you meet the Doc, does he seem mellow, satisfied?

If you can answer yes to all of the above, you're off to a good start — four out of five is pretty good. Zero out of five means you'd better get out of there.

Knowing some of you are not completely into vibrations as a means of final judgement, I'll cover some of the more tangible means of uncovering the *good* dentist.

b) What You See And Hear:

   1) The office is pleasantly decorated and has a warm, friendly atmosphere.

   2) The equipment is new and well kept.

   3) There are only two chairs, meaning that the dentist can take the necessary time to treat you individually.

4) The dentist is happy and healthy and appears to enjoy his work.

5) He is open and honest with you and his co-workers, and he does not appear to be upset and hassling with people and situations around him.

6) You have heard good things about him from your friends, and you know other people who have gotten good treatment from him.

7) His own teeth seem to be well cared for.

c) What He Does Before Any Work:

1) He has you fill out a complete health history form. (So that he will know about your general health, special health problems, or allergies which may be relevant to him in your treatment.)

2) He does his own cleaning (optional).

3) He, or the hygienist, uses flavored pumice to polish your teeth.

4) He, or his co-workers, take a full mouth set of x-rays of every new patient.

5) He — not the hygienist — does a thorough oral examination.

The first appointment need not be a bummer.

The dental office can be a friendly place to visit.

6) He offers you a complete treatment plan, with alternatives.

7) He offers you various ways of paying your bill.

8) He will admit to you what he can do, and what he cannot do. And he will refer you to people who can do the things he can't.

9) He wants to save your teeth, not pull them. And he tells you so.

10) He takes the time to talk with you, to answer your questions and to reassure you.

d) How He Performs His Work:

1) *He is painless.* He does everything possible to make you comfortable.

2) He utilizes a topical anesthetic in the area he is going to give you the shot (you can see him do this, he'll either spray it on before injecting, or swab it on with a Q-tip).

3) He warms his anesthetic solution before giving you the shot. (Ask him if he does.)

4) He attempts to hide the needle from you — this helps relieve the anxiety.

5) He injects slowly enough so that the shot *doesn't* hurt.

6) He uses Nitrous-Oxide (laughing gas) to help make you more comfortable (optional).

7) He waits until you are totally numb before he begins to work on you.

8) He will stop if you still feel anything after he begins working and re-inject to get you numb.

9) He uses a "rubber dam" (a 4x4 inch square piece of rubber with holes punched in it that exposes the teeth he is to work on but no others. It also keeps things from going down your throat. This takes him longer, but it is better for you.)

10) He removes all particles of old filling when they need replacing. (You can ask him if he does this or ask him to let you see what the filling looks like before he refills it.)

11) He places a base (an insulating material, usually white) before filling a deeply decayed tooth. You definitely should ask him if he does this.

12) He places a matrix around the tooth before filling a two or three-sided silver filling. (Again, ask him. This is nothing more than a circular band that goes around the tooth and is wedged tightly at the gum line. It prevents the silver filling from jamming into your gums and allows him to do a much better filling.)

13) He takes the time to carve the *silver filling* to the shape of the original tooth. (You can tell if he does this, because after he is finished filling the tooth, he will carve it with a knife-like instrument.)

14) He checks your bite after doing each filling to see if it is too high. (He'll have you bite on a piece of inked paper like heavy carbon paper, to mark any high spots on your teeth after he fills them. He will then grind off the high spots until your bite is perfected.)

15) He does not leave gaps between teeth after putting in a silver or gold filling.

16) His fillings do not fall out and he will tell you how to take care of them and how long they should last.

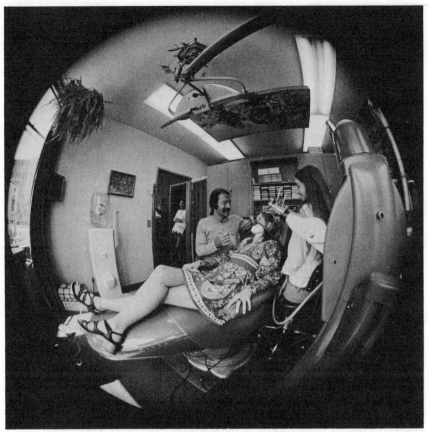

A fisheye view of the operatory.

17) He polishes the silver fillings — usually on the appointment after the fillings are done.

18) He uses the new (1972) quartz-type fillings for the small fillings in your front teeth. (Ask him if he does.)

19) He uses porcelain baked on metal for capping front teeth (Ask him — it costs a little more, but lasts a lot longer than anything else available now.)

20) He works sitting down — easier on him and it results in your getting better work done.

21) He has a second person to help him work on you who sits on the opposite side and is always there to assist.

22) The dentist (this is super important) does such good work that it doesn't have to be done over. This, coupled with your knowledge of how to take care of your mouth means you should have no new decay and that, my friend, is not only a sign of a good dentist, but also of a good patient.

So, if your dentist has scored twenty-two, you've struck gold. Stick with this guy and tell all your friends about him. Even if you get nineteen out of twenty-two, you've got a winner. By knowing the above criteria for judging good dentists, and by combining it with the knowledge in the first part of this chapter, you can raise even a mediocre dentist's score to twenty-two. Tell him what you want. You are the one who will either benefit or suffer. Speak out.

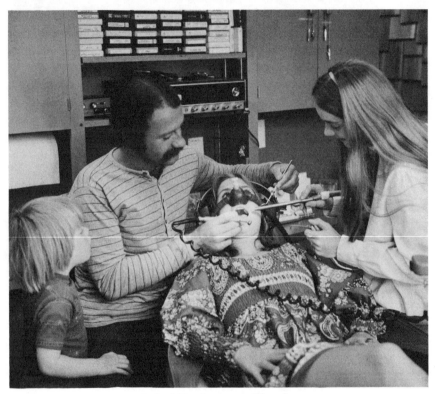

Relax! You're in good hands.

WOMEN IN DENTISTRY

One question which people might ask is, "Do women make good or bad dentists?" The answer is that women can be good dentists or bad dentists. You, with the aid of this book, will have to be the judge of that.

But the truth of the matter is this: there are very few women in dentistry in the United States, although women dentists are relatively common in many European countries. There is certainly nothing in dentistry that prevents women from doing the work. As in anything else, the fault lies in our society's teaching of sexist roles, and in our continuing to support these roles without thinking very much about them. The fault lies, too, in more specific areas; i.e., dental schools have discriminated against women solely on the basis of sex. Likewise, as children, we are taught that the dentist is a man.

Our language itself makes it difficult to speak of a single individual as anything other than "he" when the sex is undetermined. Thus, it becomes doubly easy to think and speak of the dentist in the masculine gender only. But this should not be allowed to stand in your way of picking out a dentist. If you should find one who is a woman, and if she passes your tests of how to judge a good dentist, you should have no reservations about having her to the work. Personally, I really believe women would make good dentists ... if only given the opportunity.

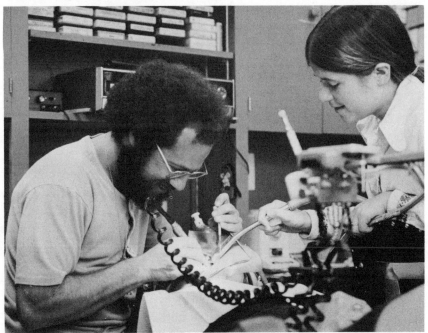

Dr. Joseph Arancio and friends, we shared an office in 1972. Thanks Joseph!

THE BAD DENTIST

Unpleasant as it is, I have to talk about this most disreputable of all characters. He is responsible for all those sadistic and painful cartoons you see about dentists. (Ever see a cartoon showing a good

181

dental trip? Fat chance!) He is the sole reason why there is a need for a book of this type to be written. And most of you have no doubt already met him.

The bad dentist must either be rehabilitated or outlawed. But you can't do either until you know exactly how to recognize him. If you are unlucky enough to find one, you could give him a chance to clean up his act, but if he won't or can't, then report him to the ADA and warn your friends about him. Don't keep going to a bad dentist. You not only suffer, you continue to support his bad act. I'll run through some of the things to watch out for. They are:

1) He has a sterile, plain, smelly, old-fashioned office and equipment. (Remember, if your dentist has 1870 equipment, he is probably doing 1870 work, but charging your current prices. Without the proper tools, you can't do proper work. Ever try and cut down a tree with a jack knife?)

2) He has up-tight, grouchy employees.

3) He never explains to you how to properly take care of your mouth.

4) His first — and sometimes only — priority is money; his second priority is your health; his last priority is your comfort.

5) He'd rather pull a tooth than save it.

6) He has three or more chairs, and is constantly rushing from room to room.

7) He stands up when he works, and seems always on the verge of leaving.

8) He doesn't do a complete oral examination.

9) He doesn't have you fill out a health history form to check for allergies, etc.

10) He doesn't offer you a complete treatment plan of the best work available.

11) He doesn't take a full set of x-rays.

12) He has that authoritative attitude, like you're a dummy and he knows it all.

13) He treats you like you are not a human being with feelings.
14) Your fillings fall out.
15) His shots hurt.
16) He uses old-fashioned and outdated plastic fillings that wash out or stain horribly.
17) He totally freaks out if you show him the *Tooth Trip*.
18) Every time you go back, something needs to be done and he never seems to tell you why.
19) Your gums are always painful and/or bleeding, and he never tells you why or how to change this.
20) He ends up filling the same tooth again and again.
21) You had more teeth when you first began going to him than you do now. In other words, instead of helping you save your teeth, he helps you get rid of them.

So, if your present dentist, or the one you will be going to, fits the above description and your attempts to retrack him have failed, stop fighting it and look elsewhere.

Any dentist who fits the above description does not deserve your faith or trust. He sees you as a wallet, and if you've ever felt his wrath when you missed a payment, you'll know what I mean.

The *bad* dentist needs you much more than you need him. You are his financial food and it's time he starved a little. The day the bad dentist finds his office empty of patients is the day he may begin thinking about becoming a *good* dentist.

You should now have a clear picture of what the bad dentist looks like. You should also have a desire to either change him (for your benefit and that of your fellow man), or dump him and report him to the ADA. The sacred responsibility of knowledge and power is now yours. Use it wisely. And remember that it can easily be abused. Ask the bad dentist about that!

13

DENTAL EQUIPMENT: NEEDLES AND STUFF

X-RAYS
THE CHAIR
THE DRILL
CAVITRON
RUBBER DAM
LIGHT
AIR AND WATER SYRINGE
CHAIRSIDE DENTAL ASSISTANT
WHAT ELSE

The piece of dental equipment that causes people the most concern and the most pain is the needle (syringe). So, let's talk about that first.

The needle will not hurt you if *handled properly.* A discussion of the needle and why it is needed will help you understand its place in dentistry, and, hopefully, lessen your fear of it. Also, the very best way to avoid having the dentist give you a shot is to prevent tooth decay in the first place — you know what I mean?

The teeth have nerves similar to the nerves of the rest of your body, and when these nerves are bothered the result is pain. Nerves do not care what causes their trauma; heat, cold, a bruise or severing them — it can all result in pain. Although it is true that different people react to pain differently, a majority of people (most likely you) do not like to experience any pain. If a tooth is drilled, the nerve in the tooth is traumatized; the resulting pain is generally considered to be the most intense pain the body can experience.

In order to prevent you from feeling the pain of decay or of the drill, dental researchers figured out that certain solutions (anesthetics), when applied on or near a nerve, would stop that nerve from

184

sending pain impulses to your brain. Thus, if the nerve is numbed, though a tooth still suffers trauma, you won't feel it.

It so happens that the nerves that enter the teeth are usually found fairly deep under the skin. If these nerves are to be numbed, the numbing solution (most of you know it as novocaine) must have a way to get to the nerve. The needle is simply a tube for carrying the anesthetic solution beneath the skin to the nerve.

The capsule containing the numbing solution is placed into the syringe or body of the needle, like a bullet in a gun, and a needle is screwed onto the other end. The handle of the syringe acts as a plunger and pushes the solution down the tube of the needle under pressure. That's basically how it works, and if done right, it's far out. I, for one, would rather have a shot (painless, of course) than have to feel the pain of the drill.

What I'm saying is that the needle will not hurt you if injected correctly. I discuss this on page 192. So, if a dentist hurts you, tell him what you read about pain and needles in this book.

X-RAYS

I've covered the reasons why x-rays are needed (page 144), but not what they are, so for those who wish to know, here goes.

An x-ray is nothing more than a photographic record of an object produced by the passage of x-rays through the object (the tooth or whatever) to a film behind it.

That's simply what x-rays do, and here's how they do it. Hang on, it'll be short, but if you don't get off on the why's of things and think they're too technical, you can skip on — the machine will work whether you know how it works or not. Knowledge is far out.

X-rays are nothing more than a type of radiant energy, like light from the sun. Also, like light rays, x-rays travel as wave motion, and the size of this wave length can be measured. The feature that makes x-rays a valuable diagnostic aid is the fact that their wave length is extremely short, about 1/10,000th the length of light waves. It is a simple physical fact that the shorter its wave length the easier these energy rays can penetrate an object. It is this fact that allows x-rays to penetrate teeth and gums that would normally absorb or reflect other waves of longer length.

So, x-rays have every property that light rays have but in a different form. Some of their special properties that are of value to dentists are:

1) X-rays can penetrate the teeth and gums.

2) Film is affected by x-rays, which allows a "record" to be produced when the film is developed. Much like taking a picture with a camera.

3) Substances of differing densities, like hard teeth or soft gums, allow more or less of the x-rays to strike the film. This means different substances are easily differentiated on x-ray film.

4) X-rays can cause changes in genes, especially in the reproductive areas. Therefore, caution must be used when taking x-rays. The dentist should use a lead shield to protect your reproductive areas. This is another good reason to keep your teeth clean; the dentist won't have to x-ray as often.

THE CHAIR

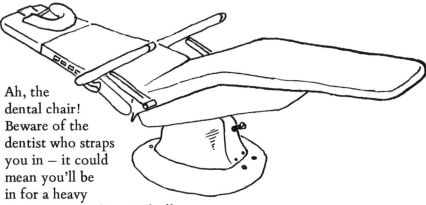

Ah, the dental chair! Beware of the dentist who straps you in — it could mean you'll be in for a heavy session! (I'm joking.) Ideally, the chair should be contoured and adjustable. This is for your comfort, but it also allows the dentist to position you so he can work easily and efficiently.

Modern dentists usually work sitting down over you tilted to a prone position. If your present dentist has an old 1800's chair and works standing over you, it could mean his dentistry is ancient too. Go elsewhere; it's not worth it. Keep it in mind that good, new equipment does not automatically make a good dentist, but it's a good sign.

Most good dentists use two drills:
1) A slow speed belt-driven
handpiece for polishing your
teeth, polishing fillings and
taking out decay that's close
to the nerve. You can tell
this one because it's driven
by a belt and makes very
little noise. Remember, these
slow jobs are only valuable for
polishing and for other finishing work
requiring slower speeds for safety. If your
dentist uses one of these old and slow babies
for *all* his work, including major drilling,
you, my friend, are in the wrong office.

2) High speed drill. Today high speed turbines (air-driven handpieces) can turn a bur (the drill bit) at speeds up to 400,000 revolutions per minute. This makes dentistry much easier for everyone, but it can have its side effects — especially in a shaky hand. Many previously time-consuming types of drilling can be eliminated by the high speed drill. For example:
a) The removal of old fillings is many hundred
times easier and less traumatic on you and
the tooth.
b) The reduction of teeth that are to
be capped or crowned is much easier and
faster.

HIGH SPEED DRILL

Some of the side effects of the high speed handpiece are:
a) Excessive heat is generated by the high speed drill from

friction. This heat can damage or kill a nerve. Consequently, the high speed drill should be used intermittently, allowing the nerve a chance to cool down. Watch for this; if a dentist keeps constant drilling pressure on your tooth, ask him to periodically give it a chance to cool. Though you can't feel it, your tooth is probably suffering. High speed drills can also be used with water as a coolant. If you are going to have extensive drilling done, ask your dentist if he will use the water spray. Nothing in the body can live very long at temperatures higher than 120° Fahrenheit, including the nerves of your teeth.

b) Excessive noise. If the dentist doesn't have earphones, bring cotton with you and plug your ears before he drills. Or ask the guy to supply earplugs.

Word to the wise — many bad dentists have been aided by the high speed drill; with it they can do shallow drilling painlessly and without giving you a shot. You may think he is fast and painless, but the truth is he's doing an inadequate job, because many teeth do not need filling unless the decay gets through the outer enamel. There are no nerves in the enamel, and with high speed drills he can cut into the enamel almost painlessly. But, in order to remove all the decay that has gone into the dentin (inner tooth), he must cut into the dentin with the drill. The dentin has nerve endings in it that radiate out from the central nerve (see page 193). Thus, drilling into the dentin causes pain. What the bad dentist does, so he can get done faster, is stop drilling while still in the enamel. He then quickly fills the tooth. You, of course, are impressed. But sadly for you, the decay that he left in the dentin will keep right on decaying the tooth, eventually either causing a painful eruption or killing the nerve and making a root canal necessary. Don't be fooled by the speed merchant. Follow all guidelines I've given you for finding a good dentist. Also, if you don't trust a guy, have him show you your x-rays and point out the areas of decay to you. (I show you how to read x-rays on page 144.) If you see that the decay goes into the dentin, you know it'll hurt unless you get a shot, so if it doesn't hurt, he didn't do the filling correctly. If he tells you he has to do a recent filling over again because of decay under the filling, it is *his* fault. You shouldn't have to pay for that. If he hassles you, you can threaten to sue him. You have a good case. Make sure you discuss this with him before he refills the tooth, for if you decide to sue, you need evidence, and the evidence is the decay left in your tooth and visible on your x-rays.

CAVITRON

This gadget is used by many dentists to clean your teeth. It is very effective and less traumatic than the old scraping method. The Cavitron is electrically driven and works like a tuning fork. The tip develops ultra-sonic vibrations, which actually *vibrate* the tartar and plaque off your teeth. It developes high heat and requires a water spray to cool it down. It is often the case that you receive some of the spray — quite refreshing!

Sometimes the pitch of the vibrations can irritate a nerve, but this is more traumatic than painful; somewhat like scraping your fingernails on a blackboard. Of course, the worse the condition of your gums, the more sensitive they will be to any form of cleaning, so don't blame your pain on the Cavitron.

FOOT PEDAL

Also, the Cavitron does not completely clean the teeth; they must be polished after it is used.

RUBBER DAM

This is a four-by-four inch square piece of rubber that has holes punched in it to allow the dentist to isolate the teeth that he'll be working on. Most good dentists use the dam routinely. Some advantages are:

1) Isolates the teeth to be drilled and keeps them dry.

2) Prevents tooth debris, old fillings and other dental material from going down your throat.

3) Keeps the tongue and lips out of the way and prevents possible damage to them.

4) Allows the dentist to do better work more efficiently. This means you get a better job.

I use the dam whenever possible, about 85% of the time, and I don't think you could consider a dentist good unless he does. If yours doesn't, ask him why.

RUBBER DAM

Some helpful hints about the dam:

1) Many dentists use a rubber bite block to hold your mouth open. Once it is in place, you can bite down upon it. Not only does it keep your mouth open, it is also less traumatic on your jaw muscles.

2) Breathe through your nose. When the dam is in place, you'll find that's much easier.

3) When the dam and bite block are in place, you may think you cannot swallow. But you can with a little experimenting. This is important, for the amount of saliva produced while you are in the dentist's clutches is many times greater than normal. If you do find it too difficult or impossible to swallow, ask the dentist to use the *saliva ejector.* This is a little tube with a plastic tip that ejects your excess saliva, but it's not very comfortable.

LIGHT

"Let there be light" is a Number One prerequisite for good dentistry. That big, round, oblong, square, or whatever shape it may be, light allows the dentist to see what's happening inside your mouth.

The newer lights provide much brighter and more concentrated light and when you can see better, you can work better. You'll most likely notice it is easily adjustable, an important characteristic, for it allows the dentist the freedom to change his position when working in different areas.

The importance of the light can be more readily appreciated by attempting to examine your mouth without light. See what I mean? Good lighting is another sound reason for choosing a dentist with new equipment.

AIR AND WATER SYRINGE

This gadget is not unlike the nozzle on your garden hose, except it lets you spray air separately or imagine a dental you to rinse and dry high standards of and water together. I can't office without one. It allows a tooth thoroughly, thus maintaining dental hygiene and efficiency. Again, if your dentist doesn't have one of these, I'd find one who did.

CHAIRSIDE DENTAL ASSISTANT

As I've told you, if your dentist works sitting down, the chances are he'll do a better job than the one who stands up. If he also has a full-time chairside assistant to help, that's better yet. A good dental assistant:

1) Mixes impression material, cements, and temporary filling material.

2) Holds the vacuum cleaner that sucks water and garbage out of your mouth.

3) Seats you and gets the equipment ready.

4) Adjusts the light and chair.

5) Develops x-rays.

6) Passes instruments to the dentist.

7) Generally allows the dentist greater efficiency by freeing his attention from mechanical details.

WHAT ELSE

There are other items that the dentist uses, some of which I discuss in the chapter on "Survival in the Dental Office," pg. 143. However, no dental equipment is any good, regardless of how new or old, unless there is a GOOD dentist behind it. It should be your first and most important concern to find a GOOD dentist. Keep trying until you do. If you have further questions about equipment, ask him to explain things to you. Every day dental manufacturers come out with new gadgets and new variations on the old stuff. When you see something I haven't explained, ask your dentist about it. You're paying him enough; he can take the time to explain his equipment to your satisfaction.

14

ELIMINATING DENTAL FEAR, DENTAL PAIN AND OTHER ANXIETIES

NEEDLES AND DRILLS
ANESTHETIZING THE UPPER TEETH
ANESTHETIZING THE LOWERS
GAS
PRE-MEDICATION
OTHER THINGS THAT HELP RELIEVE FEAR

Dentistry does not have to be painful, except in exceptional cases like an extreme tooth abcess or wisdom teeth infections. Even this type of pain can be controlled or minimized a great deal. If your dentist causes you pain, either in giving you that "fearful and dreaded" shot or while drilling on you, he is not only causing you *unnecessary* suffering, but he is working to reinforce dental decay and disease by supporting your worst fears of what can happen in the chair. The dentist you should be looking for is painless and works to promote your confidence and security about your teeth and your relaxation while in his office. Here are some tips to help you relax and possibly enjoy your dental visit.

NEEDLES AND DRILLS

If your dentist hurts you, tell him you know pain can be avoided and that if he continues to hurt you with the shot or while he is drilling on you (because he gave you a shot that didn't totally anesthetize you) you will go to another dentist. If he asks you what you think he should do (and he just might), tell him:

1) Use a topical anesthetic before injecting anesthetic
2) Warm the anesthetic solution to body temperature before injecting it
3) Use small, new and sharp needles
4) Inject very slowly so the solution doesn't hit your nerve under such pressure that it bruises the tissue and causes pain. (This is important because the opening at the tip of the needle is very small. If he injects the solution into you rapidly, the force

of the solution coming out of the tip of the needle will bruise the tissue.) This means the injection will hurt when he gives it, but will also hurt later due to the bruise.

It may help lessen your fear of shots if you understand something of how anesthetic works in your mouth, and the problem of injecting it. Probably the biggest cause of fear is mystery, so let's de-mystify the "shot" a little.

ANESTHETIZING THE UPPER TEETH

The bone surrounding the upper teeth is thinner and more porous than the bone of the lower and this fact allows the dentist to numb each tooth individually if he so wishes. The porosity of the bone allows the anesthetic to infiltrate through the bone and numb the nerve of that particular tooth. It takes a minute or two for this to happen, so if the doc is in too much of a hurry ($$) and drills too soon, you'll still feel the drill. Ask him to please wait a few minutes.

Some dentists like to give shots into the roof of the mouth. I don't think they realize how much this can hurt if not done correctly. The nerves that this shot numbs go to the gums surrounding the inside back part of the upper teeth and, except for extractions in this area, are not usually needed. I am noted for painless dentistry and have not given one of these shots in my whole career. Most bad dentists don't know how to give this shot anyway, and it's the one people are most afraid of. If your dentist tries to give you this shot, tell him nicely that perhaps he's forgotten what it feels like and that you'd like to try to do without it.

ANESTHETIZING THE LOWERS

Numbing the lower teeth poses a different problem. The bone here is much too thick to let the anesthetic filter through. Therefore, the nerve must be numbed before it enters the jaw. If these nerves, one on the left side of the lower jaw and one on the right, are numbed before they enter the jaw, all the teeth on that side will be numbed. For example, even if the dentist is only filling one tooth on the right side, he must numb all the teeth on that side just to work on that one tooth.

This lower nerve is hard to find, so you may feel the dentist poking around. Don't worry. If he waits two or three minutes before drilling and you still feel pain, be sure to tell the dentist. Sometimes up to three injections are needed. These lower shots aren't as easy to get as the uppers. Just make sure you don't let him keep on drilling without first trying to numb you again. No matter what excuse he gives you, and it's not just in your head (!), if he won't keep trying to numb you, he's in too great a hurry — bad sign.

Remember, if done correctly, the injected needle will not hurt and if a dentist hurts you, it's time to move on.

Another point, you must do your share. You should recognize and be aware of the difference between pain and pressure. I could gently press on your cheek and you'd feel pressure — you'd know what I was doing, but it wouldn't hurt. On the other hand, if I pinched your cheek you'd feel pain. The point I'm making is that even good dentistry means some pressure will be applied, but don't freak out from the pressure and confuse it with pain.

GAS

The better the dentist, the more likely are the chances that he will use gas (nitrous oxide, sometimes known as laughing gas). As I've mentioned, gas is an anesthetic and when used in moderate amounts is *safe* and really is effective in helping to relieve dental anxiety. Try it — have him start on "low"; you can always tell him if you want more. Mentally it's a trip and if you like getting stoned, you'll really get off on gas. As I mentioned before, I don't think that I'd go to a dentist that doesn't give gas; you shouldn't either but you may not have any choice. Alas! I'm not saying that a dentist can't be painless if he doesn't give gas, he can. But, by having gas available for you, he probably cares about your feelings that much more. And, remember, it also helps alleviate the fears. Try it.

PRE-MEDICATION

If you are really freaked out and nervous, you can ask for even more things to help eliminate your fear, like a pill to relax you. You'll have to ask for this one; dentists aren't mind readers, and most could care less about your fear or anxiety.

The best pill I've found that does this, and with very few side effects, is a pill called Quaalude, made by Rorer. It relaxes you and makes you feel good, yet you still function and stay alert. However, I'm not pushing pills; you should take these only if you really can't relax and feel comfortable in the chair.

OTHER THINGS THAT HELP RELIEVE FEAR

1: A nice pleasant office, nice people and a *dentist that cares.* If he cares, he won't hurt you and if he doesn't hurt you, you'll begin to feel at ease in his chair. It's only from a base of relaxation that confidence and trust can grow.

2: Earphones plugged into a stereo set or cassette tape set and tuned to a comfortable volume can be very relaxing to many people. Such a system "softens" the environment considerably for you in the chair and does not represent such a large investment for your dentist. Suggest he install a music system for his patients. You can tell from his response how much he is in tune with other people's feelings! Every little bit helps.

3: Breathing, plain old ordinary breathing, if properly exercised both in the waiting room and when you first get in the chair can do a great deal to settle and refocus your attention back on yourself and away from anxiety, fear of pain or noise or of the unknown. As you sit in the waiting room, simply begin to breathe normally *from your abdomen,* without forcing your breath in or out. When you get afriad, you breathe from the chest in short, shallow pants. Therefore, the first step in relaxation is to move your breathing back to your abdomen. Breathe gently with your diaphragm (lower part of your stomach). Focus your attention on your breath. Forget about the other people or objects in the waiting room. Close your eyes. Just breathe. Better? Now, as you focus on gentle, regular breathing, think about the distance from the top of your head to the bottom of your feet. With your body, just *feel* that distance. Pay attention to your breathing and to feeling your size and let all the other stuff slide away. After a couple of minutes, you are in a new head, no longer feeling so anxious or afraid as a moment before. Practice facilitates the speed and depth of your relaxation. This technique works whether you're standing, sitting or lying down. Try it in the dental chair. In fact, stop where you are reading this book, and try it *right now* . . . isn't knowledge far out? Knowledge in itself can get you high, just think of what happens when you add proper breathing . . . off you go . . . .

15

PORTRAIT OF THE DENTIST AS CON ARTIST

THE DENTIST'S MONEY HANGUPS
BAD DENTISTS LOOSED UPON THE WORLD
HOW THE PUBLIC CAN PUT BAD DENTISTRY OUT
LEVERS AND LEGISLATION

As a child, I used to be what the bad dentist today calls a bad patient, but I was a bad patient only because the dentist caused me more pain than I'd ever before experienced. Damn right, I was a bad patient by his standards; but he made me one. So, even though the dentist feels he is not at fault, he actually is. Your responsibility lies in learning how and what you can do to make him responsive to your needs. By your not knowing what he is doing (good or bad) you give him the freedom to do anything he desires any way he pleases, and then if anything goes wrong, you get blamed because you were a bad, complaining patient. And how can he do good work on a bad patient? Bah, humbug! You may have been conditioned to believe he does the best he can, or that his conscience will not let him knowingly cause you pain or suffering. Well, it sounds good on paper, and in thought, and it is nice to have such powerful faith in your fellow man (dentist). But it just ain't deserved here.

The above situation allows the dentist to continue doing bad work with a clear conscience, all the time thinking it is you who caused the problems, not him. So, again, it comes down to you. Until you become aware of what is going on and then use this new knowledge to deal with and change the bad dentist, you will continue to be exploited.

You see, as I have pointed out earlier, it is an easy matter to learn how to prevent dental disease — if only someone would teach you. In fact, the most important function of a dentist is supposed to be to eliminate, repair and *teach* you how to prevent dental disease from recurring. It is evident that if dentists were performing this function properly, the dental problem would be decreasing and we would then know dentists were actually doing their jobs. The results would prove this, and your faith in the profession would be justified. It is also true that if the present enormous dental problems were being solved, there would be no need for this book. I would remain silent, and be thankful for it.

What are the facts? Well, they say that dentistry is not doing the job it is supposed to do and that dentists know how to do and that you are paying good, hard-earned money for less than mediocre dental work. It also means that whatever dentists are doing to solve (your) dental disease is *not* working, regardless of the dental profession's desires, motives or intentions. The facts speak for themselves and these facts convict the dental profession not only of failing to solve the problem, but of making it worse. The profession is not curing you, but is exploiting you and is getting a big fat bank account in the process. The end result is that you lose your teeth, health and a lot of money to boot. How much of the more than four billion dollars paid to dentists last year did you contribute? How much of his Cadillac did you pay for? How much of the dentist's trip to Europe did you subsidize? And just what did you get out of it? Did you get your money's worth? Probably not! Because you still have to keep going back to him. You're still suffering and you're still paying.

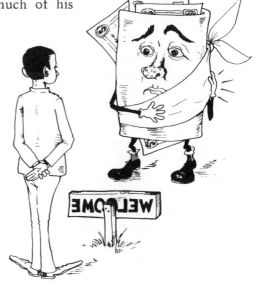

A very simple test you can use to assess the type of dentistry you have been receiving from your dentist is whether or not you have to keep going back to him to have more work done. In other words, are you continuing to suffer from dental disease? You shouldn't be, you know, and if you are, you've got a bad dentist, or you're not doing what you should in the way of prevention. You see, if your dentist was performing the service he should be, he would have permanently repaired your problems. Then he would have taught you how and why you should not ever have any future dental complications.

Today, dentistry can beautifully repair almost anything. With the spaceage technology available it is an easy matter (if you have the money) to get movie star teeth, a beautiful bridge, or nice plates. But again, the profession has completely failed because few dentists are interested in *cure and prevention*.

THE DENTIST'S MONEY HANGUPS

One reason dentists demand so much money is that they are used to having it as children. It is no coincidence that most students who are accepted into dental school are sons (and rarely daughters) of dentists or doctors, or sons of other rich people in the higher income brackets. This also is the reason why most people want to become dentists. They are used to having lots of money and they think dentistry can give it to them.

Another reason dentists charge so much is that it costs a hell of a lot of money to get into and through dental school, and once you've paid out that much money, you naturally want to get it back. Not only does it cost about $10,000 to $20,000 to go to college, but it will cost about $40,000 to get through dental school. Add about another $50,000 to set up practice after getting out of school, and you can easily see that there are not many average families who can afford $100,000 to get their kid started. This is exactly the way the dental profession wants it. The prohibitive cost of schooling eliminates a great many prospective students — and for sure they do not like the poor one or two who sneak in.

The poor student (relative to the average dental student) can become a definite threat to the status quo of the dental profession. After all, the poorer student is not used to having much money and may not need as much money to live on when he graduates. Thus, he just might do better work for less money. And that would freak the money-hungry dentists out. No, they do not dig changes, for it is the bad dentist's intention to make sure that the prospective dental student comes from a family background that has had money, still wants it, and enjoys spending it. This way, the people controlling entrance into dental school can be sure they won't let someone in who is too idealistic, or someone who might want to rock the boat.

Okay, so we now know most dental schools want you to come from a background that is money-oriented, but there is even more, for *politics* also play a big part in who gets into dental school. The dental schools interview you to see if you fit their mold ($) and then they make sure you have the proper *recommendations.* The recommendations must be from a respected dentist, a person with influence and power, or someone who has given a lot of money to their school.

It should be getting clearer who gets into dental school and how they get in. By the time a student gets into dental school, he will (hopefully) fit the complete dental mold those in power want him to fit. (As I've said, some lucky ones who don't fit the image get by, but they are in the minority, probably less than 10%.)

Whatever idealism the dental student started with is quickly and very efficiently destroyed by the old established dental order. The bad dental instructors are committed to the status quo and do everything in their power to maintain it.

Not only is dental school difficult and time consuming, but a good 50% of the time is wasted on trivial tasks, and on archaic, outdated and useless techniques. Added to this wasted time is the time that must be spent kissing many of the instructor's egotistical prima donna butts, especially if that prima donna is in a position of power.

The student is forced to spend hundreds of hours of time (time he could be spending learning techniques of value) polishing teeth he will never polish when he gets into private practice. (The laboratories do the polishing.) He also must spend precious time (hundreds of more hours) perfecting a technique (gold foil, if it means anything to you) that not only went out with prohibition, but that less than 1% of the recent dental graduates would *ever* perform on a patient in private practice. This is just a waste of time that could be spent teaching *prevention*. If the gold foil filling I speak of was worth the time the student must spend, I would not complain. But, a gold foil is an unsightly filling, difficult to do, and so traumatic on you and your tooth it kills 50% of the teeth it is done on. Porcelain (or quartz) fillings for front teeth far surpass the gold foil filling.

Not only does the student have to become proficient with gold foil in order to graduate from dental school, but also in order to pass the State Dental Examination. The whole gold foil learning trip requires about five hundred hours of the student's time in dental school. All this time and energy spent on learning a useless and destructive technique!

Prevention — the singularly most important phase of dentistry by any standard — is shoved to the bottom of the list of subjects; and money-making is pushed to the top. I think I cleaned about three patient's teeth in dental school and was never required to explain to them how and why to prevent dental disease. My instructors never thought it important enough to tell their students about prevention! What I've learned about prevention has come from years of practical application and research on actual patients.

We were never required to totally treat a patient in dental school. We had only to get enough points for gold fillings and the school made the most money from them. This made our instructors, and the school's money controller, happy, and they were the ones who allowed you enough points to graduate (not as a complete dentist, but as a complete salesman, knowing how to talk people into having work done but not knowing how or willing to talk them into prevention). Thus, after we got the things we needed out of the patient (fillings that earned us the most points) we either dumped them or passed them to a student in a lower class. Some dental school patients that I know spent five years trying to get work done that would have taken a few months in private practice to complete. And unless the patient loudly complained, which rarely happened, no one cared. As an aspiring young dentist, one soon learns the secret of dental school success. You must choose between yourself and the patient – and when you've invested $50,000, it usually turns out to be you that survives. The students who didn't learn this principle – survival of the fittest – just didn't make it out of school. This is the attitude a dental graduate takes with him into private practice. It's either you or him.

At the time of graduation, if the student makes it, the chances are that the graduated dentist will:

1) Be a nervous, unhealthy, paranoid wreck.

2) Feel that after the dental school experience he will deserve every cent he can earn. A psychiatrist told me this need to feel justified in making money at someone else's expense and suffering is a conditioned response – a created one. Yeah, a response created in dental school.

3) Be totally ignorant about the most important aspects of dentistry – prevention and cure.

4) Be unable to show respect for the patient (you), because his instructors had none for him or their patients and considered them as objects, not humans. In fact, many dentists have learned to blame the patient for their (the dentist's) inadequacies.

5) Learn to not be unconcerned about inflicting pain. The patient that goes to dental school is willing to put up with anything, including pain. Because he puts up with this, he gets work that costs less. The dental student soon learns that it takes

too much time to eliminate pain and educate the patient, and time is points needed to graduate. So, the student learns that it doesn't hurt him to cause pain, and he stops worrying about it and concerns himself with the task of graduating by whatever means he can.

6) Feel heavy guilt for having wasted a great deal of time in dental school and is probably bitter as hell about it. The dental student usually ends up taking his bitterness out on the patient when he gets into private practice. It is this bitterness, combined with his concern for money, that causes the bad dentist to cause you pain, my friend; this is why *you* suffer dental pain.

It takes more time for the dentist to fulfill your dental needs painlessly. The dentist's hurry means pain for you, discomfort for you, and mediocre work for you. That situation means that you avoid the dentist like the plague, the result being dental neglect and eventual loss of your teeth, so even though you don't go back, you still lose.

BAD DENTISTS LOOSED UPON THE WORLD

After investing maybe $50,000 for an office (and if he goes the way most dentists are going today, the recent graduate will have an office with three chairs and probably at least two or three girls to help him), the average dentist will be facing the problem of how to meet basic office expenses which begin at something like $2,000 to $4,000 per month. Add to this the money he needs to carry out his personal money trip: like new cars, a house in the best area of town, a summer home, personal investments, maybe alimoney for his first wife (dentists have a very high divorce rate), insurance, vacations, clothes, children and their education, entertainment, booze, etc. All these additions will jack his monthly expenses up to a level of $4,000 to $8,000 per month — or roughly $40,000 to $100,000 per year. Dentists have to see quite a few patients every day to earn the money needed to meet those kinds of expenses. Remember, the bad dentist experiences no other form of gratification. How can he when he charges for inflicting pain and then uses the money he gets to buy material things in order to try and calm his tormented conscience? The results, as I've said, come down to either you or him, and he makes damn sure he utilizes all available techniques to insure his own survival.

The bad dentist hires people to come by and figure out how much money he needs to earn per hour in order to maintain his life style. One of the main things this *cost accountant* tells the dentist is that it is not *financially* rewarding for him to clean his patient's teeth, do ideal dentistry and educate the patient. The dentist on this trip is conditioned to think that cleaning teeth and educating the patient is not only beneath his dignity and intelligence, but also won't make the money he needs. Some of my worst dental instructors indicated to me that if I did the cleaning, and then taught the patient how to prevent dental disease, it would mean I would lose that person as a future patient. If he cleaned everyone up so they wouldn't have to come back, except for periodic exams and cleanings, the foolish man wouldn't be able to make the money he feels he requires. What a dilemma!

The cost accountant also tells the bad dentist that he could and should cut other corners, like seeing more patients and consequently seeing each one for a shorter time. This means eliminating certain procedures — like taking extra time to give a painless shot (and they all *can* be painless), or spending a little extra time getting to know you, trying to understand and help you deal with your fears. Remember how nice the dentist was to you before he built up his practice and got too busy? Ever think about that?

Regardless of how good the dentist thinks he is or was, it is a fact that he can only work so fast, see so many patients, and still do ideal dentistry. *And ideal dentistry is what you are paying for.* You won't find a fee schedule in a dentist's office that adjusts the charges so that you pay less for bad dentistry. They can charge you for the best and give you junk. The bad dentist's quest for the almighty dollar causes him to revert to survivalist instincts, and those instincts are void of the higher human feelings of compassion and sympathy.

So, now you've a pretty fair idea as to why the shot hurts. Your dentist can't *afford* to take the time to do it *painlessly*. You also know that he can't take that little extra time to numb you again if he's in the middle of drilling and the first shot wears off, or he didn't get you numb on the first one. You all have probably experienced that — the tooth starts to hurt and you indicate this, but he seems to pay no attention to your needs and your pain, and keeps right on truckin'; time = money, time = money.

Now you know better why that filling keeps falling out and has to be redone — at your expense, of course. It takes more time to do a filling that lasts, but time is money, and your dentist can't afford to do it right. Only a bad filling falls out. Your dentist knows it shouldn't fall out. But has the bad dentist ever told you it was his fault that it fell out? Fat chance! You should know that almost any excuse he gives you for it falling out is untrue.

You should also understand a little more about why your teeth get infected and why they may have to be pulled out. It is often because the bad dentist has been in a hurry, and probably left decay under the filling. As I've proven to you, unless all the decay is removed, which takes a little extra time, the tooth will keep right on decaying. It comes down to the fact that you've paid the bad dentist to leave the decay in, and you will later have to pay him to take it out again. Who suffers? Gets monotonous, huh? Leaving decay under a new filling is often premeditated dental crime of the worst kind, since it robs you not only of money and time, but usually of your dental health itself.

You should also now better understand why you never get a complete oral exam. Time — too much time — and you don't complain. How can you be expected to complain about what you don't know? The bad dentist loves the fact that you don't know. It makes him water at the mouth. Your ignorance results in his wealth. And folks, if you haven't guessed already, that is what dentistry is all about: *MONEY*. A never-ending supply of money — your hard earned money — money that you earn at $3 — $5 per hour and the bad dentist demands at $50 — $75 per hour. You can be pretty damn certain that this type of retarded dental economics all but guarantees that you will not find many Florence Nightingales or Albert Sweitzers in the dental office. Not many. Mr. Bad Dentist far outnumbers Mr. Good Dentist. But the good ones do exist, and with your new knowledge, perhaps you can change some bad ones into good ones.

HOW THE PUBLIC CAN PUT BAD DENTISTRY OUT

The last thing the dental profession wants is to have legal restrictions imposed on it. Boy, that would really bum them out. They would be forced to do good dentistry. Satan forbid! As much as they'd hate this, they seem to be doing everything to cause that very thing to happen. They have abused the trust, faith and respect given them by the people they are sworn to serve, and when the day of reckoning comes, there's going to be plenty of freaked out, wailing, bad dentists.

The dental profession will not change from the inside. History has proven this, for the dental health problem has only gotten worse over the years. The bad dentists are financially committed to bad dentistry and have talked themselves into believing that their fat bank accounts are well worth your pain. You, the patient, are the only one who can change the dental profession's bad trip. This can be accomplished by not letting your dentist screw you, by *demanding* the care and treatment you pay for, and by not accepting less than the best.

You must tell your dentist what you now know about dentistry. He is so freaked out about getting sued that he spends hundreds of dollars a year on mal-practice insurance to protect himself. So if you think your dentist is screwing you, tell him you will get an attorney and sue him unless it is worked out. You and only you have power over the bad dentist. He knows this, and as you've seen he does his best to keep you from learning this fact. The power of knowledge is needed to make a bad dentist responsive to your needs; and with knowledge you can turn your previously negative dental trip around. Use this knowledge to stop bad dentistry now.

Finally, to help you change the bad dentist, always take this book with you to the dentist's office. Refer to it often and let your dentist know that you know what's going on. Ask him to read it and awaken him from his selfish slumber. Let him know that it feels good to help people. Maybe, just maybe, he's forgotten that experience.

LEVERS AND LEGISLATION

I am enclosing two form letters that you can cut out and mail to your senator and the President of the State Board of Education. As you can see, it will make them aware of the problem and the need for changes in the dental profession. The first will put pressure on the dental schools, dental societies and private practitioners to get themselves in gear or pay the price of legislation and governmental controls.

The second letter is included for your State Board of Education to allow you to inquire as to why there is no law that states all school children must receive a thorough education on preventive dentistry and will also ask why preventive education is not mandatory in all high schools. Children are the age group this new awareness should reach, before it is too late.

Be sure you get a response from the people you write to and if you don't, write them back and inform them that if they wish to be re-elected, they'd best listen to you and respond.

*   *   *   *

Senator
Senate Building
Washington, D.C.

Date: _____

Dear Senator _____ :

As a very concerned individual and voter, I would like to pass on to you some very startling facts concerning the present state of dental disease in the United States. Although I do not accuse the dental profession of any particular wrong doings, other than perhaps excessive greed and lack of concern, I will instead let the facts speak for themselves and allow you to draw your own conclusions.

The chances are excellent, as you will see, that you yourself are a sufferer of dental disease. Hopefully, this regrettable point shall make the facts I'll present somewhat more pertinent.

The figures and statistics I offer you are the most recent ones available, most of which come from the U.S. Department of Public Health and can be easily confirmed.

1) 98% of the population of the United States (about 205 million people) suffers from dental disease.

2) Twenty-five million American people are presently without a tooth in their heads.

3) Twenty-four out of twenty-five young children suffer some form of dental disease by the time they reach school age.

4) Nine out of ten people reaching the age of sixty today will not have any teeth of their own.

5) Fifty-six million teeth were pulled in 1969 alone.

6) There have been estimates which say that today (1972) more than nine hundred million cavities need filling in this country.

Startling statistics, I'm sure, but how about the cost involved — everyone relates better to ($$) money, I know:

1) Americans spent four billion dollars on dentistry (1971 figures) and it is predicted that this figure will continue to rise in the future as it has risen in the past.

2) Add to this three hundred million dollars that is spent on dentifrices and the one hundred twenty million dollars that is

spent on toothbrushes, and you have a lot more than pocket money involved.

3) The total amount of money spent by Americans on dentally-related subjects is said to total more than is spent on *all man's other diseases combined.*

As my representative, I urge you to help the public fight a disease that is the most prevalent and destructive disease of mankind. The positive aspect of this fight against dental disease is that it is also one of the easiest understood and most preventable of all diseases. But, the only hope is through factual education, and this education should be made available. May I suggest a few ways in which to begin this fight?

1) Put pressure on the heretofore sacred, immune and uncontrolled dental profession to require them to include under penalty of law, a thorough and effective course on prevention to every person receiving and paying for a dental exam. Today this is done by probably less than ten per cent of the dentists and it is a crime against the people that only legislation can correct. Perhaps under the threat of legislation, which all dentists hate, they will begin teaching dental prevention.

2) Require, at a grade school and high school level, mandatory dental education. It should consist of an innovative and totally factual program, geared to the age group, which positively informs them that dental disease can be prevented. We cannot rely on the archaic dental profession to provide this information.

The problem of dental disease has surpassed epidemic proportions, and if the dental profession is unable or unwilling to solve the problem, and the facts prove they haven't since dental disease is not getting better, but worse, then the responsive members of government must come to the aid of the people they represent.

The independence of a few thousand dentists cannot possibly be worth the oral health and in many cases, the general health, of two hundred five million Americans.

Thank you, and I trust you will look into this immediately.

A letter from you informing me of the direction and results of your efforts will be most encouraging and will show me that government officials can truly be responsible.

Yours very truly,

_____
_____
_____

Dr. _____

Head, State Department of Public Education

_____

Date: _____

Dear Dr. _____ :

I have sent a letter to our Senator _____ in Washington informing him of the very serious state of our people's dental health.

Hopefully, he shall be contacting you and you him in order to establish a practical and functional dental educational program in the public schools. I will, of course, give you some of the facts I presented to our Senator and also some suggestions:

1) 98% of the population of the United States (about 205 million people) suffers from dental disease.

2) Twenty-five million American people are presently without a tooth in their heads.

3) Twenty-four out of twenty-five young children suffer some form of dental disease by the time they reach school age.

4) Nine out of ten people reaching the age of sixty today will not have any teeth of their own.

5) Fifty-six million teeth were pulled in 1969 alone.

6) There have been estimates which say that today (1972) more than nine hundred million cavities need filling.

I'm sure you can now better appreciate the severity of the problem. Although as an individual I am quite concerned about those presently suffering from dental disease (including myself), I am even more concerned about helping others, particularly young people, who certainly deserve a better fate. Especially when the solution is so simple.

What I suggest is initiating a comprehensive, enlightening and functional program of education about preventive dentistry at two levels — grade school and high school. Both programs would, of course, only be practical if presented in a way that would stimulate the students. There does not exist, to my knowledge, a program that effectively reaches children, and if there is, it is not working — as the facts prove.

I do not feel we can any longer afford to leave this teaching up to dentists, for not only do most dentists fail to offer their patients an effective preventive program, but the exorbitant costs of dental care eliminate it for many people. Statistics show that as many as sixty million Americans, of all ages, have never been to the dentist. As there is no law requiring people to go to a dentist, but there is a law requiring education (at least to a certain age level), I strongly believe that the school is the place to do the educating. The very fact that the school is designed to educate and that it is "free" puts it at the head of the class as an ideal place for dental education.

I would also recommend that if you truly desire to help the children you are in charge of, I suggest you contact the author of the book from which I clipped this letter. It was the knowledge contained in the *Tooth Trip* that allowed me to restore my dental health. I'm sure he could help. His name and address are:

> Dr. Thomas McGuire, DDS
> c/o The Bookworks
> 1409 Fifth Street
> Berkeley, California 94710

I'm sure you'll agree that it is not just the knowledge that is important, but how it is presented that makes it effective.

I would appreciate it if you could please inform me as to what you are doing or will be doing to help solve this most serious problem — dental disease — facing our people today.

Thank you.

Very respectfully,

_____
_____
_____

16

THE MEDICAL DOCTOR AND DENTISTRY

Many people never go to the dentist until it is an emergency, but they see their Medical Doctor on a regular basis. What a tremendous service the physician could be to his patients if he took a few extra moments to examine their teeth and gums. Remember, more than 200 million Americans are now suffering from some form of dental disease.

There is no law to prevent the M.D. from doing a dental examination. In fact, the teeth and gums are found on the way to the tonsils, and a stop off to look the teeth over could be very interesting, to say the least. The physician is trained to recognize disease and infections commonly found in man, and *there is no more common disease found in man than dental disease.* Thus, with a short refresher course, or a rap session with any dentist, the M.D. could easily learn to recognize the signs of a healthy, as well as of a diseased, mouth. The only equipment that he might need, in addition to the equipment he already has, would be a dental mirror. This could be ordered through your friendly DDS or from the corner drugstore.

If you are in the patient category and you have a family M.D. whom you like but who does not examine your mouth, make him a present of the *Tooth Trip.* Who knows? He may return the favor with a free oral exam next time you're in. And if you don't feel that generous toward him, you could do this; next time you go in for an examination, ask him to include an exam of the mouth in his check-up. Do not let him tell you it is the dentist's job. It is true that the dentist is the only one who can legally perform dentistry on you, but the M.D. can and should be able to detect dental disease and give you an idea as to its severity.

If for some reason he hassles you about this, do not return the negative vibrations. Think positive, say "thank you very much," and then go to another doctor who cares a little more about your health.

17

HOW TO O.D. YOUR TEETH

ALCOHOL
DILATIN
MARIJUANA
TOBACCO S
SUGAR
ASPIRIN
DENTURE PAIN KILLERS
ANTIBIOTICS
COCAINE
OPIATES
BARBITUATES
LSD, PEYOTE, MESCALINE AND OTHER MIND-EXPANDERS
PAREGORIC
QUAALUDE
HORMONES
OTHER DRUGS

I doubt if I can say it better than the way Amit drew it, nor can I think of a worse drug to begin this chapter with than *SPEED*. Most of you are probably saying that this chapter doesn't concern you, for you don't take Speed. Well, if that's true, I'm as happy for you as you are, but before you jump up and down for joy, let's call speed by it's other names:

1) Pep pills
2) Methedrine
3) Dexedrine
4) Ritilin
5) Diet Pills (Yep, diet pills are speed)
6) Uppers

Well, did you make it by these? As is the case with anything, the more you abuse speed, the faster and more dramatic are the negative

210

side effects. As the picture shows, shooting (injecting) speed is the fastest way to see how truly bad speed is for your teeth, bones, and gums. Fact is, speed is bad on every aspect of your body and mind. They say, and rightfully, that if you shoot speed for as little as five years, you are dead, and you begin to die a little the minute you put that first needle in your vein. All of the other forms of speed can end up causing the same bad effects. It may only take a little longer.

Speed, like its name implies, speeds everything up. Sure, it may make you think you feel good, but like Newton or someone said, what goes up must eventually come down, and speed is one drug where the going up *isn't* worth the coming down! Your entire metabolism will be speeded up for however long you're on it, and this means that any destructive process that is going on is also speeded up (like gum disease or any other disease). Along with this, speed screws up the formation of bone and causes it to be less resistant to infections.

Add to this the fact that the euphoric quality of speed makes people not care about brushing, thus also speeding up the rate of destruction of gum disease.

The person taking speed in any form loses their appetite. Thus, they usually do not get the proper nutrition needed to maintain the health of their teeth and gums, as well as the rest of their body. Not only are the gums deprived of the massage and the cleansing action you would normally receive from a good diet, but also the body takes calcium and other nutriments from areas that do not immediately require them and gives them to the areas that do. So, by not eating the proper foods, the body, in essense, begins to eat itself in order to supply the vital areas with food, minerals and vitamins. It so happens that the bone that holds the teeth is one of the areas that gets *self-digested*.

In summary, a lot of bad things happen with speed — the rate of organic destruction being proportionate to the amount and type of speed used and the length of time it is taken. The damage done to the bone surrounding the teeth is irreplaceable — it doesn't just grow back when you stop using speed.

The end result is, too often, the loss of teeth from what might pass for gum disease. Although it may be the gum disease that caused the loss of the teeth, speed made it happen at a rate maybe 20—50 times faster than it normally would have occurred without that drug.

A characteristic sign of *speed disease of the teeth* is observed when the teeth seem to be spreading out and teeth that were once nicely lined up and touching each other are now separated like a picket fence and pushed outward — sort of like Bucky Beaver. An x-ray would show a tremendous amount of bone loss around the teeth, even though the gums still look like they are high up on the teeth.

What the speeder has is gum disease going at a faster pace than it would with a non-speeder.

For those of you who are taking speed to lose weight, there are other ways that are much safer. Although speed is not addictive, it is very highly habit forming. So, even after you lose your extra pounds and are slim and beautiful, you may not be able to put the speed (diet pills) away. A beautiful body and no teeth just doesn't do it.

Even the conservative American Medical Association is recommending speed be taken off the pharmacy shelves. So, if you're on the pills, get off today!

The treatment of speed-oriented gum disease is the same as any gum disease. After you find out what stage of gum disease you are in, you get going. But first, you stop speeding.

The problem with speed and tooth decay is the same as with gum disease and speed, i.e., the speeder:
1) neglects brushing his teeth
2) eats junk food — mostly sweets
3) could care less about going to the dentist

The speeder most likely won't have to worry too much about decay, for his teeth will probably have to be pulled because of gum disease long before decay does them in.

So, the message is clear; of all the ways to get a chemical high, speed is one of the worst for your teeth and gums. If you gotta dope, don't use this one.

ALCOHOL

The relationship of alcohol to teeth and supporting structures is similar to that of speed in that the abuser of alcohol, the very heavy drinker or alcoholic, usually has a poor diet and also seems to care little about oral hygiene. Thus, not only are they neglecting their mouth, but they are not getting the proper food required to maintain a healthy mouth and body. Again, this means that whatever disease exists will progress at a much faster rate than normal. Like, zoom, no teeth!

Alcohol depletes the body of many of the vitamins that are needed for healthy gums. Alcohol may not be as bad for your teeth

212

and gums as speed, but it is bad enough. Even if you can't quit (alcohol is both addicting and habit forming so in that sense, it is a habit harder to break than speed), make sure you eat a balanced diet, take plenty of vitamins (especially B complex) and rigidly follow my "Home Care" instructions. And, of course, visit the dentist regularly.

A moderate amount of booze, taken occasionally, is not, in my opinion, unhealthy for you. Like wine with meals or a few beers. The fact is that some characters in London showed that some booze helps kill the germs causing decay. I'll tell you one thing, I'd much rather rinse with a beer than any "soft drink."

Keep in mind that the biggest problem with excessive amounts of booze is that one's diet becomes inadequate and the boozer is usually so crocked he could care less about brushing.

DILANTIN

This is a drug given to help those suffering from epilepsy. It does a fantastic job in helping to control epilepsy, but one of its negative side effects is that it makes the gums swell tremendously. Not much can be done about this, at least not today, but research has shown that Dilantin's effects are much greater on gums that are already infected, and healthy gums do not swell as much. So, those of you taking Dilantin must be even more careful and diligent about home care. Make sure you follow your doctor's advice and make sure you get your teeth cleaned at least twice a year. Then, check out your gums, using my chapter on Evaluating Your Gums, at least once a week. When gum swelling occurs recognize that it is not just the drug's fault; it is the drug aggravating an already existing gum disease. Then go ahead and cure the disease.

MARIJUANA

As the "man" treats just about everything he wants to as a drug, so shall I treat marijuana as one. All who have tried it know of its positive aspects and for thousands of years it has been used by billions of people for a variety of ailments and maladies. It is recorded that George Washington grew and used marijuana. Anyway, there are many excellent books that cover marijuana very thoroughly. Kaplan's *Marijuana, The New Prohibition*, published by World Publishing Company, New York, is about the best and most complete I've read.

Dentally speaking, there are only three things I must caution you about, and they are relatively minor things:

1) It can stain your teeth and irritate the salivary glands to produce excess saliva. The staining is relatively harmless, but the saliva flow can increase the rate tarter is formed on the teeth. As grass and eating usually go hand in hand, I'd *make sure* I brushed after I smoked and ate. Besides, it's a gas to brush while stoned.

2) Marijuana, like tobacco, causes certain trace minerals, mainly manganese, to be used up at a rapid rate. This is said to be a cause of the lethargy sometimes associated with the heavy smoking of the weed. Make sure you take your vitamins and eat well. 3) Also, like tobacco, it causes vitamin C to be used up twice as fast in your body as if you didn't smoke. This is especially true if you are a heavy smoker. If you do smoke a lot of grass, double your daily intake of *natural* vitamin C. I would recommend about 500 – 1000 miligrams daily with meals.

TOBACCO

Aside from causing cancer, tobacco also increases the flow of the saliva, stains the teeth, increases formation of tarter, and depletes the body's supply of vitamin C and some minerals. If you gotta smoke, switch to grass; it's healthier and not physically addicting like tobacco. Also, take natural vitamin C.

SUGAR

I've been rapping about sugar all through the book and especially in the chapter on kids, page 105. So it'll be enough to say it is a *very, very* harmful drug, most assuredly to the teeth, and also to the rest of the body; use honey or substitute fresh fruits to satisfy your craving for sweets. Recent studies link sugar to cancer and heart disease.

ASPIRIN

I've also talked about aspirin and its side effects, page 124; although it happens to be the drug of first choice in relieving the pain of a toothache, it is not without its side effects. Aspirin should not be taken if you have:

1) Anemia
2) Gout
3) Ulcers
4) or if you are taking anti-coagulant drugs

If you're allergic to aspirin, Tylenol is an effective substitute in most cases. Aspirin has also been proved to cause bleeding from the stomach and kidney damage if used for prolonged periods. Remember, aspirin is to be taken internally, *never* dissolve an aspirin in your mouth — NEVER!

DENTURE PAIN KILLERS

These are mostly ointments of assorted names. They can help relieve the pain of an ill-fitting denture, but not the cause. The sores will continue if the denture is not redone properly. Just because you now don't feel it, it doesn't mean the sores have gone away. I would only recommend their use as a temporary and emergency procedure until you get to a GOOD dentist.

ANTIBIOTICS

Some antibiotics will stain the membrane that surrounds your child's erupting teeth. Others, if used in large quantities, can actually stain the forming teeth. Antibiotics are over-used a great deal and many people have built up allergies to them. Many more have used them so much that they are no longer effective.

If your doctor prescribes any antibiotic for your child, especially during his tooth-forming ages, up to age sixteen, make sure he justifies their use and avoid, if possible, the ones that cause staining — most often the tetracyclines.

COCAINE

This drug does more harm to your nose and brain, but also indirectly can effect your teeth and gums.

Usually, people who use excessive amounts of cocaine eventually get sinus infections. These can become serious enough to effect the teeth, cause secondary pain to them and may even cause them to die. Cocaine is a pain killer and also constricts blood vessels; excessive use can cause the blood supply to the upper teeth adjacent to the sinuses to be cut off and the teeth affected will eventually die. This is more likely to happen if you snort it.

Many cocaine users rub the "coke" on their gums. This can and does cause sloughing off of the gum tissue, irritation and recession of the gums, eventually leading to sensitivity of the teeth.

Coke is the best pain killer for the teeth and if you have some, and also a toothache, I would recommend you place a small quantity in the decayed cavity and get to the dentist. Best not tell him what you did, though. Dentists are mostly conservative uptight cats and they think they are the only ones who should use drugs.

Most dental anesthetics are derived from cocaine.

OPIATES

Opium, heroin and morphine. Although these may not directly affect your teeth, they can affect your baby's. If you are a mom, strung out, and give birth to a child at this time, the child will also be strung out.

A more subtle effect, but less publicized, is the effect on your gums and teeth due to the euphoric action of the drug. Most addicts could care less about brushing their teeth and eating good food; thus the teeth and gums suffer. So even though the opiates may not directly cause oral problems, the result is the same — bad.

BARBITUATES

Downers, reds, yellow-jackets, zonkers what have you. They cause dental problems in the same way as opiates because users forget to take care of their mouths. Barbituates are more addicting than opiates and cause more damage — leave them be.

LSD, PEYOTE, MESCALINE AND OTHER MIND-EXPANDERS

No known damage to the teeth or gums results from moderate use of these drugs. One friend told me that while he was high on acid, he flashed that he was not properly caring for his body, and when he came down he immediately began to increase his health care, including care of his teeth. This may be an exception, and you certainly do not have to take acid to get your Tooth Trip together.

216

PAREGORIC

Paregoric was used as an old remedy by mothers to stop a child from crying when he or she was teething. It worked, but what they didn't know was that paregoric is an opium derivative and your kid could get strung out. So the problems with this one amount to the same as with other opiates.

QUAALUDE

This is a hypnotic drug. It is of note only because it is a drug that helps alleviate the pain and apprehension of a dental visit. If you're freaked about seeing the doc, ask him to prescribe this to you. It has no known bad side effects when not abused.

HORMONES

Certain hormones, and other drugs, which must be taken regularly over a period of many years, can destroy teeth by dissolving the tooth's enamel. If you find this happening to you, you can have your dentist cap the teeth (with gold or porcelain) before they get too bad. This will protect the healthy part of the tooth from the acids which would otherwise eat into the enamel and dentin and kill the tooth. Most doctors don't consider this when giving you a lifetime prescription of hormones or other drugs and most dentists don't have enough of an imagination to come up with the preventive solutions. So, you will have to take the initiative, if you want to save your teeth. *Always* make your doctor totally explain any drug he may prescribe for you — especially if you must take it for any extended period of time.

OTHER DRUGS

Any drug that is abused will cause problems, so watch it. Better to get healthy and stay healthy Naturally (see "Diet," page 126) than depend on any drugs to hold it together for you. Never continue any drug beyond its prescribed period.

18

FLOURIDE, THE HOT POTATO

Here are a few facts about fluoride and fluorine (the parent element of fluoride):

1) Natural fluorine is found in every plant and animal.

2) Fluorine is believed to be necessary for the normal healthy body.

3) Fluorine can make your teeth more resistant to the acid that helps cause tooth decay.

4) Slightly more fluorine than is ideally used to help prevent tooth decay can cause staining of your teeth.

5) A fluoride compound very similar to the one used to fluoridate water supplies is commercially sold in higher concentration as rat poison.

6) It is estimated that the average American consumes 0.2 to 0.3 miligrams of fluoride daily. This does not include any water we may drink that contains fluoride.

7) The amount of fluoride the body needs is so small and the fluoride is so easy to get from natural sources, that fluoride deficiency is almost an impossibility.

8) Fluoride administered over an extended period of time in experiments using rats resulted in an increase in the ratio of missing teeth, compared to the ratio of missing teeth in animals not given fluoride. In this same experiment, the kidneys of the rats receiving fluoride were found to be damaged.

9) The fluorine atom takes the place of the phosphate atom to make teeth more resistant to acids which contribute to decay, but after the teeth are formed (young adult), this exchange cannot take place. Thus, the positive value of fluoride is diminished as you get older.

10) Tests have shown that decay still exists in those areas where the fluoride concentration in the water is at least 1 ppm (parts per million), the safe and effective level recommended by the U.S. Public Health Service. Other tests show that people in areas where no fluoride was found had no tooth decay. Apparently, then, the existence or non-existence of fluoride in the water is not the only thing that determines whether or not people get tooth decay.

11) *No amount of fluoridation will prevent gum disease. And it is gum disease that causes more teeth to be pulled than does tooth decay.* In fact, four out of five teeth that need to be pulled must be pulled because of gum disease.

12) Fluoride that is applied directly to the teeth (topical application) does not chemically combine with the tooth to any effective degree. Thus, its effect, if any, is only temporary.

One of the largest supporters of fluoride as a cure for tooth decay is the *Sugar Research Foundation.* How nice of them, since sugar causes more decay than almost all other foods combined. Sort of like the guy who shoots you then offers to take you to the hospital. The sugar industry is a multi-billion dollar a year business and it is increasing its production every year. Guess who is eating all of this sugar? Right on, brother: YOU!

In the early 1800's, *every* person in the United States consumed about ten pounds of refined sugar per year. Before the first third of the 1900's had passed, the amount of refined sugar every man, woman and child consumed reached 120 pounds per year. This consumption rate continues to rise. Could it be, then, that the sugar industry supports fluoridation because they want to find something that will stop tooth decay while not affecting the sale of sugar? The point is, who really benefits from fluoride, and is it really necessary to have it put into our city water systems?

The U.S. Public Health Service recommended that the fluoride content of water supplies should range from 1.0 to 1.5 ppm (parts per million). This they consider to be the maximum amount necessary to increase the tooth's resistance to decay and not cause negative side effects. If your total intake of fluoride via the water route goes past the 1.0 to 1.5 ppm, you may start getting unwanted side effects. It should now be pointed out that if you consume one liter (less than a quart) of water per day and that water contains 1.0 ppm of fluoride, you will receive approximately one miligram of fluoride. This is about five times more than the average daily diet naturally consists of. Even though most of the excess fluoride you receive is eliminated rapidly, some is still stored in your body. Because of this, you would need to take excessive amounts of fluoride for many years, probably at least eight years, before enough could be stored in your body to cause bad side effects.

Knowing that 1.0 to 1.5 ppm fluoride is ideal, let us see what happens if you receive more. Taking 2.0 to 10.0 ppm fluoride (3-15 miligrams) daily for many years (beginning from early childhood, the formative years) will result in the unsightly mottling (irregular staining: brownish areas mixed with chalky opaque areas) of the teeth. Decay is reduced; but what a price to pay!

If your daily intake ranged from 20-80 miligrams (one ounce of fluoride contains 28,000 miligrams) and you consumed this amount for at least eight years, there would be a good chance that you'd suffer from crippling skeletal fluorosis and gastric disturbances. Also, I should add that you'd again have reduced tooth decay, but is it worth it?

If you took one dose containing 250-1000 miligrams of fluoride, (1/8 of an ounce) you could expect severe nausea and vomiting. Now, for the heavy one. By taking a single dose of from 3,000 - 10,000 miligrams of fluoride, you could expect to die. That is less than half an ounce.

First glance indicates that fluoride can be both safe and beneficial (when taken in small trace amounts and from natural sources) yet harmful enough in larger doses to cause death. And this can also be said of many things, from salt to aspirin to penicilin.

If you're a parent, you may be giving your child fluoride tablets at the suggestion of your MD or dentist. Do you know how much fluoride your child is getting per day? Do you know if your city's water supply is fluoridated and to what extent? If the water supply is fluoridated, you must add the two amounts together — the amount in the pills and the amounts in the water.

What is your new fluoride total now? (Ask your doctor how much fluoride is in the tablets and call your city manager or Mayor and see if your city's water contains fluoride and how much.) Keep in mind that in some areas of the U.S., most notably in the southwest, (Texas, New Mexico, Arizona and Colorado) and the north, (principally North and South Dakota, Iowa, Indiana and Ohio), fluoride is found naturally in water supplies in concentrations ranging from 2 to 13 ppm (3-18 miligrams). To the two sources just named, you must add the amount of fluoride found in the average diet (2-3 miligrams). Most seafood contains more than the 2-3 miligrams and a cup of tea alone contains about .12 miligrams of fluoride. So some of you, depending on where you live and the other factors just given, may be giving your child much more than the 1-5 miligrams (1.0 to 1.5 ppm) recommended daily by the U.S. Public Health Service. Best get this together.

The following four points describe where I stand on the fluoridation issue:

1) I am not denying that fluoride, when controlled and used properly, is effective in fighting decay. It is.

2) I am saying that it is *not needed* if you follow a good oral hygiene habit.

3) Also, you must fully understand that even if you or your child does not suffer the ravages of tooth decay (assuming fluoride helped your teeth resist decay), you would still need to brush two or three times per day to prevent gum disease.

4) Because of this, and the danger of side effects (if given excessively) fluoridation is not a cure-all for dental disease. It is only a commercial effort to try and do what only diet and knowledge of prevention will do. Don't be fooled by it.

I would not be as critical of fluoridation had the public first been exposed to the other, more logical, positive and less harmful methods of decay prevention. Were this the case, you would at least be offered a choice, and you can't ask for more than that.

Tooth decay is man-made and it can be corrected by a good oral hygiene program and of course made easier by watching your diet.

Yet, the dental professional pushes fluoridation instead of education for the prevention of tooth decay. The government (state, local and national) pushes fluoridation, following the dental profession along like blind men, doing experiment after experiment, spending tax money and yet never looking toward preventive education as a solution.

I feel it is time to make clear the fact that nothing beats good home care and prevention as explained in Chapter 6, page 66, and if you don't get that worked out, all the fluoride in the world won't help you.

By following the simple guidelines contained in the *Tooth Trip,* you can get it together and keep it together without fluoride. Thus, by avoiding the unknown pros and cons of fluoridation, you can take another load off your mind. Today's existence is definitely complicated enough.

Many of the ideas in this chapter are based on the work of Fred D. Miller, D.D.S. whose book *Open Door To Health* I highly recommend. It was published in 1969 by Arc Books, Inc., New York and sells for $1.45.

19

STATISTICS

YOU AND THE NUMBERS GAME
A STATISTICAL LOOK INTO THE DENTAL PROFESSION

Statistics are meaningless to most of us. We've had figures shoved down our throats so often that in order to protect our sanity, we tend to look only at the number and not the fact that there is a real, live, human being behind every number. We are conditioned to *dehumanize* statistics so well that most of us forget that *we* are the ones who make up the numbers that become statistics.

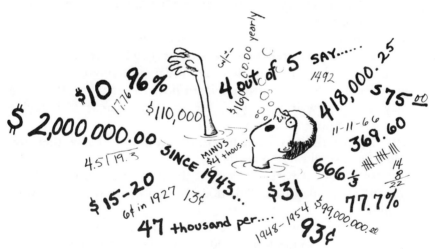

YOU AND THE NUMBERS GAME

For those of you who need to see it to believe it, here you are:

1) Almost every source I checked agreed that about 98% of Americans have suffered or will suffer from one form or another of dental disease. Also true of most other nations that eat the same food we do.

223

2) That 98% amounts to about 205 million people – or just about everyone!

3) 25 million living Americans have no teeth left – not *one*.

4) If you make it to 60, the chances are excellent that you will not have any teeth. Nine out of ten don't – that's 90%.

5) You began your adult life with thirty-two free teeth in your mouth. In your lifetime (average American's) you will lose from six to ten teeth because of cavities, and most of you will lose the rest to gum disease. Guess you can say that if your teeth didn't cost anything to begin with, you've nothing to lose – yep, guess you could, but . . .

6) A recent government survey showed that there are today from 800,000,000 to 1,000,000,000 unfilled cavities. Eight hundred million to one billion. Depends on how you write it as to how big it looks. In reality, it doesn't matter how you look at it – that's a lot of cavities!

7) In 1970 alone at least 60,000,000 teeth were pulled – any of yours?

8) Conservative figures say that about 42,000,000 people have never been to the dentist – not even *once*.

9) There are about 100,000 dentists at work for 210,000,000 people. It is projected that by around 1992 there will be only 5,000 more dentists than there are today and about 70,000,000 more people. So, if you don't learn how to get it together, you may end up waiting a year for an appointment and paying through the nose for it too.

10) By the time you reach 35 there is a 30% chance that you will have lost all of your teeth.

11) In 1970 Americans spent about $4,000,000,000 (four billion) at the dentist's. This doesn't even count how much time or money they lost taking off from work.

12) If everyone were to have all their dental work done today, it would cost $54,000,000,000 – you can stop wondering why dentists live in big houses and drive big cars and buy expensive clothes. They really get off on spending your hard-earned bread. And what do you get out of it besides a painful shot and a reduced bankroll?

13) It is not unrealistic for you to spend at least $6,000 in a lifetime for dental work alone.

14) And guess how much the "average" dentist's "net" income was in 1970 – over $30,000! How much did you make and how much of it did they get? Only M.D.'s, as a profession, made more.

They plan on you spending more next year — what do you say to that?

A STATISTICAL LOOK INTO THE DENTAL PROFESSION

1) The average dentist not only dies about five to seven years sooner than the average person, but also has one of the highest "professional" rates of suicide and alcoholism — dentists can't be too happy — money helps for sure, but that ain't all there is.
2) There are only about fifty dental schools in the U.S. and only eight of them can be found in the western half of the U.S.
3) At least four qualified applicants are turned away for each one that is accepted into dental school.
4) There are almost no "minority" groups found in the dental profession and here's why (aside from the fact that most dentists are, I think, racists, and for sure prejudiced).
5) It costs about $45,000 to $55,000 to finish four years of dental school, not including the cost of college. Not much hope for low-income minority people, is there?
6) In almost every survey I looked at, only whites were used in compiling the statistics. I constantly see things like: "This survey does not include non-whites." How's that grab you? Just think, if the "whites" suffer this much, what do you think the "non-whites" go through?
7) For you women libers, only 1½% of the dentists are women. And if most dentists had their way, the figure would be 0%. I wouldn't exactly call 1½% a representative figure, would you, Miss Steinman? I personally feel that a woman dentist cares more and relates to patients much better and there should be more.
8) Most dentists are located in rich areas. The dental associations publish booklets to show you where you can practice to make the most money.
9) Dental care of even poor quality is almost non-existent for non-white minority groups.
10) Everyone suffers dental disease; rich, poor, old and young, and so-called intelligent and unintelligent are all included in the statistics. (Thank goodness this is one area the rich get equalized.) The main difference is the rich can afford even bad dentistry and thus usually keep their teeth a bit longer than their poverty-stricken brothers. Not much, though.

11) More money is spent on dental disease than any other disease.

12) 52% of the dentists who died in 1966 died of heart attacks. (White bread, greed, and stress, no doubt.)

13) $300,000,000 was spent on toothpaste last year — how much food could that buy?

14) $120,000,000 was spent on toothbrushes — freaky!

15) An army survey showed that every 100 inductees into the army (age range 17-25) require:
   a) 600 fillings
   b) 112 extractions
   c) 40 bridges
   d) 21 crowns
   e) 18 partial dentures
   f) 1 full denture

Sad, and so young — am I speaking of you????????

Had enough? It's bad enough. Perhaps, though, if you get into the *Tooth Trip* the way I hope you will, you'll be able to stay outside these statistics. It all starts at home, get it together and stop paying for the old Doc's Cadillac.

20

THE BATHTUB

Fully realizing that all of you do not have a bathtub, nor do all of you who do possess a tub want to read in it, nevertheless, I want to enlighten you on the art of reading in the tub.

Also, I feel I want to write about something other than dentistry. You could all probably dig that. Along with this, I want to pass along my little invention to you on how to make the device that will completely restore your faith in bathtub reading. As you can see, this

fellow in the drawing is really getting off on the idea. He, of course, has added some extras of his own; so could you. Whatever, just remember not to drown or stay in too long unless you'd like your skin to look like a prune. Moderation in everything.

The advantages of reading in the tub lie in privacy and in the fact that you can relieve aches and pains and clean your body at the same time.

Sometimes a change of pace is just what you need, and since you've read this far, a nice warm bath is just what the doctor ordered – me being the doctor, of course!

Another solid reason in favor of tub reading is the fact that you'll no doubt be reading other books in the future, maybe even newspapers and comic books, or the Pentagon papers or whatever, and this information could come in handy. Besides, as I keep pounding into you, any knowledge that in itself is not physically harmful is worth thinking about.

There is also the outside possibility that you could make some money by patenting my little invention. I was going to do it for years, but never got around to it. I still haven't seen one on the market, and it will work. So, first come, first served.

Here are the tools you will need:

1) A tub
2) Some water – warm, hot or cold – as you wish
3) You
4) Soap – optional
5) Bubble Bath – anything like that – optional
6) Someone to scrub you down and dry you off – beautiful! But again optional
7) A towel – optional in a warm climate
8) A book – any kind or flavor, even the TOOTH TRIP
9) Anything I've forgotten

I'm leaving a great deal up to you, but don't go out in the cold after your bath or stay in the water too long or go to sleep in the tub or drop your book. The *Tooth Trip* is far out, but it's not water proof.

Also, keep in mind that the tub is not the only far out place where you can read the *Tooth Trip* or any book or magazine. You should now have the general idea – if you started reading the *Tooth Trip* from the back, you have, potentially, a great deal of tub reading in store. If you've read it from the beginning, you've only a few pages to go. Regardless, happy reading and good health!

Oops, almost forgot my book holder for the tup-reading design. You do-it-yourself freaks should really get off on it, even if you don't patent it.

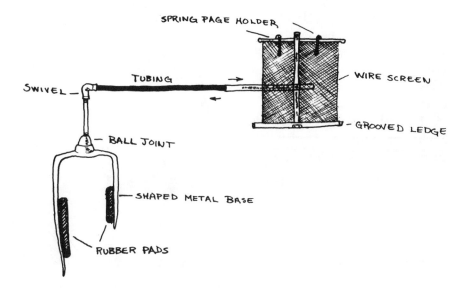

HOW IT CAME TO BE

I think the best title for this section would be "Introduction to Writer's Cramp," because my fingers are sore from all this writing, and it's about time to stop. But first I want to tell a little about how this book got going, and mention some of the people who helped.

I got the idea of making a book about preventive dentistry very slowly. Several years ago I got interested in diet, vitamins and health foods. I had been out of dental school and into practice for some time and had begun to ask why decay, why gum disease, and what could be done that really works. I began to experiment on myself; I had my share of dental problems. Whatever I learned I would try to pass on to my patients. Soon, each time a new patient came in, I would rap with him about "preventive" ideas. This made everyone high, because these ideas were working.

One day I got the idea of making a tape of this rap which the patients could listen to, then ask me questions about while in the chair. Then I thought of making a movie instead, for patients to view while still in the waiting room. I never got a chance to try this out, however, for new ideas kept coming in and the basic rap was always changing.

One thing I wanted to talk about, which I couldn't put into the tape or movie, had to do with the way you were taught in dental school. I covered that thoroughly in the chapter "Portrait of the Dentist as Con Artist," so I won't go into it further here. But dentists who were not taught preventive dentistry in dental school, would not think about it in their practice — and this is what was happening.

Finally I got the idea of writing all this stuff up in a pamphlet, but that never happened either, for soon I was writing this book.

In September 1971 I wrote to Ralph Nader about these ideas. After some delay, I received back a discouraging letter. Then I wrote to Stewart Brand after seeing his rap in the back of the LAST WHOLE EARTH CATALOG about how they made their book. I received a phone call from Dick Raymond of Portola Institute, who referred me to Bookworks. Now I was encouraged. I sat down that same day and composed an eleven-page letter to Bookworks. Don Gerrard called me in several days. About a week later — this would be in November — he and Eugenia came down to the office in Monterey. The first major problem was solved — I had a publisher. It was like getting a shot of pure energy; I was on my way.

I began to put all my ideas together. One thing troubled me. How would the reader, somewhere in Ohio (you perhaps?) or elsewhere, be able to relate to what I was saying? It was not the same as rapping in person. Then I got the idea for the drawings. Good drawings could help convey what I was feeling, and would make people smile. As I cast around for an artist, I was introduced to Amit Pieter by a beautiful friend, Jeanine Spring. After Amit and I talked a bit, he left only to return in a few days with drawings much better than I had hoped for! Our communication was very good and so a second major problem was solved.

About this time I took a place in the country, in Carmel Valley, and began to settle down to the writing. This place was owned by Miss Candace Knapp, and she helped a lot at this point. Having never written before, I was optimistic that it would be easy. This was my spirit in December and January, 1972. After a few months, I could still say far out! But soon the work began to be exhausting and the problems huge. I was in the middle of the tunnel now, but the other end still seemed far off. That's when I met Bev Horn, who offered to type the whole book for me, and did it too.

My partner at this time, Joseph Arancio, shared an office with me. Bev was a patient of his. We worked it out so he traded her dental work for the typing she did on the book. Thanks Joseph! Without Bev, I might still be typing.

In the month of March, I took off to write full-time and finish the book. Many of my friends, who had been skeptical at first, now became excited as I wrote the last chapters. In April and May the final editing was begun and the typing completed. Then the book went to the typesetters in Hayward, and even the most skeptical were believers.

I was beginning to believe it too.

A lot of people helped me get the book together; many more added value in intangible ways. A few deserve special mention here. There's Karen, Susan, Pamela and Debbie, who all work in our office. There's Hal Bennett, who did editorial work and Joel S. Thomas, who is a super photographer. Then there's the Heron family, the Faxon family, Liz Van Doernik, Ellen Beatty, Roger Hambly and Sebastian Davi. My family too. And just at the end, Linda Bennett came along with the super cover idea for the book! Thanks to everybody!

Looking back on it all, it seems that maybe the reason I went to dental school, really, was so I would be able to do this book. I never had the intention of graduating and then setting up the standard dental practice. In a way, this book has pulled it all together.

This knowledge got me high; now I pass it on to you. As you use it, let's rap about what you find. Send me your ideas, suggestions and feelings. You can reach me by writing to:

Thomas McGuire D.D.S.
c/o The Bookworks
1409 Fifth Street
Berkeley, California 94710

See you.

ORAL HYGIENE KIT

You can order an Oral Hygiene Kit from your dentist, from the company that makes them or get one in a pharmacy. The kit consists of: toothbrush, plastic dental mirror, dental floss and disclosing tablets. The retail price is $2.95, but you should be able to get some discount from your dentist, or by ordering direct. Be sure to specify the standard three-row brush and the disclosing *tablets* (they also have a liquid, which is harder to use) when you order. Best to read my rap on these things in the chapter on "The Home Equipment Trip."

Use this address to order from, or to tell your dentist about:

Professional Products
Pacemaker Corp.
P.O. Box 16163
Portland, Oregon 97216

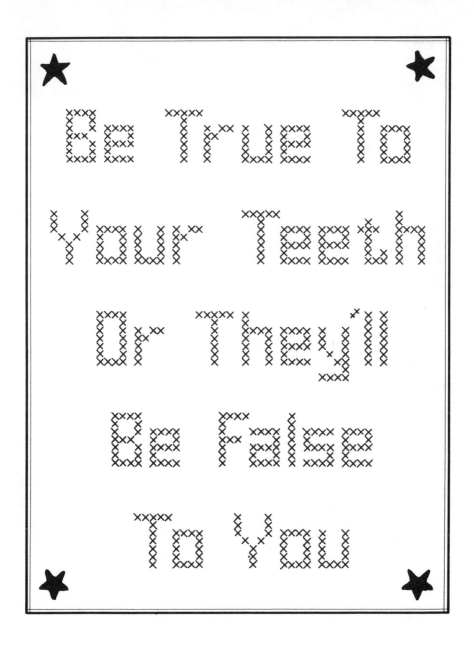

Be True To
Your Teeth
Or They'll
Be False
To You

THEATRE LIBRARY ASSOCIATION

The Theatre Library Association is a non-profit organization established in 1937 to advance the interests of all those involved in collecting and preserving theatrical materials and in utilizing those materials for purposes of scholarship. The membership is international and includes public and private institutions as well as librarians, curators, private collectors, historians, professors, theatre designers, actors, writers, and all other interested persons.

The Theatre Library Association meets annually to conduct its business in the fall of each year. It presents a day of conferences and programs during the annual meeting of the American Library Association, usually in late spring or early summer.

It publishes Broadside, *a quarterly newsletter,* Performing Arts Resources, *an annual journal, and occasional conference compendia.*

It is governed by a constitution which provides for a board of directors elected by the membership and officers elected by the board.

THE THEATRE LIBRARY ASSOCIATION BOOK AWARDS

Two awards are presented annually for books of unusual merit and distinction in the fields served by the Association.

The George Freedley Award, *established in 1968, honors work in the field of theatre published in the United States. Only books with subjects related to live performance will be considered. They may be biography, history or criticism.*

The Theatre Library Association Award, *established in 1973, honors a book published in the United States in the field of recorded performance, which includes motion pictures, radio and television.*

Works ineligible for both awards are textbooks; anthologies; collections of essays previously published in other sources; reprints; works on dance, ballet and opera; plays and similar dramatic works. Translations of significant works, other than play texts, will be considered. Entries will be judged on the basis of scholarship, readability and general contribution of knowledge to the fields served by the Association. No galley sheets or proofs will be accepted. Books nominated for awards must be published in the calendar year prior to the presentation of the awards and must be received no later than March 1 of the year following publication.

Nominations are to be submitted in writing to the Chair, Book Awards Committee, in care of the Theatre Library Association, 111 Amsterdam Avenue, New York, N.Y. 10023.

PERFORMING ARTS RESOURCES, *the annual publication of the Theatre Library Association, is designed to gather and disseminate scholarly articles dealing with the location of resource materials relating to theatre, film, television and radio; descriptions, listings, or evaluations of the contents of such collections, whether public or private; and monographs of previously unpublished original source material.*

All manuscripts to be submitted must be typed cleanly, on one side only, double-spaced and adhering to the style and method described in the MLA Style Sheet, Second Edition. *Photographs and other illustrations will be used at the discretion of the editors.*

Please submit manuscripts with covering letter and return postage to:

Performing Arts Resources
c/o B. N. Cohen-Stratyner
300 Riverside Drive
New York, New York 10025

PERFORMING ARTS RESOURCES

Edited by Ginnine Cocuzza
and
Barbara Naomi Cohen-Stratyner

VOLUME TEN

Published by the Theatre Library Association

The Library of Congress catalogued this serial as follows:

Performing Arts Resources
    Vols. for 1974 — issued by the Theatre Library Association ISSN 0360-3814
1. Performing arts — Library resources — United States — Periodicals.
I. Theatre Library Association
Z6935.P46   016.7902'08   75-646287
ISBN 0-932610-07-2

Produced by BookCrafters, Inc., Chelsea, Michigan
Manufactured in the United States of America

TABLE OF CONTENTS

ILLUSTRATIONS

FROM THE EDITORS

Resources for the performing arts can be as varied as the topics itself. A student, scholar or interested layman might need information on a play or film, its production history, mise-en-scene, casting or advertising campaign. The material that answers the query could be a memo, a letter, a contract, a videotaped commercial or an actual lighting instrument. It may be stored in a collection devoted to a single production company for live theater or film but may be found in the archives of a union, advertising agency or equipment firm. The Editors of *Performing Arts Resources* are pleased to devote Volume Ten to company and corporate archives of interest to the librarian, student and scholar of the arts.

In preparing this volume, we sought a wide range of subject matter, form, material and location. We offer articles on the business and production collections of two of Hollywood's most important film studios, each donated to a Los Angeles university. Two New York-based organizations with bi-coastal and world-wide impact have little-known archives of major significance. The Labor Archives of New York University include vital material on the theatrical unions while the corporate papers of the J. Walter Thompson agency offers information on the selling of the performance media and other products to the public. Articles on the collections of two innovative theatre companies cover issues on the placement of archives. While the papers, photographs and publications of the Pasadena Playhouse are stored in a nearby Public Library, those of the Dublin Gate Theatre are available in Mid-Western United States. Finally, we are pleased to publish an international trio of articles on lighting design and equipment archives. William Allison, who wrote on his Penn State Archives, kindly steered us to correspondents in Canada and Great Britain whose collections include manuscripts, journals and entire dimmer boards.

There are accessibility restrictions on each collection. The curatorial staffs have asked us to remind readers that permission-in-advance is required. Please note the addresses, telephone numbers and restrictions following each article.

Performing Arts Resources will continue to make available reference material to augment library collections and to give researchers access to rare material. We will publish conference papers, articles and essays that will enable librarians, archivists and scholars to locate, identify and classify information on theatre, film, broadcasting and popular entertainment. Our next volume will contain translations by C. Thomas Ault of late 18th century treatises on scenery design and construction, published originally in Paris and Copenhagen. Projected volumes include sheet music holdings, theatre buildings and architecture, dance resources and film technology.

TWENTIETH CENTURY FOX CORPORATE ARCHIVE AT THE UCLA THEATER ARTS LIBRARY

by Audree Malkin

Due to the generosity of the film industry and the studios' recent concern for the preservation of film history, UCLA has acquired a wealth of specialized sources of value to historians and researchers. One of these is the Twentieth Century Fox Corporate Archive, which consists of four main categories — scripts, stills, production/story files and legal files. Twentieth Century Fox, which is one of the few major studios still in existence whose production spans the entire history of filmmaking, has made their archives available to researchers. The files in this invaluable archive are a formidable mountain of data from 1915, when William Fox ran the Fox Film Company, to the present.

The Fox Film Company became famous with the Theda Bara vamp pictures, the Tom Mix and the Buck Jones westerns, and for big budget films such as *What Price Glory?* (1926), directed by Raoul Walsh, *Nero* (1929), John Ford's *The Iron Horse* (1924), and *In Old Arizona* (1929). The Company pioneered the Case-Sponsable sound-on-film process in 1927, which was renamed Fox Movietone, and bought the patent rights on the German Tri-Ergon sound process.

The Twentieth Century Fox Script Collection consists of approximately 6,000 feature films and about 35,000 scripts. Each title may have some, or all of the following: synopses, treatments, story outlines, rough drafts, revised drafts, final shooting scripts, post-production continuities, dialogue scripts, master title sheets, production material, memos, and correspondence.

The scripts go back to about 1914 when the "star system" was beginning to take hold and Fox press agents popularized Theda Bara and the vamp pictures. Theda Bara made enormous sums of money for Fox and ranked third in popularity behind Mary Pickford and Charlie

---

AUDREE MALKIN serves as the Head of the Theatre Arts Library of the University of California, Los Angeles.

Chaplin. Of the forty films she made, *A Fool There Was* (1941) is the only one to survive. The Fox Script Collection has that play, by P. E. Brown, a screenplay and synopsis by B. McConville, and a continuity; however, there are no stills in the Fox Still Collection. For her greatest hit *Cleopatra* (1918), there are the synopsis by H. Rider Haggard and the outline and scenario by Adrian Johnson. There are no stills in the Fox Collection, but in our Jessen Still Collection, there are 37 shots of Theda Bara as "Cleopatra."

From the John Ford films of this period, there are the August 31, 1920 scenario for *Just Pals,* the synopsis and screenplay for *The Face On the Barroom Floor* (1923), and a scenario for *The Iron Horse* (1924).

The period of transition from silent to sound films, 1926 through 1929, left only eleven scripts which appear to have been written exclusively with silent narrative. Title books are not always clearly distinguishable from dialogue continuity scripts, and many indicate that they were written for *Fox Movietone Specials,* which incorporated some sound elements.

Two important films from this period are Friedrich Murnau's *Sunrise* (1927), and *City Girl* (1929). Murnau was brought to Hollywood and given a free hand to make *Sunrise,* which was considered an artistic triumph, but Fox was appalled at the size of the budget. There is the original story by H. Suderman, a synopsis by M. H. Stein, scenarios in English and German, and the stills keyset. *City Girl* was made as a silent film, but parts were reshot by another director in sound, as Murnau would have nothing to do with sound. Willis Goldbeck, Marion Orth, Clover Roscoe, John Booth and Berthold Viertel all contributed treatments; there is also the shooting script, the continuity, the dialogue taken from the screen, the stills keyset, loose prints, and set stills.

Of the scripts from the later Fox Film Corporation, 1929-1935, the period just before William Fox was ousted from his own company and Fox was merged with Darryl F. Zanuck's Twentieth Century Pictures to form Twentieth Century-Fox Film Corporation, there is *Strong Boy* (1929), starring Victor McLaglen. A box-office success, it was released with a music track. There is the original story, a treatment, the adaptation and revision, four versions of the outline, the continuity and revised continuity and a keyset of stills. Spencer Tracy made his film debut in John Ford's *Up the River,* with Humphrey Bogart. Although MGM, Warner Bros., Universal and Fox had all turned him down as being unsuitable, Ford signed Tracy to a contract after seeing him in the Broadway play *The Last Mile.* For this film, we have the synopsis, outline, draft, dialogue, continuity/dialogue, final shooting script dialogue and continuity from the screen. In addition to John

Ford, a number of producer/directors emerged at Fox during this period—Irving Cummings, *The Johnstown Flood* (1926), Howard Hawks, *Road to Glory*, Frank Borzage, *The River* (1928) and *Seventh Heaven* (1927), Raoul Walsh, *What Price Glory* (1926), Allan Dwan, *Frozen Justice* (1929), *Lightnin'* (1930) and *Liliom* (1930).

The House of Rothchild, Twentieth Century Pictures most successful film both financially and in prestige, established George Arliss as the finest actor of the "talking screen." A top hit of 1934, it had its last sequence filmed in color. Zanuck assigned comic writer Nunnally Johnson to write the screenplay for this dramatic film. Its success was attributed to the climate of the times, the rise of Hitler and the Nazis to power, along with the anti-semitic subject matter. This was the beginning of Zanuck's dealing with sensitive and controversial topics. The Fox Script Collection has the play, outlines by Maude Howell and Samintz, outlines by Howell and Nunnally Johnson, the temporary and revised temporary scripts, the cutting continuity and the dialogue continuity, and "Suggestions by Mr. Arliss." The Fox Still Collection has stills and negatives in addition to the keyset. Zanuck produced other films for Twentieth Century Pictures, such as the classics *Moulin Rouge* (1934), written by Nunnally Johnson, and Henry King's *Lloyd's of London* (1936) with Kenneth Macgowan, who was founder of the UCLA Department of Theater Arts, as associate producer.

In 1935, The Fox Film Company merged with Twentieth Century Pictures to form the Twentieth Century-Fox Film Corporation. Whether Twentieth Century Pictures would produce for the Fox Film Company the ten films already selected for 1935-36 release through United Artists was one of the many points for negotiation. Included in the ten were *Ivanhoe; The Man who Broke the Bank at Monte Carlo,* starring Ronald Colman and directed by John Ford from a scenario by Nunnally Johnson; *The Diamond Horseshoe,* starring Lawrence Tibbett; and *Shark Island,* starring Fredric March. The first film to be produced after the merger was the pleasant comedy, *The Man who Broke the Bank at Monte Carlo* (1935), for which the Library has stills, Zanuck's notes on the story, a synopsis, temporary and final scripts, dialogue and continuity from the screen.

Zanuck took over immediately as production head of Twentieth Century-Fox, a position which he held until 1956. During the Zanuck years, 1935-1956 and 1962-1971, many outstanding films were produced, important directors and writers emerged, and many prominent stars reigned. His stable of directors, among them Henry King, Elia Kazan, Joseph L. Mankiewicz and Henry Hathaway, created roles for stars, such as, Shirley Temple, Tyrone Power, Henry Fonda, Betty

Grable, Gregory Peck, Spencer Tracy and Alice Faye. Some of the best remembered films are those directed by John Ford—*Stagecoach* (1939), *Young Mr. Lincoln* (1939), *Drums Along the Mohawk* (1939), *Grapes of Wrath* (1940), *Tobacco Road* (1941), *My Darling Clementine* (1946), and *What Price Glory* (1952). Zanuck films ranged from the musicals of Alice Faye, Betty Grable, and Fox's most successful and highest paid star, Shirley Temple, to religious epics, *The Song of Bernadette* (1942), starring Jennifer Jones, and *David and Bathsheba* (1951), starring Gregory Peck and Susan Hayward, and directed by Henry King. During the war, there was King's *A Yank in the R.A.F.* (1941), starring Tyrone Power, *A Wing and a Prayer* (1944) with Don Ameche, Dana Andrews and directed by Henry Hathaway and *Crash Dive* (1943) with Tyrone Power, Dana Andrews and Anne Baxter. In the later postwar years the studio turned out controversial films, making social statements such as *Gentlemen's Agreement* (1947) of which Zanuck took complete charge, *The Snake Pit* (1948), and Elia Kazan's *Pinky* (1949).

In order to offset the drop in audience attendance in the 1950's because of the inroads made by television, Fox developed the wide screen. The first feature film they made with this new technology was *The Robe* (1953) for which the Library has the various drafts of the screenplay, including the shooting final, the dialogue and the dialogue/continuity, conference notes and Zanuck memos. There is also the keyset of stills, prints and negatives, make-up and wardrobe stills, and photos of all activities before and during the opening, including footprints at the Grauman's Chinese Theater, window displays, luncheons and the premiere.

Overseas location shooting was a very expensive habit which also contributed to the financial problems of the Studio. The $40 million *Cleopatra*, which was shot on location in Rome, was a disaster which almost destroyed Fox. For *Cleopatra*, the Library has numerous outlines, drafts and revised drafts of the screenplay by a variety of writers, including Sidney Buchman, Ludi Claire, Nigel Balchin, Nunnally Johnson, Dale Wasserman, Lawrence Durrell, Ranald Mac-Donald and Joseph Mankiewicz. There are memos and conference notes; added scenes, an outline of the death scene; a comparison of Mankiewicz and MacDougall scripts; legal comparison of the script and book; the title book; Italian translation of the script and treatment; and the dialogue/continuity. The Fox Still Collection has 17 boxes of black and white prints, the keyset of stills, color stills and negatives, layouts, make-up and wardrobe stills, color wardrobe, shots of the premiere and press party, negatives and prints of Elizabeth

Taylor and Peter Finch before his replacement by Richard Burton. From another Collection, there are artists renderings of the sets. Also part of the Script Collection are 278 boxes of scripts in various drafts for feature films never produced by Fox. For *Kitty Foyle,* directed by Sam Wood for RKO in 1941, there are Dalton Trumbo's estimating script, 7/10/40, a final 8/13/40, and a final 10/8/ 40. Along with *The Gay Illiterate,* by Louella Parsons, there are Darryl F. Zanuck's suggestions for the story adaptation; a treatment and suggested storyline by Wanda Tuchock, 1945; a Zanuck memo, 1/ 20/45; Anita Loos' first treatment of May 1945, screenplay in June and July 1945, and a revised treatment, undated; then back to Wanda Tuchock with screenplay in December 1945, January and April 1946. Robert Kennedy's *The Enemy Within,* producer, Jerry Wald, has general notes and specific notes, a treatment 12/4/61, first draft 4/16/ 62, and a final 8/20/61. For Woody Allen's *Play It Again Sam,* released by Paramount in 1972, there is Woody Allen's play, revised play, December 1968 and revised final play, undated; Joel Lieber's first draft screenplay, undated; Charles Grodin's first draft, December 1970, and first draft screenplay February 1971.

Twentieth Century Fox Still Collection

In addition to the film footage shot, a still photographer is on the set taking still pictures which follow the action of the production and chronicles the off-camera action of the director, cast and crew. They are used for publicity to promote the film in newspapers and magazines, and as lobby card and poster displays in the theatres. There are also the stills that document the production, such as make-up, wardrobe and hair stills, set and scene stills. It has been estimated that the Collection consists of approximately four million of such stills and negatives for the years 1915-1984, including material never released. There are photographs of previews, premieres and studio activities — everything from the 1935 Fox Women's Golf Tournament to the premiere of *How to Marry a Millionaire* to Khrushchev's visit to the Studio. The 71 "Fox Star Boxes" consist of portraits and head shots of executives, producers, directors, writers, actors, actresses and authors. There are such greats as Darryl F. Zanuck, Gregory Peck, Henry King, Joan Crawford, Gary Cooper, Marlon Brando, King Vidor, Charlton Heston, John Steinbeck, Betty Grable, Shirley Temple, Spyros Skouras, George Stevens, Jr., Traville (designer), Jerry Wald, Raoul Walsh, and Joseph Schenck.

Taking advantage of a patron's research on photographs of stars putting their footprints and handprints in the cement in front of the

Grauman's Chinese Theater, duplicates were made and kept together as a separate collection. The property department has just turned over six five-drawer cabinets of keysets of set stills.

Twentieth Century Fox Television Collection: Stills/Scripts

In addition to the feature films there are scripts and stills for a number of television productions, including *James at Fifteen, The Time Tunnel, Voyage to the Bottom of the Sea, Young Dan'l Boone, Lost in Space, Swiss Family Robinson, Judd For the Defense, The Ghost and Mrs. Muir, Trapper John, Anna and the King of Siam, Land of the Giants, Room 222, The Fall Guy, M*A*S*H*, and a number of pilots that have and that have not been produced.

These scripts are clean, include various versions and drafts, and are without any production material. Supporting these scripts are color and black and white stills and negatives for pilots, presentations, press kits, parties, premieres and publicity stills for 49 productions.

In addition to the scripts for *Room 222* in the Fox Collection, there is the *Room 222* Collection donated by Irv Tunick, which consists of various annotated drafts, casts lists and schedules, and architectural drawings.

Larry Gelbart, writer of the award winning series *M*A*S*H*, has donated his scripts, notes, correspondence, and research for the series, and its sequel *After M*A*S*H*.

Complementing the scripts in the Fox Collection, the Library has complete runs of both *Judd for the Defense* and *Peyton Place* series, which were received from other sources. Unlike the clean scripts in the Fox Collection, the scripts in these collections include annotated drafts and production material.

Irwin Allen, producer of *The Time Tunnel, Lost in Space, Voyage to the Bottom of the Sea, Land of the Giants,* and *Swiss Family Robinson,* has donated his scripts and production materials for these television productions. Each episode has annotated drafts of the scripts, cast lists, schedules, production information, research, and original sketches which are particularly interesting. Researchers will find this collection fascinating and invaluable.

Legal Files

722 boxes of legal files have recently been added to the collection. There are contracts, correspondence and other legal documents in the Production Files (405 boxes), Music Composition Files (253 boxes) and Music Scores (64 boxes).

The Production Files consist of literary property rights, copyrights

and renewals, title registrations, scenarios, writer's contracts, screen
credits, distribution, production budget agreements with independent
companies, censorship reports, correspondence, and reviews as relevant. However, the documentation for a particular production varies
considerably.

One group of Music Files is arranged by name of the song or music
and contains contracts, licenses, correspondence, and usually a copy of
the music; i.e., the song from *Bus Stop* is filed under *The Bus Stop
Song;* the La Strada theme is filled under *Love Theme From La
Strada.*

The other group of Music Files is arranged by title of the film and
consists of Inter-Office memos, composer agreements, contracts with
recording companies, royalty statements, music score agreements,
music cue sheets, producers cue sheets, licenses, and song books.

Story Files

The Fox Story Department deposited its 1) call sheets and construction reports, 1971-1983, 2) Synopsis Files, pre-1969, 3) Contract
Synopsis Files regarding produced and unproduced properties and
purchase of literary material, and 4) Correspondence which includes
letters from agents concerning properties, synopses, and Story Editor's comments and coverage.

At almost 6,000 linear feet, the Fox Collection caused a major
space problem. The Theater Arts Library could not accommodate a
collection of this size. However, the UCLA Library had recently
acquired an off-campus facility to house the overflow of the Library
System; this solved our problem. The material is on delayed paging
and depending upon when the request was made, is available the
same or next day.

For the Script and Still Collections, we are using Xerox copies of
Fox's catalogs which are alphabetically arranged by the release title
of the films. The script catalog is an excellent reference work. The
cross references and working titles of the films are particularly valuable. You can trace the evolution of the script from outline to final
shooting script, and to the continuity. Each draft, its date and its
author, when available, is given.

The Still catalog, on the other hand, was not immediately deci-
pherable. The letter symbols had meaning only to the Head of the Still
Department and defied all attempts to "break the code." However, it
all made sense — I think — after I was told that the letter 'M' means
'match-ups,' which means negatives that are filed with their matching prints; 'L' is for boxes containing loose prints; 'S' for star shots and
miscellaneous events; 'SS' are set stills, and 'EP' are Executive Sets,

which are a keyset with a smaller selection of stills compiled for an executive. There is also the 'plain digit' numbered section which is another problem. There may be 10 boxes with the same number, containing three different film titles without any indication as to which title is in which box. When we are confronted with this situation, we add a letter to the box number and record the change on the catalog card.

The Legal Files have box numbers only and no record of which titles are in which boxes. Until we have time to go through all 722 boxes (1,113 linear feet) and make a record for each file, we must ask Fox for the box number of the file each time we have a request. Before a box is reshelved, we make a card for each of the files in the box. In that the Legal Files may contain information which Fox may consider sensitive or confidential, prior permission is required. Copying of any material in the Archive is not permitted without the permission of Twentieth Century Fox Corporation.

The first step in the conservation process of the Archive has been completed. Instead of the hot, wooden bungalow that housed the stills on the Fox lot, and the soundstage where the scripts were kept, the Archive is now in a cool, temperature-controlled facility. Some of the negatives had deteriorated and some prints seem to be permanently tubular. The scripts and legal files are in good condition but must be transferred to acid-free document boxes. The stills have been removed from the dirty, broken, taped together boxes and transferred to acid-free document boxes, the boxes labeled; the catalog is being updated. But, this is only the beginning.

In addition to the Fox Corporate Archives, the Theater Arts Library's general collections of screenplays, television scripts, stills, posters, programs, original sketches, contain a great deal of material relating to Fox films. In the Screenplay Collection, there are approximately 1,500 scripts for Fox films, including treatments, story outlines, rough drafts, revised drafts, final shooting scripts, and title sheets from films produced from 1924 to the present.

The Stills Collection includes nearly 190,000 publicity and production stills, portraits, keybooks, proof sheets, rolled proofs, and transparencies for Fox films from around 1917 to date. There are the personal papers of directors, writers, and miscellaneous collections which also contain material from Fox productions. 120 Fox films are represented in the Thematic Cue Sheet Collection, which contains cue sheets for silent film accompaniment. A wealth of information can be found in the extensive file of clippings from newspapers, magazines and trade publications from 1918 to the present.

The importance of the Archive is directly measurable by the importance of the Studio, which is one of America's major film companies. It is a valuable resource in that it documents the sociological history of the country as well as the history of filmmaking. The scripts offer an education in writing for films and television. Graphic artists, publicists, sociologists, and psychologists study the poster, pressbooks, stills and other advertising material which are a treasury of cinema history; they show the artwork of the period, the advertising methods, the slogans. Virtually every aspect of the business of filmmaking is available for study. These thousands of original documnts and scripts are an excellent complement to the 14,500 books and 300 periodical titles. Together they offer a combination or resources which allow students and scholars with a wide variety of interests to study the history and business of filmmaking.

Please contact:
The Head, Theater Arts Library, 405 Hilgard Avenue, University of California, Los Angeles, California 90024.

"VERBAL MESSAGES CAUSE MISUNDERSTANDING AND DELAYS (PLEASE PUT THEM IN WRITING)": THE WARNER BROS. COLLECTION

by Joanne Yeck

It may be impossible to imagine James Cagney cast as Robin Hood instead of Errol Flynn, to visualize Ronald Reagan, Ann Sheridan, and Dennis Morgan starring in *Casablanca*, or to believe that George Raft turned down the role of Sam Spade in *The Maltese Falcon* because he wasn't willing to take a chance on first-time director, John Huston, but this is only a sampling of the buried treasure of film history hidden in the Warner Bros. Collection now housed by the University of Southern California.

In 1977, when Warner Communications, Inc., first decided to make a gift of nearly forty years of Warner Bros.' studio records, the plan was to divide the collection among the major cinema libraries in Los Angeles. However, at the time, only USC could meet the space requirements which the studio prescribed to catalogue the material. During the next year, while fifty people organized and inventoried the more than 4,000 boxes of paper, Warner Communications rethought their original idea and offered the entire collection to USC.

The contents of this unmatched collection, maintained by archivist Leith Adams, reflect the studio's operations from the late 1920s, through the height of the studio system and the rise of independent production, ending in 1967. Files survive from the story department, research, legal, production, advertising, and publicity. Scripts, still photographs, interoffice memoranda, correspondence concerning censorship from the Production Code Administration, and communications with other studios are represented as well.

JOANNE YECK, presently teaching film studies at the Art Center College of Design in Pasadena, used the Warner Bros. Collection while researching her dissertation, "The Women's Film at Warner Brothers, 1935-1950," for the University of Southern California.

Unfortunately, much of Warner Bros.' early history predates the collection. Sam, Harry, Albert, and Jack Warner began making moving pictures in 1912, exhibiting them in a converted store in New Castle, Pennsylvania. By 1919, the brothers moved their production west and built a studio on Sunset Blvd. in the heart of Hollywood. On April 4, 1923, Warner Bros. was incorporated and with the spectacular success of the *The Jazz Singer* in 1927, the studio became a major influence in the motion picture industry.

While many scripts in the collection date from the early days of the studio, the correspondence is relatively thin in the years before 1934 and what does survive provides little documentation on the transition from silent pictures to sound or Warners' early and significant contribution to the gangster film and the musical. However, the materials after 1934 offer detailed evidence of the studio's commitment to producing more grade "A" productions and to building up one of Hollywood's largest companies of contractual talent.

During the studio's heyday, each piece of Warner memo paper was printed with the following directive: "Verbal messages cause misunderstanding and delays (Please put them in writing)." This policy obliged personnel to confirm all types of conversations in writing. The resultant paper legacy offers the researcher an understanding of corporate and creative decision making from the point of view of the individual — a level of detail which is often sketchy or non-existent in other studio collections. In addition to the studio-wide policy which preserved interaction on paper, historians can be particularly grateful to Hal B. Wallis (the studio's executive producer from 1933-1942) and later to writer/producer Jerry Wald, both of whom were prolific memo writers.

The files are organized by personality and by film title. They range in thickness depending on when the film was made or how long the individual was involved with the studio.

For example, the file on Bette Davis is voluminous. It covers a seventeen year period with letters to and from the actress concerning her work, contracts, payroll slips and notices of suspension, etc. One illuminating memo from a studio executive reflects Warners Bros.'s interest in changing Davis's screen image in the late 1930s: "In other words, where the average glamour girl fears to tread, Bette Davis steps in and 'takes over.' . . . Bette Davis is a female [James] Cagney and if we give her the right parts, we are going to have a star . . ." The "right part," as it turned out was the soon-to-be-produced *Jezebel* which won Davis her second Academy Award for Best Actress and made her an unqualified star.

The existing papers on films released between 1934 and 1968

constitute the bulk of the correspondence in the collection. Most of the material concerns "A" budget productions; there is minimal information on cartoons, shorts, and "B" pictures. However, for the studio's important feature films, preproduction, production, and some postproduction phases are well represented. While not every title contains all of these materials, many files are surprisingly complete. Hundreds of memorable and significant films such as *Captain Blood, Jezebel, The Adventures of Robin Hood, Casablanca, Mildred Pierce,* and *A Streetcar Named Desire* are extremely well documented.

Beginning with the studio story analysts' evaluations and the purchase of a property, the files from the story department are among the most thorough. The original source of the screenplay is often available — this includes unpublished treatments as well as hard to find short stories or magazine pieces. For most properties, various drafts of the screenplays have survived, which in many cases reflect contributions by ultimately uncredited screenwriters.

The files reveal that for *Casablanca* one such uncredited contributor, Casey Robinson (who adapted *Dark Victory, Kings Row, Now, Voyager,* etc.), added much of what is memorable in the film today when he was called upon to strengthen the "love interest." In a seven page memo to the film's producer Hal Wallis, Robinson in his concluding remarks writes, "[W]hen Rick sends her away on the plane with Victor . . . he is not just solving a love triangle. He is forcing the girl to live up to the idealism of her nature, forcing her to carry on with the work that in these days is far more important than the love of two little people." Today, Robinson's unacknowledged suggestions can still be heard, almost verbatim, in Rick's last speech to Ilsa.

Additionally, letters from authors concerning the adaptation of their works, critical input from writers, directors, or producers who never became directly involved in the project, or notes by those who were, may be discovered. One example reflects the sentiments of playwright Tennessee Williams who wrote to the studio attempting to preserve what he called the "dignity, poetry, and pathos" of his play, *The Glass Menagerie.* Williams writes, "The heartening message in the character of Laura is to those thousands of girls who do not find the dream-boy who sets everything magically right in the final sequence. This . . . can be underscored and played up in the screen version without violating the essential meaning and truth of the play . . . ."

Other stages of preproduction such as the business of casting or contracting talent from outside the studio are all documented in production files. Materials from the research department for a period picture can be quite extensive, in addition to the routine matters for films with contemporary settings.

Once actual shooting began on a production, the front office received daily reports on the film's progress. Along with notations on which scenes were shot that day and which members of the cast and crew were present, the unit manager often added comments as to the general work environment. These remarks range from perfunctory to illuminating, depending on the personality of the unit manager and the percentage of difficulties on the set. In addition to these daily reports, interoffice communications continued throughout production as script changes were circulated and producers commented on "rushes."

Evidence of postproduction activity includes some cutting notes and many dialogue continuities, as well as cue sheets and scores — with the complete orchestral parts — from the music department.

Because the advertising for the Warner films was done "in house," the exploitation materials are particularly rich. Not only are pressbooks, thousands of stills, and press releases preserved, but extensive clipping files were maintained which contain comprehensive reviews from New York and Los Angeles daily papers. Clippings from industry trade papers, magazines, and newspapers columns from other regions are also represented. Therefore, it is possible to study relatively complete ad campaigns for such films as *Angels With Dirty Faces, Now, Voyager, High Sierra, Johnny Belinda,* or *The Big Sleep.*

Additionally, correspondence between the studio and the Production Code Administration, the so-called "Breen Office" which administered Hollywood's self-imposed censorship during the 30s, 40s, and 50s, exposes the censors' complicated process. The studio's long series of submissions to this organization frequently began with a treatment or synopsis of a proposed screenplay and ended with a decision on the film's "final cut." In many cases, letters from the P.C.A. reflect the office's concerns throughout preparation, production, up to and including their scrutiny of the finished film.

The files on *Beyond the Forest,* for example, show the Production Code office's cautious exorcism of even the smallest hint of immorality, demanding deletions of any unpunished "prostitution, lust, abortion," or "adultery." Still, despite the censors' watchful eye, the Bette Davis vehicle was eventually condemned by the Legion of Decency. Just two years later correspondence concerning *A Streetcar Named Desire* illustrates the censors' position on the filming of such issues as "sex perversion," "nymphomania," as well as Stanley's "justified and unpunished" rape of Blanche. All of these topics were unthinkable under the Code, yet *Streetcar's* release in 1951 significantly contributed to the gradual breakdown of censorship in Hollywood.

In addition to the files generated in Burbank, the collection contains evidence of the constant communication between Warners' west and east coast offices. By the 1930s the company had long since established a bi-coastal organization. Jack Warner acted as production chief, running the studio in California, while president Harry Warner managed the company's administrative affairs — including general legal matters, distribution, exhibition, and advertising — from New York. This structure, used by several studios, kept the company situated in the nation's financial center and close to European distributing offices, while benefiting from the climatic advantages of a production facility located in California.

These coast-to-coast communiques (predominately from the 1940s) contain information concerning U.S. and foreign distribution, censorship at the state level, plans for reissues, etc. The business papers from Warner Bros.' New York office are housed with the Theatre Collection in the Princeton University Library (see below).

As the old studio system gave way to increased independent production, Warner Bros. expanded their own production to include filmed television series. The collection includes stills, various drafts of teleplays, and some interoffice memos from every television series the company produced. *Hawaiian Eye, 77 Sunset Strip,* and *Maverick* are just a few of the titles represented. Documentation concerning Warners' unproduced series is preserved as well.

The studio collection has already been put to a variety of uses. Some of the editors writing for the University of Wisconsin's published series of Warner Bros. screenplays have used documents housed at USC to write their introductions and annotations. Additionally, the papers have lent historical support to such scholarly works as Nick Roddick's *A New Deal in Entertainment: Warner Bros. in the 1930s.* In *America's Favorite Movies: Behind the Scenes,* Rudy Behlmer includes chapters on four Warner titles: *The Adventures of Robin Hood, The Maltese Falcon, Casablanca,* and *A Streetcar Named Desire.* His use of the Warner Collection brings these histories to life with accurate day-to-day details of the films from conception through completion.

The most extensive use of the collection to date is Rudy Behlmer's *Inside Warner Bros.,* which reprints actual archival material from the studio files spanning a period from 1935 through 1951. Behlmer has selected, edited, and generously annotated a cross section of story conference notes, casting memos, production reports, telegrams, private correspondence, etc.

Other authors who have relied on the Warner Collection include: Tony Thomas *(The Films of Ronald Reagan* and *The Films of Olivia de Havilland),* Donald Spoto *(The Dark Side of Genius: The Life of Alfred Hitchcock),* Bernard F. Dick *(Hellman in Hollywood),* Patrick McGilligan *(Cagney: Actor as Auteur)*, and Clive Hirschhorn *(The Warner Bros. Story)*. Charles Higham utilized the collection in four recent popular biographies, including a collaboration with Hal B. Wallis.

Additionally, a growing number of masters theses and doctoral dissertations are making use of the collection.

Non-print projects have benefited from the papers as well. Ronald Haver copies photographs from the collection for his still collages in the reconstructed *A Star Is Born* (Warner Bros., 1954). Haver also utilized the film's music cue sheets.

The preservation of the music recently made possible a new, full orchestra recording of the complete score for *The Adventures of Robin Hood* (Varese Sarabande records), produced by George Korngold, the son of the composer Erich Wolfgang Korngold. The orchestra parts from Max Steiner's music for *Adventures of Don Juan* were relied upon for the scoring of *Zorro, The Gay Blade*.

Set drawings and set stills have been used in several recent film productions. *The Favorite Year* used drawings from *The Adventures of Robin Hood* to recreate the castle staircase, and the *Casablanca* television series meticulously copied the interior of Rick's Americain Café. *Fandango,* Ken Reynold's feature film based on one of his USC student projects, utilized the set drawings from *Giant*.

In addition to scholarly use, the collection is frequently accessed by Warner Communications for ongoing studio business.

The collection is extremely well indexed. A 1,474 volume microfiche inventory contains a detailed entry for each item in the collection. This inventory has several indices: volumes 1-38 by "Film Title," volumes 39-62 by "Name," volumes 63-113 by "Subject or Title." A twenty-six volume appendix organizes the Warner filmography by title, staff and cast, film type, theatrical category, film source, production company, and by produced or unproduced titles. In 1977, an additional five volume supplement on new materials was added to the index; its volumes are organized by film title, name, and subject or title.

Since the material itself is housed off campus, researchers intending to use the Warner Collection need to provide archivist Leith Adams with a minimum of several days notice. Use of the papers is restricted to a separate Special Collections room in Doheny Library. With exception of screenplays, photocopies may be made of most of the materials, but only with prior permission from Warner Communications.

For further information contact: Robert Knutson, Archives of Performing Arts, University Library, University of Southern California, Los Angeles, CA, 90089-0182. Phone: 213/743-6058.

THE WARNER BROTHERS COLLECTION AT PRINCETON UNIVERSITY LIBRARY

By Mary Ann Jensen

The Warner Bros. Archive at Princeton University Library contains business records from that studio up to 30 June 1967. Housed in three separate locations in the Princeton area, it is the largest single archive in the holdings of the library's Theatre Collection. Its contents are made up of contracts and other legal files as well as some distribution information. These materials are not available to the general public, but may be used by qualified scholars and researchers by appointment only.

Because of the size of the archive (there are nearly six thousand cartons of material), we request that researchers arrange an appointment by letter at least three weeks in advance of their visit to Princeton, detailing in writing the specific area of research and the materials they wish to use. No photocopying is permitted.

Hours of the collection vary, depending on whether or not classes are in session at Princeton University. There are no weekend or evening hours at any time of year, however. For further information, write to the Curator, William Seymour Theatre Collection, Princeton University Library, Princeton, New Jersey 08544.

I. Theda Bara in the title role of *Cleopatra* (Fox Film Corp., 1917).
Jessen Collection, UCLA Theater Arts Library.

II. Fox Cathay Circle Theater, Los Angeles. Promotional photograph for *Wilson* (20th Century Fox, 1944). UCLA Theater Arts Library.

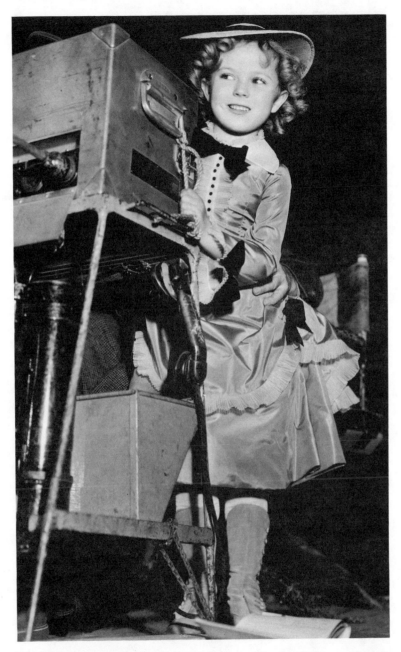

III. "Shirley Temple tries her hand at sound recordings on the set
during making of the new picture, *The Little Colonel,* in which
she shares starring honors with Lionel Barrymore." Photograph
and text dated Dec. 11, 1934. UCLA Theater Arts Library.

IV. " 'Bill' Robinson, world champion tap dancer, shows Warner Baxter an intricate step on the *One More Spring* set. Robinson will appear in *The Little Colonel*, Shirley Temple-Lionel Barrymore starring picture for Fox Film." Photograph and text dated Dec. 27, 1934, in photo-file for *The Little Colonel*. UCLA Theater Arts Library.

V. Ezio Pinza (r) and Jimmy Durante in front of Grauman's Chinese Theater, Hollywood. Los Angeles *Daily News* Collection, UCLA Theater Arts Library.

VI. Sid Grauman helping John Barrymore with the wet cement in front of Grauman's Chinese Theater, Hollywood. Los Angeles *Daily News* Collection, UCLA Theater Arts Library.

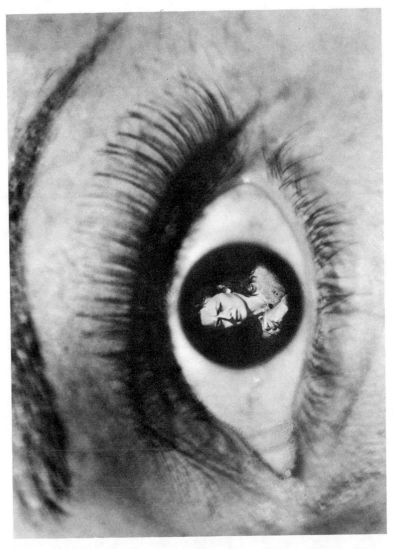

VII. Promotional photograph of Olivia De Havilland in *The Snake Pit* (20th Century Fox, 1947). UCLA Theater Arts Library.

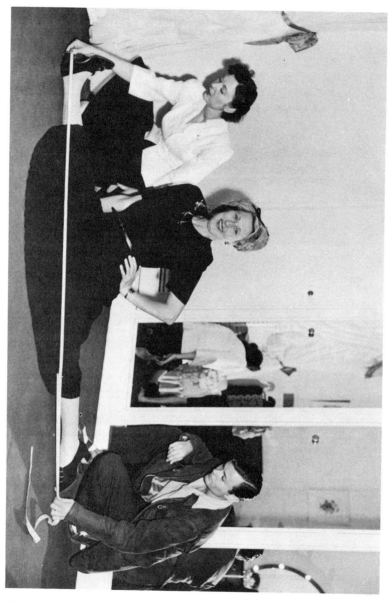

VIII. Promotional photograph of Charlotte Greenwood in her famous split. UCLA Theater Arts Library.

PERFORMING ARTS COLLECTIONS AT THE ROBERT F. WAGNER LABOR ARCHIVES

by Steve Nelson

A labor archive may seem an unlikely place for a performing arts collection. While union records are not often thought to be of great interest to theatre scholars, there is an exception to be found on the 10th floor of the New York University library. The Robert F. Wagner Labor Archives, housed in NYU's Bobst Library, is developing a research collection on performing arts union and service organizations. These presently include the records of the Actors' Equity Association, the American Guild of Variety Artists, and the American Federation of Musicians. In addition, the Archives has a detailed catalogue of available research for the Equity Library Theatre and a survey listing of materials at The Society of Stage Directors and Choreographers and the American Federation of Television and Radio Artists. The Archives is also engaged in surveying the records of other performing arts unions.

The project had its beginnings in 1982 when The Actors' Equity Association donated 157 file drawers of material to the Wagner Archives. In 1983 a grant was provided by the Equity Foundation to begin the considerable task of processing the records. My first encounter with this theatre collection to-be was both daunting and intriguing. I was led through the stacks to a motley assemblage of dilapidated cabinets and damaged transfiles, all of which were covered with a layer of dust at least as old and formidable looking as they were. I opened a drawer at random and pulled out a folder. Inside was a 1923 petition by a young actor named Freddie MacIntyre Bickel, who for some reason wanted to change his name to Frederic March. A second cabinet yielded an extensive file on *The Miracle* and another on a young singer named Jeanette MacDonald. I began to realize that

---

STEVE NELSON, is currently completing his dissertation on Billy Rose for the Department of Performance Studies, New York University.

there was a good deal more to this pile of dirty boxes than claim forms and routine union paperwork.

The brief overview which follows is intended only to give a general sense of the materials available and is by no means a comprehensive survey of the collection. Since Equity's records are presently both the most extensive and fully processed segment of the project, I have chosen them to introduce potential researchers to the sorts of materials contained in a performing arts union archive. The Equity Collection consists of documents in five separate categories.

General Files

By far the largest segment of the Equity Collection in terms of volume, these records cover a broad range of general union activity from 1946 to 1975. There is a wealth of interesting membership and internal correspondence and a series of files detailing the various contract disputes of the period. Besides extensive information on Broadway productions, there is a good deal of material on regional and touring companies as well. As they are still being processed, access is somewhat limited at the present time.

'Settled Claims'

These are the records of the Association's Legal Dept., roughly from 1915 through 1950, with the period between 1919 and 1940 constituting the most extensive part of the collection. These materials are a far cry from the dry record keeping normally associated with matters of this kind. The files include correspondence, contracts, salary claims and various disputes between Equity members and producers. There are numerous letters detailing working conditions and some very candid assessments of productions by cast members.

In addition to the usual run of theatrical lawsuits and contract squabbles, there are a good many offbeat cases, such as a chorus girl's $10,000 claim in 1923 against a producer who promised to publish photographs of her in *The Saturday Evening Post*. While this may seem a routine show business affair, the principle allegation was decidedly unique:

> That greatly to the plaintiffs discredit, damage and humiliation and in violation of the terms of the plaintiff's contract, defendant did not publish or otherwise set forth plaintiff's picture in said periodical except that he used, published and otherwise set forth a reproduction of plaintiff's body, and upon said body set forth, published and otherwise produced a head other than that of the plaintiff.[1]

Complaints received by Equity often amounted to sour grapes against colleagues who were enjoying a measure of success, as this ribald 1923 lambasting of Arthur Hammerstein and Frank Tinney indicates:

Recently Arthur Hammerstein made the complaint that Frank Tinney his star caused him to lose $80,000 . . . We doubt this statement. Hammerstein is a wise man — loves himself — women — and is not losing any such sum. If he did lose money because Tinney was drunk, there is no one to blame but the aforesaid Hammerstein . . . He knew that Frank Tinney was a bum and a dissolute character before he engaged him . . . this same Frank Tinney who committed MAYHEM on a little chorus girl by biting off completely one of her breast tits in a drunken all night affair in Chicago . . . further, it is a well known fact that Hammerstein conspired with the so-called authors of the Frank Tinney musical play in stealing the entire plot of said play from a manuscript submitted to him . . . he steals the play, puts a bum like Tinney into the stolen play, and cries, "I lost money!" This Hammerstein is some fine gentleman, along with his pet Friml, who chucked his wife for a night with Trentini . . . Why should he not lose $80,000?[2]

Often the producer is on the complaining end, as in Florenz Ziegfeld Jr.'s responses to the claims of some of his more notable performers:

[to Fanny Brice] Before making a demand you should read your contract. I never have been accused of breaking the terms of a contract or of failing to carry it out, no matter how exhorbitant [sic] the salary.[3]

[To Equity re: Fred and Adele Astaire] Am I to be forced to respond to this unjust claim of the Astaires? When blackmail like this succeeds, it is a sad day for the theatre.[4]

[To Equity re: Eddie Cantor] What is your policy on two faced actors who go in pictures and sit in the studio from six in the morning until eight o'clock at night and yet claim they are too ill to appear on the stage, thereby evading their contract. Kindly let me hear from you.[5]

The selections above are not intended to convey the impression that all of the collection's holdings are restricted to the frequently overblown prose of litigation. There are currently files on nearly 400 different productions, ranging from such famous Broadway denizens as *Blossom Time* and the *Ziegfeld Follies* to chestnuts with titles like *Helen of Troy New York, Making Mary, Divorce A la Carte,* and the no doubt aptly titled *Fools Rush In*. Production related materials include programs, flyers, clippings, box office reports, and the frequently detailed descriptions given by actors and producers in their depositions and complaints. In addition to the extensive records of New York productions, the Settled Claims series contains numerous files on the regional companies, touring and tent shows, variety acts and other entertainments that dotted the American theatrical landscape in the first half of this century. The often colorful exploits of these troupers should be of significant interest to scholars and historians of American popular entertainment.

The files on individuals are equally as rich and include the correspondence, contracts and assorted papers of a host of theatre luminaries. They range from a Tallulah Bankhead tiff with the Shuberts to a series of charming letters for W.C. Fields when he was an Equity deputy. There are files on promising young actors such as Clifford Odets and Helen Hayes. Though their records predominate, actors are not the only noteworthy personalities on hand. There are also producers, directors, opera singers, agents, designers, dancers and countless other theatre professionals chronicled in this collection. Together with the production files, these papers offer a vivid and hitherto unseen glimpse into the stage careers and lives that make up 20th century American theatre.

Off-Broadway and Showcase

These files document activity on Off-Broadway stages in New York from the early 1950s through 1978. They are divided into two series, one which deals with records prior to the creation of the Showcase Code in 1966, and the second which covers Off and Off-Off Broadway shows produced under the auspices of the Showcase Program. While much of the correspondence is routine, there is a good deal of useful production information including programs, flyers, cast lists, contract information and general correspondence. Materials are generally filed by show title or name of producing organization.

Union Publications and Minutes

This segment of the collection contains Equity's founding papers and minutes of the initial meetings at the Players Club in 1913 that led to the creation of the union. *Equity* magazine is also included as are the initial issues of *The Actors Equity News of Hollywood*, a newsletter put out by the union's West Coast office. Contract negotiations, numerous updates of the Equity constitution, and a variety of materials from the various actor strikes are also available. There is also a collection of letters, speeches and other materials pertaining to the career of longtime Equity President Frank Gillmore, which chronicle the numerous disputes he undertook on behalf of the union.

Miscellaneous Files

These include a collection of performer resume photographs from the '60s and '70s, 8 × 10 black and white headshots of both famous and lesser known actors and actresses. The photograph collection also contains a small number of older pictures of theatres, performers, and such notable union extravaganzas as the 1919 strike benefit produced by Hassard Short. There is a manuscript collection covering Alfred Harding's notes and various drafts for his account of the union's formative period, *Revolt of the Actors*. One of the early versions is written on the back of a prompt script for *Little Women*. Other files in this series document Equity's role in the 1939 and 1964 New York World's Fairs and other 20th century expositions. There is an interesting 1939 study on the potential impact of television and a similar treatise on the future of actors in the video age. This series also contains a good deal of material on the McCarthy era, including a well publicized red-baiting episode from the fifties involving AEA council member Frank Fay (who originated the role of "Harvey" on Broadway).

Equity Library Theatre

A detailed catalogue of archival materials at New York's Equity Library Theatre was recently compiled with the assistance of the ELT staff. Available records include files on every ELT show since its inception in 1946 as well as an extensive collection of prompt scripts, photographs, clippings, correspondence and other production related materials. Those wishing to use these materials should contact the Archives directly, **not** the ELT office.

The Archives has recently undertaken surveys of other performing arts unions and related organizations in the New York area. Under a grant from the National Historic Public Records Commission, the Archives will compile a listing of New York area labor union records with an eye towards materials of historical interest. This survey has enabled field workers to catalogue in some detail important materials that cannot at present be accessioned. Foremost of these from the standpoint of theatre researchers are the Actors' Fund, with records stretching back to the late 19th century, and the Directors and Choreographers Society which maintains a fascinating tape collection of round table discussions with notable theatre professionals.

The materials covered thus far constitute but a small fraction of the performing arts union holdings at Wagner. Future plans call for the acquisition of additional materials and the development of an oral history project. Though much remains to be done, the project is already shaping up as a significant new performing arts collection. It promises to be of great interest to scholars and students of both the performing arts and American labor history.

Those wishing to use the collection should address inquiries to:
Director, Performing Arts Collections
Robert F. Wagner Labor Archives
Elmer Holmes Bobst Library
70 Washington Square South
New York, New York 10012
212-598-3708

Notes

All materials quoted are from the files of the Actors' Equity Theatre Collection, Robert F. Wagner Labor Archives.

[1]New York State Supreme Court summons, September 4, 1923.

[2]Letter to Actors' Equity New York Office, signed J.R.K., February 17, 1923.

[3]Telegram from Florenz Ziegfeld, Jr. to Fanny Brice c/o Actors' Equity New York office, March 13, 1922.

[4]Letter from Florenz Ziegfeld, Jr. to Frank Gillmore, April 10, 1930.

[5]Letter from Florenz Ziegfeld, Jr. to Frank Gillmore, April 2, 1927.

PERFORMING ARTS ON MADISON AVENUE

by Cynthia G. Swank

J. Walter Thompson Company may not be familiar to most people but its products are — advertisements and commercials seen and heard around the globe for such clients as Ford, Kodak, Burger King, IBM, and Rolex. J. Walter Thompson Company is the world's oldest and largest advertising agency. Twenty-five to fifty years ago, the Company's name also was unfamiliar but the radio and television programs it created for its clients were among the most popular on the air. The Company played a major role in the development of these popular entertainment media.

Early commercial radio programs, more often than not, were created, produced, and directed by advertising agencies for their clients. In fact, many of the country's favorite radio programs incorporated the names of their sponsors — *Kraft Music Hall, The Royal Gelatin Hour with Rudy Vallee, The Chase and Sanborn Hour with Edgar Bergen and Charlie McCarthy* to name a few. Early television followed the same development pattern. Advertising agencies adapted radio shows to television and created new programs. It was not until the late 1950's that the networks and independent producers usurped the sponsors' and advertising agencies' role in the creation of television shows.

The J. Walter Thompson Company Archives, among its many collections, contains records that document the Company's activities in radio and early television. These materials include thirty thousand scripts of more than two hundred radio and television programs dating from 1928 to 1958. They include the three radio shows already mentioned as well as such favorites as *Lux Radio Theatre* and *One Man's Family*. Among television programs are *Kraft Television Theatre, Medical Horizons, Hour Glass,* and *Lux Video Theatre.* Often

---

CYNTHIA G. SWANK has served as Archivist for the J. Walter Thompson Company since 1979. She holds degrees in Archival Management from Muhlenberg College and New York University.

information about the production or execution of the programs accompanies the scripts. For example, radio scripts include an analysis of the individual program by a staff member of the agency's Radio Department. The analysis contains a rating of the script, the performers, the audience, and the transmission as well as descriptive comments. The television scripts often include staging instructions and rehearsal times.

These records are on microfilm, not by choice but happenstance. The Company began microfilming some of its records in the late 1930's and continued until 1960. In almost every case, the original documents were destroyed. Even though the 16mm reels are on silver halide film, the longest lasting type, the filming and processing was inconsistent and the quality of the images is not good. Moreover, the reels were stored in unsuitable conditions for a number of years, accelerating their deterioration. The Archives staff's first step, after determining that the records had archival value, was to have duplicate reels made. The Company stores one set in cold storage off-premises and keeps the other set in the Archives in acid-free boxes under environmental controls.

The bulk of the Archives collections are in hard copy form, including records that supplement the scripts. Print advertisements often promoted radio and television programs. For example, the Archives contains the advertisements as well as the scripts to a radio show hosted by Eleanor Roosevelt and sponsored by Cheesebrough-Pond's. The Archives' Lever Brothers' advertisements include one for an episode of *Lux Television Theatre* starring Ronald Reagan and Jane Wyman. The Company newsletter collection contains descriptions of many programs and photographs of the performers. Biographical information about Company staff members, and their reminiscences about working in the Radio-Television Department provide details about the creation and production of the shows. Full-time staff members included script writers, directors, and producers, some of whom went on to fame and fortune in the theatre and movies. The Archives also has minutes of staff meetings from the late 1920s and early 1930s that describe the Company's first steps in commercial radio and what its competitors were doing.

The Radio-Television Department materials document an aspect of the Company's business that by the late 1930s accounted for a third of the corporation's revenues. Notable staff members, officers, and directors of the Company worked in the Radio-Television Department, including a former President and Chairman of J. Walter Thompson Company. The Company has retained as clients many of the companies whose radio and television programs it produced. These clients frequently request information and are amazed at the

Archives staff's ability to respond to their requests. All these materials are available to outside researchers although there are restrictions against photocopying some collections. Despite the Archives' efforts to alert outsiders to the existence and availability of these materials, external use has been minimal. Academics from communications, history, and women's studies programs have used the collections. Journalists, producers, and individuals who were themselves radio or television performers have sought information from the collections.

As the Archives' primary responsibility is to serve J. Walter Thompson Company, internal use is of especial concern. The Archives exists to collect, preserve, arrange, describe, and make available for use by the Company those materials that we consider to have archival value. Archival value means not only historical worth but also informational, legal, fiscal, and administrative value.

Internal use of the Radio-Television Department materials mirrors the type of inquiries the Archives generally receives. Questions fall into two categories, what and why. What questions ask for specific facts: What were broadcast billings in 1955? Who starred in the first *Lux Radio Theatre* broadcast from Hollywood? When did the first television dramatic program air? Why questions involve interpretation of the original documents. One recent inquiry sought a description of former chief executive officer Dan Seymour's contributions to the Company. Seymour headed the Radio-Television Department during a critical transitional period within the Company as well as within the television industry. The Archives staff does the research and provides the answers to both types of questions. An answer may consist of one word, two hundred pages of photocopies of original documents, or a six page synopsis of our findings. The interpretation of our archival records clearly is an expansion of an archivists's traditional job responsibilities.

Interpretation of archival holdings also is an integral part of the Archives outreach activities. The Archives staff writes histories, prepares slide presentations, and creates exhibits regularly. Senior management, when it established an archives five years ago, wanted to convey its pride in the traditions and heritage of the Company to employees. The Company has a philosophy, an attitude about itself, its staff members, and its prominent position in the advertising industry. The Radio-Television Department records as well as other collections enables the Archives to transmit J. Walter Thompson Company's corporate culture to new generations of staff members.
Contact:
Cynthia G. Swank, Archivist, J. Walter Thompson Co.,
466 Lexington Avenue, New York, NY 10017

THE PASADENA PLAYHOUSE COLLECTION

by Lee R. Nemchek

The illustrious history of the Pasadena Playhouse of Pasadena, California, an internationally-recognized leader and innovator in the community civic theater movement from 1917 to 1969, is well documented.[1] Considerably less known is the fate of the untold wealth accumulated by the Playhouse over its lifespan in the form of its documentation, a significant collection of archives and original theater research material. The bulk of this precious matter has, over time and in various forms, come to rest in the Reference Department of the Pasadena Public Library, where it is considered part of their substantial local history holdings, and where it is collectively known as the Pasadena Playhouse Collection.

At the height of its activities and reknown, the Pasadena Community Playhouse Association functioned as a legally incorporated, nonprofit organization with a Board of Directors, full staff and business department, over twenty active committees, and thousands of individual subscribing members. The Playhouse School of the Theatre, established in 1929, was touted by *Variety* as being 12:1 over any other single-unit training facility in America in training people for the entertainment field.[2] It awarded degrees of Bachelor and Master of Theatre Arts to its graduates, and possessed a library containing over 3,600 volumes.[3] During its first twenty-five years of operation, the Playhouse produced 477 world premiere productions, and further distinguished itself as the first theater in the United States to present the complete theatrical works of Shakespeare.[4] Five separate performance areas operated under the direct supervision of Playhouse management, not including off-site performance locations. With a

---

LEE R. NEMCHEK, is currently Assistant Law Librarian at Manatt, Phelps, Rothernberg & Tunney, Los Angeles. As a student, she participated in the Pasadena Playhouse Collection organization project (1980-1981) and designed a community analysis study on the Collection at its present setting, the Pasadena Public Library.

year-round production schedule of at least two plays monthly between its various stages, the Pasadena Playhouse lead the entire world in the number of plays mounted by a single producing unit.[5] The Playhouse was designated "State Theatre of California" by the State Legislature in 1937, and appears on the California Inventory of Historic Resources. In addition, the property is a Pasadena Cultural Landmark and is listed on the National Register of Historic Places.[6]

As might be expected from an important and diversified organization such as the Playhouse, an enormous quantity of records, documents and memorabilia built up during the years of its operation. While the Playhouse flourished under the leadership of its founder — actor-director-producer-"theater visionary" Gilmor Brown — the archives of the Playhouse and documentation of its activities were organized by the Playhouse Association and safe-guarded within the Playhouse building. However, following Brown's death in 1960, the theater entered a decline. Inflation and rising production costs finally forced the Playhouse and its school to close their doors in bankruptcy in 1970, after several unsuccessful attempts to raise funds and transfer ownership. All Playhouse assets, including an extensive costume inventory, stage equipment, building and grounds, and the library, were sold at public auction. This occurrence might well have been the beginning of the end for an important body of recorded theatricana. Fortunately, however, events have coincided favorably for much of the Playhouse archives.

The bankruptcy auction necessarily fragmented the original collection of materials into several smaller parcels. The collection of theater books formerly housed in the Playhouse Library, which included class and production work texts, play manuscripts and many rare, out-of-print publications, was first purchased in its entirety by an individual, then later resold to California State University at Long Beach. Cal State, in turn, sold approximately 1,000 duplicates from the collection to a local used book-dealer, from where, in 1980, they were repurchased by the Pasadena Playhouse Alumni and Associates organization.

The non-book resources of the Playhouse — its archives and theater memorabilia — were purchased by a different group, consisting of representatives of the original Pasadena Playhouse Association. This material was brought together and stored for safekeeping at the Pasadena Historical Society from 1970 to 1973. The Pasadena Public Library was approached thereafter and asked to provide a temporary home for these materials, as it was believed that the collection could be more properly exhibited there. Furthermore, the collection would benefit from the professional skills of the library's special collections staff in organizing and protecting the materials and in making them accessible to the public through reference services. This arrangement was based on an understanding that the library would only serve as a caretaker of certain materials until the Playhouse reopened and resumed control.

The collection was indeed transferred from the historical society to the public library in 1973. Since then, the library has from time to time received gifts from different Playhouse-related sources, the majority of which consist of valuable theater memorabilia which were added to the now-established Pasadena Playhouse Collection.

This collection consists primarily of non-book items which fall into one of two descriptive categories — pictorial or printed. Approximately 5,000 photographs, stills, portraits, negatives and slides are classified according to whether the depiction is of personalities, productions or Playhouse activities, and alphabetical files are maintained accordingly for each of these sub-categories. For example, photographs of Gilmor Brown may be found (1) under his name ("Brown, Gilmor") in the People section of the photograph file; (2) under the titles of the many plays he acted in, filed alphabetically in the Production section; and (3) in folders holding photographs of Playhouse activities that he participated in, e.g., School of the Theatre graduation ceremonies. The card index to the collection provides cross-referencing to the various categories and file locations of pictorial materials. The collection also includes several framed photographs, some theater posters, a few original design sketches, and an impressive oil portrait of Gilmor Brown.

An added attraction of the pictorial section is a special collection within the special collection. The "Uncle" Billy Haas Collection of photographs given to the library includes hundreds of portraits of stage and screen stars taken between 1900 and 1930. Most of them are autographed to Mr. Haas, a one-time theatrical agent who later took up residence in Pasadena and became involved with the Playhouse. Many include his handwritten notes on the back, detailing the person's measurements, character type, background notes, and personal comments relating to the actor's identity and/or how he knew him or her.

The extensive collection of printed materials can be classified as either archives — documents generated by the business machinery of the Playhouse Association and School of the Theatre — or memorabilia. The archival materials include corporate records of the Playhouse Association, financial statements, box-office statistics, news releases and publicity brochures, drama school records and catalogs, and the personal correspondence of Gilmor Brown and other Association board members.

Perhaps the most valuable part of the collection is composed of memorabilia in the form of playbills, programs, clippings, scrapbooks and production scripts. These are the important raw material from which social as well as theatrical history can be reconstructed. A record of the mainstage productions is available through the publication *Playhouse News,* which uniquely served as both a performance program and a theater periodical. In the early days of Playhouse operation, programs were printed on single sheets providing only the necessary details about the current production and coming attractions. In 1923, the basic program expanded into a four-page single-fold paper called the *Playhouse Bulletin,* and by 1925 had expanded again to an eight-page paper called the *Playhouse News,* complete with private advertising and short informative pieces.

In its later years, the *Playhouse News* gained a national reputation as an educational publication, with a circulation throughout the United States of over 200,000 a year.[7] Each issue, of up to thirty pages, featured an introduction to the current production and the playbill; short biographies of the actors, director and playwright; a preview of coming artistic offerings at the Playhouse and in the community at large; and the names of the staff, patron and sustaining members of the Playhouse Association. Additionally, articles on interesting items of theatricana frequently appeared in the pages of the *Playhouse News,* bearing titles such as "Wig-Wearing and Wigs"[8] and "Sword Play as an Accomplishment and an Exercise."[9] Multi-part scholarly treatises were printed, such as Ralph Freud's "A Short History of the Theatre in America,"[10] as well as book and film reviews and reappearing thematic columns, such as "American Star" (biographical), "Stage Whisper" (gossipy current doings), and "Theatricana California" (historical). The Pasadena Playhouse Collection is fortunate in holding an almost complete run of the *Playhouse News* from 1925 through 1961. This set is further supplemented by various other Playhouse publications: *Playgoer* continued the *Playhouse News* from 1961-1970; *Playbill,* a single-fold paper that featured only the particulars of the current mainstage production; *The Playhouser,* a quarterly publication designed primarily for the Pasadena Playhouse Associates and students; *Curtain Call,* a single-fold newsletter, founded in 1950 to consolidate all the various mailing-list information into one monthly publication; and finally, playbills and programs from plays mounted by the Playhouse's secondary production areas: the Playbox, East Balcony, West Balcony, Patio and Altadena/Farnsworth Park (outdoor) theaters.

Primary source material on the staging of certain plays exists in the form of scripts and production books, many of which are marked with handwritten blocking notes. Some also contain production plots for the costumes, props, scenery, sound and lighting that were used in the shows. The collection holds approximately eighty-five scripts in all; a few are from mainstage and other miscellaneous production, and twenty-five are from plays mounted by the Playbox, Gilmor Brown's experimental theater. Fifty remaining scripts, which are in an extremely worn and brittle condition, comprise a special collection of children's theater material that was once the property of the Pasadena Department of Recreation. As part of is program of activities, the Department of Recreation put on plays for children using children as actors. Their repertoire included both original plays and classics adapted into play form, e.g., "Alice in Wonderland," "Jack and the Beanstalk," "Pinnocchio," "Heidi." The scripts currently held by the Pasadena Playhouse Collection date to the 1940's, and they provide teachers and drama coaches with a master file of imaginative and popular plays for children.

The collection is completed by approximately seventy-five scrapbooks of various sizes filled with clippings, and a comparable quantity of loose, unmounted clippings. The loose clippings are organized in a manner similar to the system used for photographs, i.e., by the name of a person, the title of a play, or a subject heading such as "History," "Theater Building," or "One-Act Play Tournament." The tedious and time-consuming task of cross-referencing in the master card file has also been undertaken with the clippings, which include reviews, pictures, advance notes, synopses and historical background of plays, biographical profiles of and interviews with Playhouse personalities, and general news items, culled primarily from newspapers published up and down the California coast during the years of Playhouse activity.

In its entirety, the Pasadena Playhouse Collection represents an important addition to the realm of known theater documentation. In some lucky instances where a complete production book, performance photographs, reviews and management data for a production have been preserved, a rich record is available for theater scholars. There are also many members of the general public who are frequently more interested in reading about the early careers of their favorite stars than in researching community theater history. The collection is superbly equipped to satisfy this type of information request. Its files on hundreds of performers who began their careers at the Playhouse school and on its stages include many who went on to real stardom, among them Victor Mature, Robert Young, Raymond Burr, Carolyn Jones and George "Superman" Reeves.

The Pasadena Playhouse Collection had been housed at the public library for several years before any real processing and organization of the materials began. In 1980 and 1981, major progress was made with the assistance of two library school students who arranged to gain practicum credit towards their degrees for working on the collection. The files and card indexes to the Playhouse materials which were set up during that time provide the only means of systematic access to the collection. Although there are still many boxes of unidentified and unprocessed items, there have been no additional volunteers, and work on the collection by library staff members has been suspended, pending major reorganization of the library's local history collection.

There has always been substantial community interest in Pasadena local history, and the importance of the Pasadena Playhouse Collection as a record of local history was verified by a community analysis research study initiated in 1981.[11]

One aspect of the study focused on determining how the collection was valued by three different categories of potential or actual users: (a) Pasadena residents; (b) local library professionals; and (c) Pasadena Playhouse Collection users. The majority of respondents in all three categories viewed the collection most valuable in terms of local history. Subsequent to the community analysis project (though not necessarily a direct result of it), the library reference staff decided that, with respect to further expenditures of staff and funds for the Pasadena Playhouse Collection, the library had a responsibility to first reorganize their general local history materials before concentrating on a related special collection with less potential for significant public interest, and with an uncertain future at the library (see discussion below).

It is probable, however, that interest in the Pasadena Playhouse Collection will intensify when the Playhouse reopens as a professional resident theater company. Serious plans and negotiations to this end have been in the works since 1975, when the City of Pasadena purchased the Playhouse property from the Bank of America, which had held the title since 1970.[12] The curtain is finally scheduled to rise again on the Mainstage Theatre after 15 years, and the opening season promises to feature four plays, consisting of "two major American theater revivals, one world premiere commissioned especially for the Playhouse and a Los Angeles area premiere."[13] It is impossible at this time to predict whether this venture will be successful.[14] However, if it is, the Pasadena Playhouse Collection will take on added significance as the theatrical archive for an extant producing organization.

Ironically, though, a new beginning for the Pasadena Playhouse may ultimately result in an end to the Pasadena Public Library's custodianship of the Pasadena Playhouse Collection. Two "rival" groups — the Pasadena Playhouse Association, which claims legitimate ownership of the materials, and the Pasadena Playhouse Alumni and Associates, which plans to renovate the original Playhouse Library as a memorabilia and meeting room — have contacted the library regarding the disposition of the collection. Future decision making with respect to the collection's permanent home may hinge on whether one environment and/or group of caretakers can provide more than others in the way of funds for storage space, personnel and supplies to continue the work of organizing the collection. Security and stability of the maintaining institution may also be taken into consideration. In any event, it is highly likely that the collection will remain within the City of Pasadena, where it will be most appreciated by the community.

Meanwhile, the Pasadena Public Library continues to protect a special theater collection that aspires to the same high standards of professionalism and public appeal that have always been espoused by the Pasadena Community Playhouse, which it memorializes. Due to the fragile nature and non-standard formats which characterize most collections of theater research material, the items are non-circulating and unavailable for public browsing. However, access to the materials will be granted to patrons with legitimate needs. The Pasadena Special Collections Librarian personally provides assistance in all Playhouse-related reference inquiries, whether made by mail, phone or in person, however appointments are mandatory if physical access to the material is desired. The library prefers that a letter be sent wherein the researcher states his or her research needs and/or interests in advance. The Special Collections Librarian will generally make a determination as to whether the information is in fact available in the collection before granting or confirming an appointment. All inquiries should be directed to the attention of the Special Collections Librarian, Pasadena Public Library, 285 East Walnut Street, Pasadena, California 91101; phone (818) 405-4054.

ACKNOWLEDGMENT
The author would like to acknowledge Joyce Y. Pinney for her pioneering work on the Pasadena Playhouse Collection, and Elaine Zorbas, Head, Pasadena Public Library Reference Section, for her assistance in updating this manuscript from 1981 to 1984.

REFERENCES

[1]See, for example, William C. Young, *Documents of American Theater History.* *Vol. 2. Famous American Playhouses, 1900-1971.* Chicago: American Library Association, 1973, pp. 101-05; May Rose Borum, *A History of the Pasadena Community Playhouse.* Los Angeles: University of Southern California, 1928. See also a set of transcripts produced under the auspices of the Oral History Program, University of California, Los Angeles. Individual titles of note include: *Pasadena, the Pricketts, and their Playhouse.* Oliver Prickett interviewed by Bernard Galm (1982); *Remembering the Pasadena Playhouse.* Lenore Shanewise interviewed by Bernard Galm (1980); *Character Parts and Community Challenges.* Maudie Prickett Cooper interviewed by Bernard Galm (1982).

[2]Oliver Prickett, tape-recorded speech on the Pasadena Playhouse. Pasadena: Pasadena Public Library, Fine Arts Series, February 25, 1976.

[3]Mary Ambler, *Classification System for Theatre Libraries.* Chicago: University of Chicago, 1939, p. 32.

[4]"The Pasadena Playhouse Revitalization: Background." Press release issued by The Pasadena Playhouse, Stephen Rothman, Executive Director (undated), p. 1.

[5]Prickett, *op. cit.*

[6]*The Pasadena Playhouse. Historic Structures Report.* Pasadena: City of Pasadena and the Arroyo Group, March 1980, p. 1.

[7]Borum, *op. cit.*, p. 124.

[8]*Pasadena Playhouse News,* March 7, 1927, p. 4, 6.

[9]*Pasadena Playhouse News,* August 2, 1928, p. 7, 10.

[10]*Pasadena Playhouse News, start date December 3, 1927.*

[11]Lee R. Nemchek, "The Preservation and Maintenance of Special Research Collections in Public Libraries: A Review of Related Literature and a Call for Community Analysis." *Public Library Quarterly* 3(4):19-32 (1982). This article serves as background and literature review for the cited research study. The project report — including hypotheses, methodology, results, analyses and conclusions — is currently in preparation.

[12]For a detailed history of the current Playhouse revival, see especially, *Curtain Up! The Revival of the Pasadena Playhouse.* Peggy Ebright interviewed by Bernard Galm and Thomas Bertonneau. Los Angeles: University of California, Los Angeles, Oral History Program, 1982; "The Pasadena Playhouse Revitalization: Background," *op. cit.*, pp. 1-3.

[13]*Stages: The Magazine of the Pasadena Playhouse* 5:2 (Spring 1984), p. 16.

[14]More problems and delays have recently been reported. See Jim Tranquada, "Final Sale of Playhouse Approved." *Pasadena Star News,* December 12, 1984, pp. A-1, A-3; Steve Hochman, "Rothman to Leave." *The Weekly,* December 13-20, 1984, Discovery section.

THE DUBLIN GATE THEATRE
AT NORTHWESTERN UNIVERSITY LIBRARY

by Ellen V. Howe,
assisted by R. Russell Maylone

Northwestern University Library has the tenth largest private university research collection in North America. The collections support work in a broad range of fields, responding to research and teaching activities in the University. Northwestern, in Evanston, Illinois, has developed collections of the first rank on Africa, transportation, economics, music, international law, the contemporary women's movement and specific areas in literature, history, and art.

The Northwestern University Library holds some 3 million volumes (about 1.7 million titles), over 300,000 manuscripts and almost 1.3 million microform units. The Library holds 43,900 phonograph records and 173,300 maps.

The Library's Special Collections Department concentrates on literature, history and art and holds more than 180,000 volumes, about 4,500 cubic feet of manuscripts and archives, 7,200 photographs, and nearly 6,000 caricatures, broadsides and posters.

Particular strengths developed and maintained as special collections at Northwestern University Library include early law books; history of dentistry; the Paris Commune, 1870; British theatre history; printed and manuscript sources for twentieth-century British and American literature; Dada, Surrealism, Art Nouveau, Futurism, and Expressionism; architecture, especially that by Frank Lloyd Wright; posters and the graphic arts; private press printing; and little magazines.

Some of the strongest and most unusual of the special collections are built around rare and ephemeral documents relating to the radical and underground movements of the twentieth century. These include the Spanish Civil War; the Dutch, Danish and Norwegian

---

ELLEN V. HOWE serves as Manuscript Assistant at the Department of Special Collections, Northwestern University Library.

Underground during World War II; the May-June Revolution of Paris, 1968; Underground Newspapers and the Alternative Press; Radical Political Literature of the 1960's in the U.S.; and the Feminist Movement (which alone contains more than 1,200 current periodicals). The acquisition of the Gate Theatre papers began in 1971 in Chicago's O'Hare Airport when the Assistant University Librarian for Collection Development, Richard L. Press, was introduced to an English bookseller who subsequently came to Evanston and enjoyed a rousing dinner at the Press home with family and friends. He quickly became a good friend to the Library. Following his return to England, the bookseller called one morning to say he was in Dublin speaking with friends at the Gate Theatre who wondered if he knew of an American university library which might wish to purchase the Dublin Gate papers. Our bookseller friend thought of us. We agreed to the terms outlined and several months later, nine large wooden crates arrived carrying the several tons of material. In 1973 we purchased more material and in 1983 we secured at auction the professional library of Hilton Edwards, one of the two founders of the Gate.

The distinguished Northwestern School of Speech's Theatre and Theatre History Departments played a large role in our deciding to acquire the papers of the Gate Theatre. They are now fully organized with access through a 170 page guide produced several years ago. The material is fully integrated into the Special Collections Department and is available to patrons during regular Special Collections hours — Monday-Friday, 8:30-5:00 and Saturday, 8:30-noon.

The Dublin Gate Theatre Papers, 1928-1979

History

The Dublin Gate Theatre was founded in 1928 by Hilton Edwards (1903-1983), an English singer and established Shakespearian actor; and Micheál MacLiammóir (1899-1978), a noted child actor, later an artist, who was born in Cork as Alfred Michael Willmore. Their company's name was suggested by Peter Godfrey's Gate Theatre in London. Edwards' and MacLiammóir's aim was to produce and interpret world drama in Dublin, both classic and contemporary, not merely the naturalistic and self-consciously Irish plays found at the Abbey Theatre.

Beginning at the Peacock Theatre for two seasons and then in the theatre of the eighteenth-century Rotunda Buildings from 1930 until the present day, the two founders, with Edwards as producer and lighting expert, and MacLiammóir as star, costume and scenery designer, gave Dublin, and other cities on tour, a long and eclectic list of plays. Through their imaginative and innovative style, the Dublin Gate Theatre produced over 400 different works from Sophocles, Shakespeare, Congreve, Chekhov, Ibsen, O'Neill, Wilde, Shaw, Yeats and many others. They have also introduced plays from younger Irish playwrights such as Denis Johnston, Mary Manning, Maura Laverty, Brian Friel, Fr. Desmond Forristal and MacLiammóir himself.

Until his death in early 1978, the year of the Gate's 50th Anniversary, MacLiammóir wrote, as well as acted and designed for the Gate, plays, revues and three one-man shows, besides translating and adapting those of other authors. Both Edwards and MacLiammóir wrote about the theatre — Edwards as an art in *The Mantle of Harlequin,* and MacLiammóir autobiographically in books about the Gate, amusing experiences at home and abroad, and notable acting associations.

The acting careers of Peggy Cummins, Geraldine Fitzgerald and Orson Welles were launched at the Gate, and other notable actors such as Sarah Allgood, Sybil Thorndike, Siobhan McKenna, James Mason and Cyril Cusack have played with the company during its long history.

Despite constant financial worries and some lean years, when Edwards worked occasionally as an independent producer and as the drama director for Radio Éireann and MacLiammóir toured extensively with his one-man show about Wilde, *The Importance of Being Oscar,* the two friends carried on their joint venture. Until Hilton Edwards' death in 1983, Gate Theatre Productions, Ltd. produced plays for the Dublin Festival and shared the actual Gate Theatre with other dynamic acting groups. Today the Gate Theatre itself is under new management, but it still occupies a unique place in Dublin and in theatre history.

The Papers

The papers of the Dublin Gate Theatre at Northwestern University are held in 384 legal size boxes, 7 large art folders of drawings, and 69 original press cuttings books. Of the 384 boxes, the production scripts and notebooks (arranged by play title) account for 316 of these boxes, the music 17, photographs 5, lighting plots 3, and plans 1. The costume, scenery and miscellaneous designs done by MacLiammóir and others are in 7 oversize folders. The theatre correspondence and that of Hilton Edwards and Micheál MacLiammóir from 1938 to 1970 are filed in 29 boxes; the manuscripts of Hilton Edwards in 2 and those of Micheál MacLiammóir in 10 with one box of miscellany. The separation of the various components of a production reflects the order in which the Gate itself held and used them. Northwestern University

Library has kept Gate numbering and divisions but superimposed its own numbering.

Productions

The 316 boxes of production materials comprise the major portion of the collection. The plays are arranged alphabetically by title and these boxes contain annotated scripts, prompt and production copies, and the detailed production notebooks of Hilton Edwards who produced and directed each play. Wherever they exist, the scripts and notebooks for revivals are also filed. The inventory lists all the separate holdings for each play as well as dates of any known productions between 1928 and 1977.

Music

The music used by the Gate for productions from 1928-1970 is held in 17 boxes. It is arranged alphabetically by title of the production, if known, or by the composer; the Gate production number is included when found. Some music was written especially for particular productions, such as some of the early revues. One group includes many original songs and another, Irish music. The largest amount of material is for *The Drunkard*, with prompt book and all the instrumental parts written out by conductor Edwards.

Photographs

The production and publicity photographs (1928-1970) are in 5 boxes, listed alphabetically by production title. The photographs are not all identified nor present for all productions. The *Hamlet* photographs of several different productions make up one of the largest folders.

Lighting Plots

The original lighting plots are arranged alphabetically in 3 boxes as held by the Gate. Though unsigned, they are nearly all by Hilton Edwards. Revivals or tours are often identified as such, as in *The Drunkard, Hamlet,* or *The Provoked Wife.*

Design-Plan Books, Time Books

One box contains set designs, lists of scenery and ground plans for a limited number of Gate productions, largely undated. The notebook numbers are those used by the Gate. Some set designs and ground plans were loose and have been placed in the production boxes where possible. The time books are only for some listed productions, 1951 to 1954, and give the running time of the acts.

Costume and Miscellaneous Sketches

This large group of diverse pencil and water color or tempera designs, mainly by MacLiammóir, 1928-1977, has been arranged and described as clearly as possible. The sketches have been identified by production, author, and title where possible, with the size and medium noted. Oversize posters of photographs, used by the Gate for publicity, have been arranged alphabetically and included here, as well as a few oversize handbills and 4 large photographs of MacLiammóir.

Correspondence

The correspondence in the papers is in 29 boxes and has been divided into "General" theatre and business correspondence of 1938-1950 (1 box), 1953-1960 (9 boxes), 1961-1970 (4 boxes); then Hilton Edwards' correspondence of 1953-1970 (5 boxes); followed by Micheál MacLiammóir's correspondence of 1952-1970 (10 boxes). It should be noted that the correspondence is arranged chronologically, and that the years covered, except for one box, are the years 1952 or 1953 to 1970. The most interesting letters are possibly those dealing with the Gate's own 25th Anniversary celebration and those with Orson Welles, 1934-1961.

Manuscripts

Hilton Edwards' manuscripts, contained in 2 boxes, include drafts and proofs of his two published books, *The Mantle Of Harlequin* and *Elephant in Flight,* a book of poetry, and many identified articles. The second box contains his articles and scripts of others used or considered during his position with Radio Éireann, 1961-1963.

The manuscripts of Micheál MacLiammóir are held in 10 boxes and are listed alphabetically by book or play title. His shorter "writings" are listed alphabetically and dated. Correspondence on the "writings" is included here as part of MacLiammóir's original arrangement.

Press Cuttings

The press cuttings books Nos. 1, 3-10, 12-66, include material from 2/10/1928 to 6/2/1971. Books 2 and 11 were missing. Much valuable information can be gleaned from the fragile clippings about productions and dates, casts, the activities, work, and public appearances of Edwards and MacLiammóir as well as press reviews. The Gate organized the press cuttings under the productions or under MacLiammóir's and Edwards' activities. Programs were usually included only in early books.

Miscellany
The papers include one box of interesting miscellany. Some of the items are biographical or historical and some are from the Gate's 50th Anniversary exhibition in a Dublin gallery to which Northwestern lent many of the treasures from the Dublin Gate papers.

Additions
In 1979 and in 1983 new Gate materials were added to the collection: production materials and costume designs for plays given 1970-1979, 71 plays annotated by Hilton Edwards for Gate production and 392 plays from his personal library.

Contact:
R. Russell Maylone, Curator, Special Collections Department, Northwestern University Library, Evanston, Illinois 60201

IX. Costume plate by Micheál MacLiammóir for "Fion's Men," in *Ford of the Hurdles*. Northwestern University Library.

X. Costume plate by Micheál MacLiammóir for "The Speckeldy Shawl," for unidentified production. Northwestern University Library.

XI. Century-Izenour Ten-Scene Preset Panel and Lighting Control Console, ca. 1951. Penn State Archives.

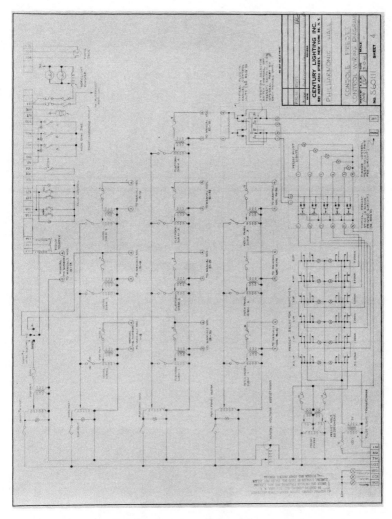

XII. Console and Preset Control Wiring Diagram for Philharmonic (now Avery Fisher) Hall, New York. Drawn by James McGowan, March 10, 1961. Penn State Archives.

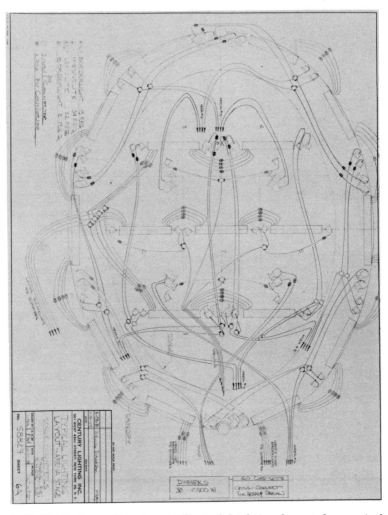

XIII. Preliminary Drawing of Typical Lighting layout for musical
tent or arena stage. Drawn by William H. Allison for Century
Theatre catalog, October 21, 1958. Penn State Archives.

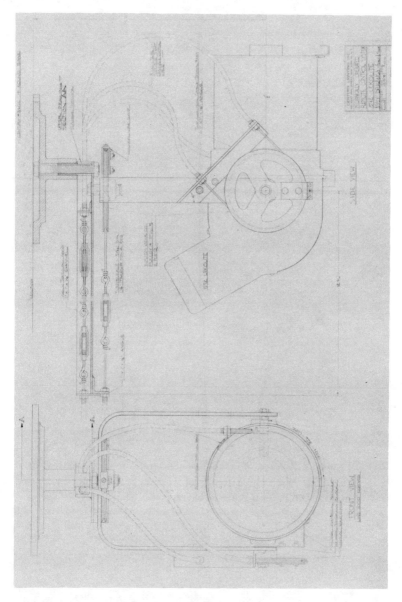

XIV. Mechanically Operated Remote Control System Lekolite (1952),
fitted for tracker-wire control. Concept by Rollo Gillespie
Williams; drawn by Wm. H. Allison, September 12, 1958. Penn
State Archives.

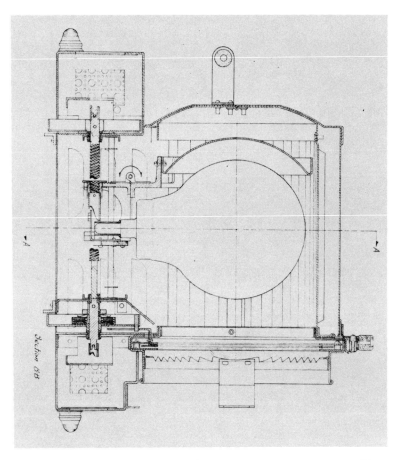

XV. Remote-Controlled Featherlite, section view on center line. Drawn by Wm. H. Allison for Century Lighting, Inc., Los Angeles, 1952. Penn State Archives.

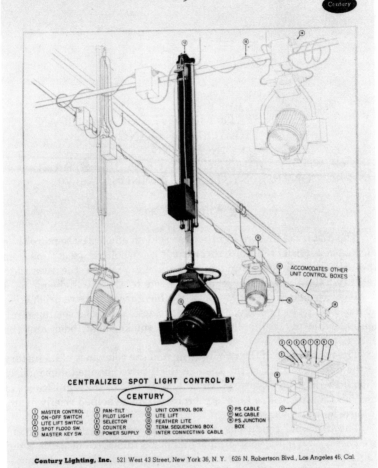

CENTRALIZED SPOT LIGHT CONTROL BY

CENTURY

① MASTER CONTROL	⑥ PAN-TILT	⑪ UNIT CONTROL BOX	⑯ PS. CABLE
② ON-OFF SWITCH	⑦ PILOT LIGHT	⑫ LITE LIFT	⑰ MG. CABLE
③ LITE LIFT SWITCH	⑧ SELECTOR	⑬ FEATHER LITE	⑱ PS. JUNCTION
④ SPOT FLOOD SW.	⑨ COUNTER	⑭ TERM. SEQUENCING BOX	BOX
⑤ MASTER KEY SW.	⑩ POWER SUPPLY	⑮ INTER CONNECTING CABLE	

Century Lighting, Inc. 521 West 43 Street, New York 36, N. Y.   626 N. Robertson Blvd., Los Angeles 46, Cal.

XVI. Remote Controlled Featherlite for centralized control of the lift, pan-tilt, on-off, spot-flood and mechanical dimming functions of a 2kw fresnel lens spotlight. Developed by Century Lighting, Inc. (West Coast Branch), 1952-1953 for NBC Studios, New York. A system comprising 90 featherlites was installed in 1953. Penn State Archives.

THE PENN STATE ARCHIVES OF AMERICAN THEATRE LIGHTING INCLUDING CENTURY LIGHTING AND CENTURY STRAND CONTROL SYSTEM DRAWINGS; 1950-70

by William Allison

The history of theatre lighting has seldom amounted to more than an occasional brief reference throughout the whole range of time from the origins of Greek drama into the early years of the twentieth century.[1] Rarely was any thought given to theatre lighting as a distinct art-related activity — mostly it has served theatre production as a necessary technology, revealing the actors and the setting minimally, while unfortunately introducing smoke, heat, odor and the danger of fire.

The importance of theatre lighting and the relevance of its history to the developing art of the theatre itself have changed enormously within the past half century. An understanding of the significance of the Penn State Theatre Lighting Archives can be helped briefly examining why that is so.

The principal conditions needed for theatre lighting equipment are these: a compact, controllable and powerful source of white light; equipment embodying the mechanical and optical design attributes necessary for most effective utilization of that source; and a control system by which light, in all of its qualities, can be varied in response to theatre productions needs. The great beginnings of Greek drama in the fifth century BC were necessarily performed under conditions of natural lighting. Two thousand years later, the renaissance theatre audiences could expect little more than minimum visibility from the wax candles and oil lamps which illuminated their indoor perform-

WILLIAM ALLISON is Professor of Theatre Arts, Associate Director of the Institute for Arts and Humanistic Studies and Assistant Dean of the College of Arts and Architecture at Pennsylvania State University.

ances. Gas lighting was introduced for theatre use in 1803, serving as the principal stage illuminant for three quarters of the nineteenth century. The electrically powered incandescent lamp was invented in 1879; it has been virtually the sole light source utilized for stage purposes in the twentieth century. The first of the essential conditions for effective theatre lighting had then become available.

Instrument design for the incandescent lamp began with adaptations of equipment which had been developed for earlier light sources. The late 1920s and early 1930s brought major optical improvements to the theatre with two new spotlight designs — one based on the fresnel lens and the other on the ellipsoidal reflector. The newly organized Century Lighting, Inc. and its chief competitor, Kliegl Bros., Inc., both in New York City, shared major credit for those developments. The two spotlights have been of central importance to the industry and to the art of theatre lighting ever since. Thus the second set of conditions for artistic control of theatre lighting was developed.

Lighting intensity control for the theatre was, at the twentieth century's beginning, a cumbersome process of direct control whereby large resistance or autotransformer dimmer units were manually controlled, usually by a crew of dimmer operators working without a view to the stage. The development of a remotely controlled dimming system in the 1940s changed all of that — slowly at first but then in a growing surge of achievement. This third essential development completed the conditions necessary for opening the potential richness of expression inherent in theatre lighting.

George C. Izenour, a theatre engineer, was responsible for developing the first satisfactory remote dimming control system, using thyratron gaseous discharge tubes operated in tandem. Low voltage control circuitry enabled remote placement of the control console so that the lighting control operator could be located with a full view of the stage. The controls were small and easily mastered for group action. A presetting feature enabled the operator to set complete light intensity levels for several (frequently ten) scenes in advance. After personally completing four installations of his new control system during the late 1940s, Izenour entered a working relationship with Century Lighting, Inc. in 1951 whereby that company built and installed the Century-Izenour Control Systems thereafter. Solid-state technology produced the silicon controlled rectifier as a superior dimmer in the 1960s and computer technology brought on infinite presetting capabilities in the 1970s.

Thus the major contributors to the Penn State collection — Century Strand, Inc. (the company's name when it began donations to

Penn State) and George C. Izenour — were greatly influential in the development of American theatre lighting during the years when great changes were made and the new art form of lighting was brought into being. My idea for the development of the lighting archives at Penn State began from working with the people who were central to the Century history, first at Yale, then as a Century employee with both the east and west coast branches of that company. Knowing the importance of what had been accomplished in the industry in the post World War II years and being aware that major changes were taking place within the company, I developed a plan and rationale for an archival collection which would receive historically significant records and materials as they became available; particularly so when they might otherwise be discarded. The purpose behind the archives has been to acquire, preserve and share significant records and examples from a newly developing field of artistic endeavor. Dr. Charles Mann, chief of the Penn State Special Collections Department, agreed in February 1970 to provide space for the Century collection. Mr. Laurence Kellermann, a colleague from my days with Century and, in 1973, appointed vice president of the company, was an enthusiastic proponent of the archives project and a generously cooperative collaborator in the project's development.

When the collection was begun in 1970, many of the materials important to the modern history of theatre lighting were still available at their source of origin. I was keenly aware of a critical time factor for beginning the project, since several of the principal contributors to that history (for example, Stanley McCandless, the Kliegl brothers, Jean Rosenthal and Thomas Wilfred) had died recently and their records had been variously bestowed or discarded. Still others then nearing retirement age were likely to welcome an opportunity for placing their records for permanent safekeeping. Several of the major lighting companies had recently moved (both the New York and Los Angeles branch offices of Century Lighting, Inc. and Kliegl Bros., Inc. being important examples). Furthermore, several major companies had recently gone through changes of management (Century Lighting, Inc., Ariel Davis Manufacturing Company, among others) or had gone out of business (Theatre Technology, Inc., Associated Lighting Service, Inc. and others). Those conditions tended to precipitate the abandonment of old records and equipment wherever their relevance to the company's future functions were uncertain. That seemed true especially since most of the significant developments of theatre lighting have occurred so recently that items of importance to that history have seldom been given due consideration.

The collection's purposes for the University have been as a research base, as a teaching resource and as a means of contact with industry leaders and outstanding professional practitioners in the theatre. The archival collection comprises materials in the following categories:

a. Drawings, including original work, sepia intermediates, and black line prints.
b. Photographs and promotional graphic art work.
c. Records of development. Research and development files and correspondence from companies and individuals.
d. Lighting instruments and control systems, including prototype units, experimental models, and major types of equipment.
e. Special lighting equipment developed for unique conditions of theatre production.
f. Taped interviews with lighting designers and industry leaders.

An understanding of the extent and the interrelations of items in the Penn State collection can be aided by examples. The Century-Izenour (C-I) thyratron tube remote-controlled dimmer system, which changed the industry fundamentally and which altered theatre lighting from a production service into a supporting art form, is represented by these items in the collection:

• Over fifty sets of drawings, documenting Century's complete output of that system, ending in the early 1960s.
• A prototype console with a ten-scene preset panel, one of four built by George C. Izenour and his staff. Built in 1950 for installation in the Carnegie Institute of Technology's Drama School theatre.
• Prototypical hand-fabricated controller demonstration assemblies, thyratron tube laboratory test assemblies, preset selectors, and other system components, all produced in the Yale Electro-Mechanical Laboratory.
• Century Lighting company catalogs, data sheets, promotional flyers and graphic art sheets, all describing the C-I thyratron tube system.
• Office files, with correspondence and laboratory design notes from George C. Izenour's professional practice (virtually complete from the 1940s through 1970s. Described in a 112-page computer printout).
• One fully operational C-I thyratron tube controlled system, installed in Penn State's Pavilion Theatre in 1963, is still in use for University Theatre productions.

- An unpublished manuscript — George C. Izenour's memoirs from the beginning of his career into the early years of his professional relationship with Century Lighting, Inc., giving a well-detailed account of his development of the C-I system.

The Century Lighting Company drawings (mostly of lighting control systems) are housed in map cases in the Rare Books Room of Pattee Library, maintained by the Pennsylvania State University Library's Department of Special Collections. There are about 10,000 drawings for 570 projects, all arranged chronologically and each identified by the job for which the system was designed, usually auditoriums, theatres or meeting halls throughout the United States, and with some for Canada, Central and South America and the Caribbean Islands. The remainder of the collection, comprising lighting instruments, equipment patterns, lantern slides, control systems components, files, categories, drawings, etc. is kept in the Eisenhower Auditorium. More extensive and more varied than the Century drawing collection in the Library, it represents donations from many sources, including Kliegl Bros., Inc. and the Yale Electro-Mechanical Laboratory.

The cataloging of the collection is maintained through a computer bibliographical and grouping system master file, which can be updated to include new items or to show new information about projects cataloged earlier. The file is coded to facilitate computer search by major subject areas. The 235-page printout of the complete catalog is available at cost, as are smaller printouts resulting from subject searches.

Century Lighting Equipment Inc. opened offices and a small factory at 351 West 52nd Street in New York City on 10 August 1929, established under the partnership of Edward F. Kook and Joseph Levy.[2] The partners moved aggressively to secure dominance in supplying equipment to the professional theatre. Kook made contacts with the Broadway show producers, architects, stage designers and engineers, developing strong working relationships which helped to shape the nature and qualities of the company. Designers such as Robert Edmond Jones, Norman Bel-Geddes, Lee Simonson, Mordecai Gorelik, Jo Mielziner and Donald Oenslager soon formed dependence on the new company — they took their problems as designers to Century and technical solutions in terms of equipment, materials and systems would be developed promptly to meet their needs; Joseph Levy saw to that. Century patented the "Lekolite" (the partners, LEvy and KOok contributing to that name) in 1933. The Kliegl brothers patented their ellipsoidal reflector version of the "Klieglight" at about the same time. Those units introduced the ellipsoidal reflector spotlight to the American theatre — the two companies each claiming primacy for that important invention.

Stanley McCandless, one of the original faculty members in the new (1929) drama department at Yale University, became involved with Century from the beginning. McCandless was already the world's foremost educator specializing in theatre lighting. A whole generation of theatre lighting specialists learned their profession directly from "Mac" or were guided by his books *A Method of Lighting the Stage* (1932) and *A Syllabus of Stage Lighting* (1931). McCandless was a major influence on Century Lighting and became director of the company's laboratory for research and development in 1945. For the rest of his professional life, nearly twenty years, he maintained his Yale professorship and his Century position by a rigorous schedule of weekly commuting. And the leadership of the burgeoning company was enhanced by a succession of Yale graduates holding their MFA degrees in theatre lighting, including Louis Erhardt, who became director of Century's west coast branch; Frederick M. Wolff, chief engineer; and Charles Levy, director of professional theatre services.

Rollo Gillespie Williams, world-renowned expert in light and color joined the company in 1959 as director of color research. In his nineteen years with the company he became its vice president and contributed importantly as author, inventor and lighting consultant.

The company's association with George C. Izenour, as mentioned earlier, was a long and important one for all concerned. The Yale connection was strengthened in that relationship. Izenour held the rank of professor of theatre design and technology and was director of the Yale Drama School's electro-mechanical laboratory. Author, inventor and the foremost American theatre engineer during the great post World War II period of theatre construction, his contributions in the development of electronic dimming control gave Century a vitally important advantage in the formative years when new technology, brilliantly designed for the demanding conditions of theatre use, changed theatre lighting into a contributory art form.

Managed in a sound and aggressive manner, Century Lighting had a firm commitment to dependable service and to the production of equipment of good quality. Attention was focused on the professional lighting designers and technicians, and Century took pride in being responsive to their needs. But more than that, Century continually sought to be foremost in finding new design opportunities and for introducing new means for achievement in the art of theatre production. The company enlarged its influence over the years, developing equipment and marketing capabilities to provide architectural and television production lighting and to command a large share of the nation-wide supply of lighting equipment to community and college theatres.

Century Lighting, Inc. was sold in 1964; Edward Kook continued as president and chief executive officer until 1969, completing forty years in leadership of the company. Ultimately the Rank organization of Great Britain, owner of Strand Electric Limited, of London, acquired the company; its name was then changed, first to Century Strand, Inc. and later to Strand Century, Inc., by which it is known to this day.

Although the Lighting Archives have predictably been most used by researchers from the northeastern states, and by advanced classes in lighting and theatre technology at Penn State, there have been interesting variations from that pattern. The U.S. International Communications Agency has borrowed several early American lighting instruments for an exhibit entitled "American Theatre Today." The exhibit was first shown in Budapest during November 1982; attendance records were broken, with over 127,000 visitors seeing the exhibit. Other bookings were requested and there were two highly successful showings in 1983; Athens, Greece (June) and Belgrade, Yugoslavia (September). In July of this year it was shown in Sofia, Bulgaria and the exhibit has recently closed (7 October 1984) in Bucharest, Romania.

Francis Reid, a lighting designer for professional theatres in London, and editor of *TABS, Stage Lighting International,* the Rank Strand Electric magazine, visited in October 1975, spending several days in study and discussion of the collection and of the problems, purposes and advantages involved in establishing a national archival collection for theatre lighting. He devoted the cover article of the *TABS* spring (1976) issue to the Penn State Archives and wrote his editorial page on the general subject of Lighting Archives. In summation, he wrote, "Where shall we preserve? In National Archives, each country having, in addition to its own full national collection, a selection of key international materials to establish reference points. Archives should not be in a central national library or museum but should be associated with an institution (? university) having an active live theatre tradition and a scenographic research structure . . . The matter is urgent. With every passing day, another valuable fragment of lighting history is lost."[3] Subsequently the Association of British Theatre Technicians began the process of establishing the British National Theatre Lighting Archives.

The Canadian Archives were initiated in 1974. Entitled the Ryerson Theatre Archive and housed in the Ryerson Polytechnical Institute of Toronto, the collection was begun by Bruce Whitehead under conditions similar to the Penn State experience; Ward Leonard of Canada, a principal manufacturer of stage lighting control equipment, was closed in 1974 and that opportunity was seized to acquire a substantial collection of important company records. The *TABS* article informed Whitehead of the Penn State collection and we have begun correspondence to augment each archive through knowledge of and cooperation with the other.

The collection of Century Lighting, Inc. drawings can be visited during the working hours of the Penn State Library's Special Collection Department at University Park (Monday-Friday, 8-5). Catalog listings of items in the collection and copies of materials can be had for cost. Donors agreement for the release of some items may be needed — it is a good policy for visiting researchers to inquire in advance, making known what copying or other services may be needed, so as to avoid possible delay during their time at Penn State. Inquiries should be made to Professor William H. Allison, Associate Director, Institute for the Arts and Humanistic Studies, Ihlseng Cottage, University Park, PA. 16802, (telephone: 814-865-0495).

Endnotes

[1] The history of theatre production is interspersed with accounts of lighting effects and of achievements by remarkably determined precursors of the modern lighting designer. Gosta M. Bergman's book *Lighting in the Theatre* (Almqvist & Wiksell, Uppsala, Sweden, 1977) is an excellent source of information on the history of theatre lighting. Fine, imaginative work has been done by artists working with light from Renaissance times onward. The gas light era had its wonders of theatre lighting effects. And the Broadway theatre of our own time still achieves miracles of lighting artistry by means of antiquated control.

No lack of respect for the accomplishments of any of those pioneers in the development of theatre lighting is intended. But ready means to the full and dependable accomplishment of all that the lighting designer imagines and wishes to achieve has made a tremendous difference in very recent times.

[2] The fresnel lens spotlight derives historically from the lighthouse beacon lens developed by the French physicist A. J. Fresnel. The fresnel lens achieves a very short focal length condition without the problems of distortion or mechanical instability which limit the stage use of the plano-convex lens. Concentric rings of glass replicating the optical characteristics of the thick plano-convex lens are incorporated in a thin lens form which accepts a wide gathering angle of light in short focus relationship to the light source. A powerful, efficient lighting instrument, the fresnel lens spotlight uses a spherical reflector to nearly double its utilization of output from the highly concentrated light source. The rear surface of the lens is pebbled to produce an evenly diffused field of light with soft edges. The lamp is adjustable in its relation to the lens, with that movement altering the size of the light beam.

[3] The ellipsoidal reflector spotlight consists primarily of a concentrated high-powered light source, an ellipsoidal reflector, beam shaping controls near the conjugate focal point, and a lens system based on plano-convex or stepped lenses of various focal lengths. The spotlight is highly efficient, utilizing approximately 75% of the light emitted from the source, and shaping it into a relatively narrow beam. Shutters, shaping templates or an iris inserted at the "gate" (a position slightly behind the conjugate focal point) result in a sharply defined beam shape.

[4] Ronald Charles Olson, *Edward F. Kook: Link between the Theatre Artist and Technician.* Ph.D. dissertation, New York University, 1978.

[5] Francis Reid, "Light Archives," *TABS,* 34(1):2 (Spring 1976).

ENGINEERING CONTRIBUTIONS TO
THEATRE TECHNOLOGY:
REMEMBERING THE INNOVATORS

by Bruce Whitehead

For every actor who treads the boards there are many technicians and craftspeople working unseen, backstage, making possible the marvelous effects often taken for granted by the average theatre goer. The contribution of these individuals deserves more recognition. So too, the contribution of the early pioneers in the electrical industry deserves proper recognition. They provided the machinery and systems which made possible the magic of modern stage lighting.

As an electrical engineer, I have long been fascinated by Edison's prolific achievements. It is quite possible that the world may never again see such an all encompassing contribution to technology by a single individual and a small group of technicians. I was therefore quite surprised to learn one day in 1968, that H. Ward Leonard, the founder of the company for which I worked, was an associate of Edison and was also a prolific inventor at the turn of the century. Both of these individuals made major contributions to the art of theatre lighting and, after almost 100 years, I think it is about time that we started to think seriously about preserving evidence of their work as it relates the theatre lighting.

The Inspiration

In the GENERAL ELECTRIC history "A Century of Light", author James A. Cox notes that Thomas Alva Edison was discouraged to learn that his name was to be dropped from that of the firm he started EDISON GENERAL ELECTRIC COMPANY, after the merger in 1892 with the THOMSON-HOUSTON CO.

"He felt a growing coolness toward the company he had originated . . . until he came to realize that his role in lighting the

---

BRUCE WHITEHEAD, P.Eng., is president of Lumitrol, Ltd, Toronto, Canada.

world had been fulfilled . . . Now it was time for the trained businessmen and engineers to polish and market the amazing magic show he had created."

Enter H. Ward Leonard, engineer extrordinaire. As Edison was inventing the carbon filament lamp, H. Ward Leonard, born in Cincinnati in 1861, was just beginning his engineering studies at M.I.T. After graduating in 1883 he joined Edison's staff of engineers. By 1888 he had become general superintendent of the WESTON ELECTRIC LIGHT COMPANY (later to become part of WESTINGHOUSE ELECTRIC AND MANUFACTURING CO.) In 1889 he patented a system of electric lighting for railway cars and formed the LEONARD AND IZZARD CO., one of the first companies in USA to engage in central system and electric railway construction. When this firm was bought out in 1889 by the EDISON GENERAL ELECTRIC COMPANY, Leonard became manager of the firm's combined interests in USA and Canada.

Ward Leonard Electric

In 1891, Leonard resigned to form an electrical contracting firm and on Nov. 24th received patent No. 463802 for a system of motor speed control, his most important invention. This development also won him industry recognition, a John Scott medal from the FRANKLIN INSTITUTE in 1903, and a Gold Medal at the St. Louis World's Fair in 1904. In 1892 he helped establish the CARPENTER ENAMELLED RHEOSTAT CO. in Bridgeport, Conn. and began manufacturing heating devices, rheostats, motor controllers and the first plate type dimmer for carbon lamps, in a former roller skating rink building. In 1894 the company was renamed WARD LEONARD ELECTRIC and operations were moved to Hoboken, N.J. When that building burned in 1897 the firm moved to Bronxville, N.Y. During those early years many more patents were obtained including one for electric elevator control. In 1898, Leonard's control on the gun turrets of the USS Brooklyn helped in the destruction of Cervero's fleet at the battle of Santiago during the Spanish American War. This was the beginning of a long association with The U.S. Navy and the U.S. Army Signal Corps.

One of the firms most important products, the improved "VITROHM" rheostat, employed Leonard's novel concept of sealing the resistance wire in a vitreous enamel whose co-efficient of expansion matched that of the wire. The wire was mounted on an iron plate to improve heat dissipation. In contrast to the earlier 'loose wire' construction, the Ward Leonard design prevented the wire from oxidizing, the assembly was mechanically more rigid, and equipment size and cost were both reduced. In 1900 the firm installed the first effective control system for moving sidewalks at the Paris Exposition in France. By 1903 the company's product line had expanded to include motor speed controllers, circuit breakers, stage dimmers, battery charging rheostats and even automobiles. The following year Leonard resigned as president of the firm to devote more time to his experimental work and his inventions. He joined The Inventors Guild in 1911 and became president in 1913. In 1912, patent No. 1042698 was obtained for the Ward Leonard gasoline-electric automobile. Models built at the Bronxville plant between 1899 and 1903 included the 24-30 H.P. "Motor Car," the award winning 3½ H.P. "Century-Tourist," and the 5 H.P. "Knickerbocker." In 1916, a year after the death of Leonard, the firm moved to its present location on South St. in Mount Vernon, N.Y.[1]

Although his over 100 patents fell far shy of the record 1,093 patents obtained by Edison during his lifetime, H. Ward Leonard made a very significant contribution to the electrical industry by developing reliable and efficient means of controlling the raw power delivered by dynamos, generators and rotating machinery.

D. M. Fraser Ltd.

Daniel MacFarlane Fraser was born in Edinburgh, Scotland in 1879, the year Edison invented the carbon filament lamp. In 1910, after graduating from the Heriot-Watt College in Edinburgh, with a degree in engineering, he and his new bride emigrated to Canada. With a letter of introduction from his College, he was accepted into the MONTREAL LIGHT HEAT AND POWER CO. Fraser later worked as an operating engineer at the Cobalt, Ontario sub-station. At the beginning of the war he tried to enlist but was rejected for health reasons. Throughout the war he proudly wore the "A&R" button (applied and rejected). From Cobalt, Fraser moved on to employment as an estimator and engineer with Edison's GENERAL ELECTRIC COMPANY at their King St. plant in Toronto. At G.E. he worked on switchgear and power generating equipment design. Three of the generator systems he designed for the Sir Adam Beck Generating Station at Niagara Falls, Ontario, are still in operation today.

After 8 years with G.E., Fraser left to set up DOMINION ENGINEERING AGENCY in Jan. 1921 as a Canadian sales agent for switchgear components. On May 23rd, 1925 the name of the firm was changed to D. M. FRASER LTD. For the next 20 years the firm operated out of a three story building at 54 Lombard St. in the heart of Toronto, offering application engineering advice, and selling switchgear and electrical control products manufactured by the CUTTER

CO. (late ITE), ALLEN BRADLEY, ESTERLINE-ANGUS, and WARD LEONARD ELECTRIC. At the end of World War II the firm started manufacturing switchgear to boost ITE circuit breaker sales, and stage lighting dimmer boards using WARD LEONARD ELEC-TRIC autotransformers. In Sept. 1945, son George M. joined the firm after leaving the Canadian Navy. George Fraser brought with him not only his naval experience and contacts, but also engineering knowledge gained before the war as an estimator and designer at AMALGAMATED ELECTRIC of Toronto. When the senior Mr. Fraser died in 1951, at the age of 71, his son took over as president of the firm. In 1953, to provide a more efficient shop layout and to accommodate his staff of 57, George bought a 3½ acre lot in Scarborough and built a new factory at 1070 Birchmount Rd. The success of D. M. FRASER LTD was well known to its suppliers. Confident in the potential growth of the Canadian market, WARD LEONARD ELEC-TRIC decided to purchase the Canadian company. In 1955 it made the first of several offers which were refused. It continued to up the ante until George Fraser felt the offer was too good to refuse. In July 1956 the name was changed to WARD LEONARD OF CANADA LTD, and Ward L. Berry, an American, became the Canadian president.

George M. Fraser Ltd.

George Fraser invested the proceeds of the sale into real estate and promptly started another firm, GEORGE M. FRASER LTD. as a sales agency for motor control, power instrumentation and electrical equipment. After almost 30 years the firm continues to prosper selling to utilities and electrical contractors across Canada, and employs a staff of 15 in Toronto and Montreal offices. The Frasers have become well known for their volunteer activities in the Canadian electrical industry. In 1916 Daniel M. Fraser was one of the founding members of the ELECTRICAL CLUB of TORONTO. In 1980 George became president of this organization. In 1963 George became the first chairman of the Canadian IEEE (INSTITUTE OF ELECTRICAL AND ELECTRONIC ENGINEERS) when it was formed as a merger of the AIEE and IRE associations.

Ward Leonard of Canada Ltd.

My first experience in the dimming industry were with the engineering department of GEORGE KELK LTD., in Toronto, where I had written instruction manuals and sales literature for TV studio dimming systems. My fascination with the field of entertainment lighting prompted me to apply for a position with WARD LEONARD OF CANADA, one of the three major firms of this type in Canada. I joined the firm as product manager for the dimming department in the fall of 1968. The year before RIKER VIDEO INDUSTRIES INC. had acquired effective control of WARD LEONARD ELECTRIC and its Canadian subsidiary.

My mentor was J. Hans Kluge, president of the firm, a man with marvelous enthusiasm and energy. Mr. Kluge had started in the industry as a wiremen and assembler with D. M. FRASER LTD. about 1951. Hans is now president of ASCOLECTRIC in Brantford, Ont., and chairman of the board of directors of the CANADIAN STANDARDS ASSOCIATION. He is active in volunteer activities as a member of the board of the Canadian Opera and several other arts organizations.

In 1968, WARD LEONARD OF CANADA was concentrating on the manufacture of dimming systems, battery powered emergency lighting and vitreous enamel resistors. The firm was also Canadian distributor for most of the parent firms' electrical components, and a line of submersible sewage pumps, an eclectic mix to say the least. The dimmer department prepared specifications, drawings and proposals for stage and studio lighting systems. It also estimated manufacturing costs, issued quotations, expedited production and ultimately commissioned the systems on site. Mechanical and electrical drawings, and bills of materials were produced by the engineering department.

The Stage Dimmerboard

Before the advent of the solid state (SCR) dimmer in 1959, our dimmer panels consisted of plate resistance dimmers or rotary autotransformers driven by motors or geared hand levers. The basic configurations had been documented by WARD LEONARD ELECTRIC in the early 1900's and a full range of standard hardware and accessories was available to us from Mt. Vernon. Our engineering department chose the details most suited to the particular needs of the customer and prepared a scale rack drawing showing how the steel angle iron and sheet steel were to be cut and welded. They also prepared schematic or wiring diagrams showing electrical component interconnections.

A typical medium size stage dimmer panel, often seen backstage in a high school auditorium, might contain 18-2400W or 3600W autotransformer dimmers with lever handles, pilot lights and circuit breakers protruding through the front panel. Such a unit would be 6 ft. high by 6 ft. long by 20 inches deep and weigh several thousand pounds. Another popular product was the motorized dimmer used to control houselights in a cinema or auditorium. This would consist of 3 or 6 autotransformers ganged together and driven by a geared down motor allowing a slow fade out in 15 seconds for example. These dimmers were sold with trade names such as "MOTORLITE", "REGULITE", "SOLITROL", "RADIASTAT", "VARISTAT". The Canadian firm also manufactured other stage equipment including patch panels, borderlights, floor pockets, and wiring battens. WARD LEONARD OF CANADA was able to produce finished systems starting with raw steel in the one factory. Facilities included a sheet metal forming, cutting and welding department, a paint booth, and assembly and test areas. Dimmers could be tested under full load using a load bank with close to 100 bulbs. Dimmers were sold to schools, churches, universities, professional theatres, TV studios, and to a wide range of users for architectural lighting control.

Electronic Dimmers

In the early 1960's, solid state dimmers were beginning to replace autotransformers as the most popular dimming means. The SCR or silicon controlled rectifier made remote control much easier and less expensive, and permitted far more flexibility. WARD LEONARD ELECTRIC, unwilling to compete with their switchboard manufacturing customers, had decided to cease producing complete dimming systems. They would continue to supply dimmerboard components such as dimmer modules and controllers. Unfortunately for WARD LEONARD ELECTRIC, many North American firms realized that they could produce their own components and dimming modules in relatively small quantities without the need for expensive tooling. Firms like CENTURY, STRAND, KLEIGL, MAJOR and METROPOLITAN to name a few, stopped purchasing components and subassemblies from WARD LEONARD ELECTRIC. Even WARD LEONARD OF CANADA found Canadian sources for many of the parts previously bought from the parent firm.

Computerized Lighting Controls

Under the guidance of president Hans Kluge, the Canadian firm began considering the concept of computerized lighting control in 1969. After several false starts we began development of the "SOLMATIC" system, a powerful remote control and memory system for larger theatres. We employed the services of the IBIS CORP., Waltham, Mass. Brent Haslam, founder of IBIS, came up with excellent hardware and software concepts and manufactured the first few systems for us. These were installed at the SHAW FESTIVAL THEATRE in Niagara-on-the-Lake, Ont., and at the STATE UNIVER-

SITY OF NEW YORK, Purchase, N.Y. Dimmers and auxilliary equipment for these projects were manufactured in the Canadian factory.

Developing the computerized systems proved to be quite a drain on the Canadian firm both in terms of time and money. As a result of the poor performance of a number of subsidiaries in the RIKER group and other financial problems, the management looked for assets to liquidate, and began reducing overheads.

Phasing Out the Canadian Division

In 1974, we were notified that the Canadian company was going to be merged with RICHMOND HILL LABS, a sister company also owned by RIKER. Only the dimmer and emergency light product lines were to be transferred. All other product lines were to be sold to other Canadian firms or returned to the control of the Mt. Vernon head office. After about 6 months it became apparent that the dimmer division was going to be phased out.

Since there were only two other manufacturers of dimming systems in Canada at that time, I felt that a marvelous opportunity was at hand. In December of 1974, I decided to set up my own company, LUMITROL LTD. I purchased most of the service equipment, repair parts, and old engineering records so that I could continue to offer service on the WARD LEONARD systems in Canada. I negotiated with RICHMOND HILL LABS and was able to work part time for the next two years as production manager while they worked through the backlog of dimmer orders.

Saving the Records

While working at WARD LEONARD OF CANADA I had begun collecting catalogs from the various dimmer and spotlight manufacturers for marketing and product design ideas. I had also felt it useful to organize records of earlier dimmer system installations for use as promotional material and for service follow-up. At that time I had no sense of the importance of maintaining company records for archival purposes. One of the records to attract my attention was the 1967 WARD LEONARD Annual Report. It celebrated the 75th anniversary of the founding of the company and provided a fascinating wealth of detail on the accomplishments of H. Ward Leonard and his firms. In the first few years with my own company I began to realize that a collection of old dimmers and theatre lights might make an excellent marketing tool. Since most of the old equipment was being thrown out after each theatre renovation, the cost of acquiring such items might be limited to the transportation costs. By the end of 1977 I was making a concerted effort to notify all of my customers of the importance of preserving such artifacts.

Ryerson Polytechnic Institute

Egerton Ryerson was Superintendent of Education in Upper Canada (now Ontario) in the 1840's and was instrumental in abolishing school fees and substituting governments grants. From that period on, education was no longer a privilege of the rich in Ontario. The college which bears his name was the prototype for the many Community Colleges now in existence in Canada. It offers degree courses in many areas of technology including aerospace, architecture, chemical, civil, and electrical engineering, photographic arts, graphic arts management, radio and television arts, journalism, interior design, etc. A number of major computer and electronics manufacturers have donated significant amounts of technical equipment to RYERSON to ensure that students receive their training on modern, sophisticated equipment.

The Theatre Department within RYERSON was established in 1971 in order to train students for careers in professional theatre, dance, and dance teaching. It offers conservatory style programs to a limited number of students who have already made a clear decision to work in this field.

Ryerson Theatre Archives

In 1978, while we were both serving on the board of a regional theatre organization, (THEATRE ONTARIO) Sandy Black, a senior member of the teaching staff in the Theatre Department, and I discussed the need for a permanent collection of artifacts. He felt that there was sufficient interest at RYERSON to establish an archives dedicated to theatre technology. I met with Sandy and Brian Meeson, chairman of the department, at the Toronto campus, and we agreed that my collection would be turned over to the newly formed Ryerson Theatre Archives, and that a classroom would be set aside for the initial displays. It is quite appropriate that the Theatre Archives has found a home at RYERSON in light of the school's relationship with the industry, and its highly regarded theatre programs.

Canada Council

In 1979 I was awarded a grant from the "Explorations Program" of the Canada Council. This was intended to cover the research costs related to my proposed publication "Stage Lighting in Canada, 1879-1979". The Canada Council is the major arts funding body in Canada and the Explorations Program was set up to encourage innovative one time cultural or artistic projects.

Collecting and Preserving

At the present the term "Archives" is a misnomer because no trained archivist is involved and the majority of the items at RYERSON are either theatrical lights or dimmers. The WARD LEONARD project records, documents, catalogs and other items so far collected are still used by LUMITROL for business purposes and for the historical research project mentioned earlier. In addition, RYERSON has no secure storage space set aside for documents. There is some urgency at the present to locate the remaining examples of earlier lighting equipment, and to convince the owners to make a donation of the item to RYERSON rather than to sell the lights or dimmerboards for scrap. Unfortunately there is not sufficient room for some of the larger items at RYERSON and we must be content with a photographic record and samples of the individual dimmer modules.

Cataloging

Documents will eventually be cataloged on the UNIX system at the BLADEN LIBRARY, SCARBOROUGH COLLEGE, as part of the "Bibliography of Canadian Theatre History, 1583-1975", compiled by John Ball and Richard Plant. This data base management system has the ability to recall entries using key words without the need to specify the particular field. No inventory of our collection presently exists, however, the majority of the WARD LEONARD OF CANADA project records, drawings and catalog sheets are filed chronologically.

Restoration

Many spotlights acquired have missing or broken parts and an altered finish. For this reason it is desirable to obtain more than one of each style in order to be able to salvage the missing parts. Early catalog sheets are useful in identifying the shape or nature of the missing hardware. Often parts can be found in the junk bin of a stage lighting rental firm, or backstage in an old theatre if one has the patience to search. In the process of restoring old equipment the decision must be made whether to attempt to remove layers of paint and markings to reach the original finish, to strip the paint off and respray to the original color (often black), or just to remove dirt, oil, baked on tape and loose rust. RYERSON students are presently cleaning and rewiring many of the fixtures and plan to plot photometric data as a lab exercise.

Other Sources of Information

We have been able to obtain microfilmed corporate records for most of the theatrical supply and manufacturing companies incorporated in Ontario, from government records, and a record of the plant locations from earlier trade magazines and phone directories. An inventory of all Canadian theatre buildings past and present is being assembled using the same sources. Retired stage-hands, and previous employees of the various firms are being sought for interviews and for contribution of printed matter related to the project. Theatre programs often list the names of the lighting designer, chief electrician, and source of the rented lights and dimmers. Also the nameplates on equipment give clues as to the location and name of the switchboard manufacturer.

Contact: LUMITROL LTD. 253 Merton St., Toronto, Ont. M4S 1A7 Attn: Bruce Whitehead, P.Eng. President

Postscript

In the 1870s, a man named Henry Woodward was working on a new idea for industry which he tested successfully at the MORRISON BRASS CO. at 87 Adelaide St. W. in Toronto, Ontario. The product worked well and he was able to obtain a patent on Jan. 4th, 1875 from the Canadian Patent Office. Unfortunately for him and for Canada, he ran out of funds and was forced to sell the rights to his patent. His product; a glass globe filled with a rarefied gas, containing a carbon element heated by electric current. The buyer: Thomas Alva Edison.

THE STRAND: ITS HISTORY AND ARCHIVE

by Frederick Bentham

The 'Strand' as the British stage lighting firm has been known to theatre people for most of its seventy years was founded, in the heart of London's theatreland, by two theatre electricians Arthur Earnshaw and Phillip Sheridan in 1914. The full name of the firm was The Strand Electric & Engineering Co. Ltd. and the trading company retained this until the takeover by the Rank Organisation in Autumn 1968. However the company had gone public as Strand Electric Holdings Ltd. in February 1936. Arthur Earnshaw and Moss Mansell retired at that time but Phillip Sheridan continued as managing director but died in the December of that year. His son Jack Sheridan succeeded him in that role immediately and held the post until the end of 1969.

The fact that Strand Electric only had three managing directors in the first fifty-four years of its life but seven in the sixteen since Rank takeover cannot be allowed to pass unremarked. There was great continuity in the old Strand, not just at the top but at all levels. People joined when young and the majority remained with no intention of making a change. And this in spite of the fact that as with many such 'family' companies the pay was relatively poor. It was as if most of us had fallen in love with Strand and the work we did there.

Although the firm did have various departments it was not until the Rank takeover that rigid job descriptions became the rule. People tended to gravitate to what they were good at. Thus when I joined Strand in June 1932 at the age of twenty-one to look after the Hire showroom of 'prop' fittings and the firm's first demonstration theatre, no one seemed surprised when I started doing R & D (research & development) as well. Three years later in Autumn 1935 the result of this work appeared as a range of new or modified lanterns (instru-

---

FREDERICK BENTHAM, for many years editor of TABS and Technical Director of Rank Strand, was first Fellow and past President of the Association of British Theatre Technicians.

ments) and lighting controls together with my invention the organ type Light Console; all this in a case-bound catalogue of 124 pages, dated 1936, devised and written by myself. This catalogue entitled *Theatrical Lighting* used a demi-quarto page whereas the prvious one was made up of smaller loose-leaf sheets and had been rather obviously based on Digby's catalogue. Thomas J. Digby had been *the* stage lighting firm in the years when the arc had taken over from the limelight as the source for spotlighting and the like. Digby, however, failed to see the challenge to his dominant position represented by the tungsten filament projector lamp in the early twenties as backed by the young Strand Electric. Another important catalogue in the archive of that time was that published by the stage lighting dept. of the large "Everything Electrical" G.E.C. It consisted of mainly, but not wholly, German Schwabe equipment. This department handed over its activities to Strand in Autumn 1932 — coincidentally I had left G.E.C. theatre consulting engineer's dept. in June that year.

It is impossible to separate myself from the Strand archive, and not only because the major part of what has been preserved is in my possession. Only I can now write down so much of the story that I have therefore set about writing a Strand biography/Bentham autobiography. Meanwhile, parts of this have been dished-up as separate articles in *TABS, CUE* and *Sightline* from time to time in recent years. The last two are a two-monthly by Twynam Publishing Ltd. and the ABTT's bi-annual journal. *TABS* is Strand's house journal and provides a unique guide to the history and technical progress of the firm; the development of its equipment and the nature of the theatre it served — and sometimes attempted to discipline!

The very fact that *TABS* was introduced in October 1937 as "Issued in the interests of Amateur Theatre" is significant. We did not expect the real theatre people to bother to read it. Those at the top were too busy or important and at stage manager or electrician level we either had, or had to make, personal contact. For this the pubs adjacent to every stage door were better than publications. Even after I took over the editorship in Sept. 1957, from founder Hugh Cotterill, I did not rumble that by then amateurs were no longer our only avid readers and the word "Amateur" was not dropped until one year later. A complete set of *TABS* is an archive in itself; all the more so because Vol. 22 No. 1 March 1964 is a 120-page history with index of the Strand Electic to that date. It was written by the editor to celebrate the company's Golden Jubilee. Complete bound sets from the very beginning are rare indeed. I have one, Percy Corry in Manchester has another and Edward F. Kook in New York has the third.

There was, not surprisingly, a gap from the April 1939 issue until that of September 1946. It could well be that there are other sets which started in the fifties for by then this little free issue (but you had to ask for it) journal of around 32-pages had become popular. Witness a letter from Eugene Braun, the chief electrical engineer of Radio City Music Hall in 1951 "I want to express my appreciation for the many wonderful copies of *TABS*. I really and truly enjoy reading the contents . . . We have nothing here to compare with it and I would feel very much let down if I could not look forward to its continued receipt." Coming from a man without a single item of Strand equipment in his famous New York theatre this was indeed a tribute!

In Dec. 1953, do-it-yourself *TABS* binders (price 6/- post free in U.K.) were made available thereby increasing the probability of sets being preserved. An Index for all post-war issues thus far appeared in April '61 and in 1969 case-bound sets were offered to cover 1967-69, and thereafter. In 1974, following my departure from Rank Strand, large format A4 was adopted instead of the A5 or the original octavo. I have always seen *TABS* as news now and contemporary history one day when bound as a book. A book of a size to take down from the shelf and read in bed should one wish. This tradition I then continued with the ABTT's *Sightline* twice yearly from Spring 1974 thru Autumn 1983. Curiously the new editor, Ian Herbert, immediately changed it from A5 or A4.

I think any would be student of Strand Electric or British stage lighting/technical theatre history would be wise to consider the book format *TABS* and *Sightline* as one series. Certainly, as their editor for over 25-years and an author in every issue from the beginning in 1937, I consider them as such. Over the years *TABS* tended more and more to deal with technical aspects of the theatre other than stage lighting. This spotlights a feature of the pre-Rank years — the provision of free advice by no means restricted to what we actually wanted to sell and hire. We offered lectures & demonstrations each Spring & Autumn; but more enduring we published booklets free.

Of one of these the reviewer in the *Architects Journal* wrote in 1962: "It is an interesting commentary on the literature of the subject (Stage Planning) that this booklet, published by a manufacturer of stage lighting equipment and issued free on application, is not merely the best of its kind, but one of the very few good books obtainable." It is not too much to claim that we were *the* source of technical instruction and information. Since the role played by academe was negligible in U.K. until the end of the sixties. In Autumn 1973, when Rank closed down our Covent Garden premises and left theatreland for Brentford, the pioneer in open staging here, John English, likened our influence to that of the Bauhaus. By that time other influences were at work. The ABTT (Association of British Theatre Technicians) had been founded in March 1961 and signalled a recognition that professionals ought to come together to attend to such matters as theatre planning, safety regulations, materials, sound, lighting and training. Not long after, the society of Theatre Consultants was started and representatives of these bodies and others, such as the Society of Theatre Research plus the management associations and the unions, began to meet regularly as the Theatres Advisory Council.

It is necessary at this point to go back to the beginnings of Strand Electric and trace its general development. In 1918 Earnshaw and Sheridan were joined by Moss Mansell, whose firm Mansell & Ogan manaufactured arc resistances, dimmers and other electrical control equipment mainly for cinemas. It was this board of only three men which was responsible for running Strand Electric until the firm went public in 1936. Nevertheless Mansell & Ogan continued to have a separate existence with their own small factory a few doors away from Strand on Floral Street. At the other end, just two minutes walk away, was the stage door of the Royal Opera House. Although there were drawbacks to being sited in the heart of the fruit & vegetable market (as Covent Garden was to remain until 1974), it was also the heart of London's theatreland. Over fifty theatres, to say nothing of cinemas, were within reach on foot and the smaller items like lamps and gelatines could be delivered by a boy on a trike.

Earnshaw and Sheridan were very different characters; the latter being an excitable Dubliner whereas it was difficult to tell what the former was thinking. It is curious that Earnshaw's son, Stanley, who joined in 1923, had in spite of his very short stature a great outgoing personality. He was to become our contact man *par excellence* with 'the' theatre people who mattered in the West End and No. 1 tours. Another person who joinded in 1923 and became a great personality almost right away was L. G. Applebee. He started the Theatre Lighting Dept. to deal with complete installations of stage and colour lighting for the super-cinema boom between the wars. There were theatre installations, usually to cope with the change-over from DC to AC current; but there was also new theatre building even in London's West End, including the Savoy (1929) and the Adelphi (1930).

What one finds right from the start is the way members of the Strand Electric became involved in the process of lighting and not just the supply of equipment, its installation and maintenance. We were, so to speak, at home on both sides of the stage door. Even the humbler employees would 'work' shows during their spare time. Of course stage lighting spilled over into other activities. Impressarios, such as

C. B. Cochran, did not restrict themselves to theatre proper and thus Strand became involved early on in displays in the Royal Albert Hall and Cochran's indoor presentation of Suzanne Lenglen, surely the World's first media tennis star, at Holland Park in 1927.

The backbones of Strand's early manufacturing career were the new compartment footlights & battens (known as X-rays in USA at that time) with reflectors and gelatine colours. The drive over here came from productions such as *Round in Fifty* using Adrian Samoiloff's scenic effects with complementary colours. Strand also specialised in optical effects — waves, clouds, snow, flames and so forth. The Wembley Empire Exhibition of 1924 and '25 used a large variety of special lighting effects. I know this from personal experience as a schoolboy because it was but a tram ride from home and therefore a favourite outing long before my own career of 42-years inside Strand.

As anonymous author of the 1964 Golden Jubilee *TABS* I could depend on three people, Stanley Earnshaw, L. G. Applebee and H. O. Jordan, for an inside view of those early years. Jim Jordan, as we knew him, joined Mansell & Ogan in 1919 became Strand Electric in 1932 when the two firms amalgamated their two factories and continued with the firm until the 1968 takeover. During those 59 years he was foreman, then works manager and finally works director.

Applebee is particularly important in an article such as this slanted towards history and archive because he was Strand's first fertile lecturer and writer. Later there were to be two others, Percy Corry and myself. Applebee had an energetic personality and a flair for attracting attention; in consequence his was the best known name outside Strand. A key example of the educational side of his work is the printed version of his *A Cavalcade of Stage Lighting* lecture delivered in 1935 to the Illuminating Engineering Society. Although he tended to favour the well established equipment like battens & footlights plus a manual dimmer control, with or without grandmaster interlocking, his lecture did cover some of my new R & D items giving advance notice of the organ console type of lighting control. Prior to joining Strand I had been assistant to Basil Davis (son of Israel Davis the super cinema pioneer here), then Theatre Consulting Engineer at the G.E.C. One way and another a feeling for playing light to music (Colour Music) had developed and this was, it must be confessed, the prime purpose of my console. However, the organ console principle which gave one man absolute control over large resources plus the organ type wiring and relay systems of the Compton Organ Co., which made it economically possible, was destined to influence Strand work until the solid-state electronic era of the 1960s and the memory control computer age which has followed.

At the remote dimmer banks the use of the Mansell magnetic clutch, invented by him in 1929, was fundamental. This enabled one motor to drive any combination of dimmers up or down; later, when an inexpensive polarised-relay became available, it could provide a simple servo system. Dimmers once driven did not have to be constantly energised to hold their levels and thus the complications of multiscene preset controls were avoided in this country. The first big Mansell clutch job to go in a theatre was the 120-way 700-kW one for Sir Thomas Beecham's 1934 season at the Covent Garden opera house. The control panel backstage on the prompt side pros. perch survived until 1964 in spite of the primitive nature of the facilities and the fact that manual shaft drive was used instead of electric motor. My Strand Light Console the following year amassed all the publicity one could have wished but did not become properly accepted here until 1949 and in 1956 a revised form of it, system CD (or de luxe system C) was to enable us to claim before long that all television studio controls were by Strand Electric: CD also became popular for the larger theatre installations.

In 1937 Percy Corry joined Strand Electric by founding our first branch in Manchester. Rather like Moss Mansell before him, he continued to run his own scenery supply firm — Fitups of Manchester (later to become Watts and Corry Ltd.[1]). Percy was, among other things, an amateur actor and director of considerable and varied experience. He immediately started lecturing and writing for us. That October the first *TABS* was published and he and his branch were featured. Incidentally the first three issues were not only crudely printed but contained two pages of our hire charges. By Vol. 1 No. 4 both these crudities had disappeared and the soft sell had begun, albeit modestly. We authors were anon in the eight issues until the outbreak of war stopped publication. Afterwards we were allowed our initials but when I took over, all authors, staff or otherwise, were allowed their full names. Anonymity then only extended to the editor and his writings in that role such as the editorials up front. Percy Corry did use a nom de plume for some of his earlier writing and often mingled humour with instruction; whereas I remained a grimly serious crusader. Happily this trait evaporated as youth receded.

Wartime provided opportunity for Percy and I to become better acquainted, mainly because he was in charge of a large project to develop and build flight simulators for torpedo attack teaching and the like. The first were for the Royal Navy Fleet Air Arm and had to provide a syncro-visual display on a great 44-ft. diameter cyclorama around a Link trainer aircraft slap in the centre. This was very difficult to do in those days but we managed, thanks to a coming together of ingenious talent and many were made for use here and overseas. Percy and I would often speculate on the kind of Civic theatres which ought to be built post-war for professional and amateur companies. Some of these ideas do appear in my first book *Stage Lighting* (published by Pitman 1950) but largely written in 1946 and 47 in a sanatorium bed. This qualification is important from the archive point of view as it means that the technical chapters are largely a distillation of British stage lighting practice of the years just before and during the early part of the war. The thoughts and ideas on theatre planning were more or less new but the lighting equipment was well established by then. What was really new in that line had to be crammed into a 2-page appendix "Recent Progress". A second revised edition followed in 1955 and a couple of others after that until a large re-write became necessary in 1968 and the title was changed to *The Art of Stage Lighting,* in its turn largely re-written for the edition of 1976. Because there was always such a large amount of detailed discussion on the design of equipment, these books do compared one with another, give a good indication of the way the author, from his privileged position inside Strand thought things were to go technically and in contrast the way they subsequently developed. By no means always the same thing! Thus from the very first I argue that the control must be a compact one man affair out front where the operator could see the lighting he was doing. There is of course no hint of the 'Memory control' revolution but there is more than a hint that such precision would have been unwelcome to that author of 1950 and 55 and his concept of a future in terms of "live lighting".

In 1949 Strand Electric published (at five shillings) a small book called *Stage Planning and Equipment* by Percy Corry. In 1953 he condensed the gist of it into the free booklet *Stage Planning.* This ran for six editions until 1971 when it seemed a good idea to combine it with another booklet *Planning for New Forms of Theatre* written for us by the late Stephen Joseph the pioneer of theatre-in-the-round in this country and first published in 1962. By June 1966 there were sufficient new and varied theatres built in U.K. to justify a special edition of *TABS* and in 1970 it became a book *New Theatres in Britain* featuring seventy-eight of them. One reviewer said that it was like our cheek not to meantion that all the installations & controls were by Strand Electric but leave the reader to assume it! Another booklet *Lighting and layout for small TV studios* had one BBC and two Commercial TV experts collaborating for us in 1967. At the other end of the scale there was Percy Corry's *Stage Lighting on a Shoestring* first issued in 1954 which showed how hard-up schools and amateur societies could acquire, in five installments of roughly £25, over the years stage lighting which could be useful and expressive from the very beginning.

Of course over the decades there have been catalogues, price lists and other sales literature. These have often taken loose-leaf form but the important ones for the archivist are the permanently bound ones written at a time of technical change. Key catalogues of this type are 1936, 1945 *(The Position Now)*, 1958, 1961 and 1963/4. The last three were condensed format to ensure the widest circulation as each heralded major changes over this period of transition. These represent times when we had to discipline our customers, so to speak, but at others 'the catalogue' would seem to be a large folder stuffed with literature, not always related in format. What with data sheets and '12-pagers' devoted to some new product or other the Strand Theatrical Lighting catalogue folder could sometimes be described as bulging with comprehensive chaos. Gazing at British Rail's neat pocket Inter-City timetable I recreated the same format devoted to the art of stage lighting and our equipment.

The result was the *TABS* Lighting Compendium of 1969 which ran to five editions until 1974. Significantly, perhaps, it died after I left Rank Strand. The 32 pages were A6 (2 ³⁄₄-ins. by 4 ¹⁄₄-ins.). Yet although tiny they contained basic advice on lighting, all important equipment with prices & accessories, schedules of filters, branches & agents and publications. Marvellous discipline and great fun to do. One could have a pocketful to give away at lectures and a magnifying glass was *not* necessary!

No mention has been made of export thus far. In the 1930s little happened in this respect; but on the other hand by then it was not necessary to import any such equipment — this country was self sufficient in stage lighting. The first really important Strand export job came in 1940 after the factory had turned over to war work and air raids and the blackout made everything as difficult as possible. Nevertheless we managed to make the complete stage lighting installation for the S'Carlos opera house Lisbon together with a 108-way Light console (our first sale) control to be placed in the orchestra pit. Having made it, we even got it to Lisbon and working on time, in spite of the decision of Hitler to bomb the London docks for three successive nights while the whole lot was awaiting shipment there.

The war over, the next big export was another opera house complete with Light Console — the new National in Ankara for Carl Ebert in 1949. From then on export grew until it formed the larger part of Strand's business in spite of the amount of new work or re-equipment in U.K. In this connection the important name was J. T. Wood, known everywhere as Woody, who joined us on demob immediately after the war. He seemed to have a genius for locating right small firms to become our agents in each European country. Our first overseas branch was set-up down-under in Melbourne in 1952[2] and one in Toronto followed in 1959. North America was a tough nut to crack but in 1969, one year after we had become Rank Strand, we acquired Century Lighting — something that would have been inconceivable while Ed Kook was still in control of his firm. To judge by the latest press announcement as I write the work of Rank Strand and Strand Century is to be linked even closer. Certainly it is much harder nowadays to distinguish between American and U.K. practice in stage lighting than it was in all the years that I was actively engaged in it. Maybe there is something of the 'Little Englander' in me or perhaps it is just nostalgia that makes me regret this. Even the last control I designed, the 240-way system DDM for the RSC at Stratford-upon-Avon 1972, although software computer based, relied on a philosophy (the rocker per channel) not taken up by anyone else since. If there is a great change in the switchboards of today, there has been a great change over the years in the instruction books and maintenance handbooks during that time. Originally non-existent since it was mechanically obvious what one had to do to work the thing or put it right, something of the sort gradually became necessary until literally some vast volumes had had to be printed at times. Only the other day I came across in the ABTT library a book, seemingly much larger and heavier than George Izenour's *Theater Design* but dealing with one type of lighting control only — the Rank Strand system MMS current in the first half of the 1970s and obsolete long since.

The rate of change now sets greater problems of archival conservation to say nothing of the preservation of examples of the more outstanding equipment itself. It seems to me personally that none of the advanced forms of storage by computer, microfiche or whatever can ever bridge the decades or the centuries in the way the file or the document itself complete with tea or coffee stains can. Anyway that is the kind of Strand Electric archive that I have at home but hope will be transferred one day to London's theatre museum. Apart from the printed material already referred to in this article and much else of that nature, the most accessible material is that in a complete set of press books with pasted-in cuttings of articles and advertisements from April 1923 until the Rank takeover in 1969. They have continued the practice of course but those books are in Rank hands: as is the large slide collection of 3½ × 3½ slides and the 35mm ones which succeeded them. Certainly during the time I was responsible for this collection its nature resembled that of *TABS* and in consequence was not confined to stage lighting and the firms work only. The collection must consist of at least 3000 slides excluding duplicates and is catalogued — albeit in a somewhat cryptic manner.

A useful feature of the press books is that more often than not they are not neat cuttings but all or a large part of a page from the journal or newspaper torn or cut out thereby giving a better contemporary evocation. The archive contains the wage books of the twenties and thirties and other books of this nature. Also the Board room minutes but these are often so sparse as just to record who was there and the fact that the equally sparse minutes of the previous meeting "were read and signed as a correct record". Soon after my arrival on the board in 1957 something known as managerial minutes were added — after all, we were at that time all executive directors. The truth is that this Strand Electric archive is more or less a personal one and therefore centres around R & D and public relations. There is little indeed about the financial workings of Strand but reasonable record of how the designs of the equipment were developed, prototyped and went into manufacture. The teething troubles encountered en route are recorded. There are memos covering the 1932-36 activity and, from 1947 thru 1953, very good minutes of the frequent R & D meetings always chaired by Jack Sheridan as managing director. This was a period of great activity and the record shows our failures as well as our successes, for example, the ergonomically popular Electronic control system based on thyratron valves which after a number of important installations had to be discontinued. As the firm's activity and turnover increased, the R & D records show Strand coasting along very nicely but the Golden Jubilee of 1964 marked a turning point. Trouble lay over the horizon; we could no longer continue as the 'family' firm; we were getting out of our depth technically and managerially. The majority of our board could not be made to realise that we could not service the ideas which flowed so freely between Strand and its friends. Crucial were the new Instant Dimmer Memory systems IDM/R and IDM/DL — the ergonomic ideas were excellent. We knew very well how stange and television lighting controls *should* work; but the board had no idea of the engineering talent needed, or the money that it required, to make these controls work with reliable precision.

When Thorn launched their Q-File control in 1966 there was still this tendency to say — but *they* do not understand theatre. Whereas the truth was not that Thorn were invading Strand Electric territory but the need to base control systems on the new technology was taking us into theirs. It is a fact that after takeover the Rank Organisation failed to take account of the technological hiatus; although there was someone who never tired, as the records show, of stressing it. Instead, it was Accountancy and Admin systems not lighting control systems which got the priority. The result was a succession of managing directors, financial controllers and marketing managers and a whole series of organisational charts which could do nothing until Rank Strand had something reliable both to sell and to replace what had been sold at the top end of the market.

It was the demonstrating of the computer software system DDM, first introduced in *TABS* of March 1971 under the heading "Lovable", that signalled Strand back on course. This sytem was installed in Stratford-upon-Avon at the end of the same year so as to be tried and tested to take on the RSC's 1972 season. Other system with wider application, such as the modular memory MMS, followed and Strand was by then so firmly established again technologically as to survive and prosper in spite of being wrenched out of the centre of London's theatreland after just on sixty years there. And with the firm's departure from Covent Garden to the Thespian Siberia of Brentford near Heathrow and my own from the firm; this bending author must put down his rough and un-able pen and cease to mangle the story he hath confined in little room.

Footnotes

[1]A Watts & Corry archive does not exist but Percy Corry has written an 84-page booklet (Neil Richardson, Manchester: 1984) on his firm's and Strand Electric branch activities.

[2]Dennis Irving of Entertech Melbourne was written a short but informative personal account of the early days of Strand in Australia.

Frederick Bentham can be contacted at 29, Shaftesbury Avenue, Norwood Green, Southall, UB2 4HH, England. The journal *TABS* can be ordered directly from Rank Strand Ltd., P.O. Box 51, Great West Road, Brentfors, Middlesex. TW8 9HR, England. The current editor is Richard M. Harris.